The Princeton Review®

Cracking the

AP®

COMPUTER SCIENCE A EXAM

2017 Edition

Matt Gironda and the Staff of The Princeton Review

PrincetonReview.com

Penguin
Random
House

The Princeton Review
24 Prime Parkway, Suite 201
Natick, MA 01760
E-mail: editorialsupport@review.com

ISBN: 978-1-101-91988-0
eBook: 978-1-101-92014-5
ISSN: 1546-9069

Editor: Selena Coppock
Production Editor: Beth Hanson
Production Artist: Deborah A. Silvestrini

2017 Edition

Editorial
Rob Franek, Senior VP, Publisher
Casey Cornelius, VP Content Development
Mary Beth Garrick, Director of Production
Selena Coppock, Managing Editor
Meave Shelton, Senior Editor
Colleen Day, Editor
Sarah Litt, Editor
Aaron Riccio, Editor
Orion McBean, Editorial Assistant

Random House Publishing Team
Tom Russell, Publisher
Alison Stoltzfus, Publishing Manager
Jake Eldred, Associate Managing Editor
Ellen Reed, Production Manager

ACKNOWLEDGMENTS

For Kristen and Alex who support me, Marie and Michael who inspire me, Meg who puts up with me, Mark and Maria who educate me, and all of my awesome AP kids who motivate me. This is truly, for me, the icing on the cake.

—Matt Gironda

The staff of The Princeton Review would like to thank Matt Gironda for his tireless work on the 2017 edition of this book and Chris Chimera, Russ Greenspan, Jenkang Tao, Debbie Silvestrini, and Beth Hanson for their contributions to this title.

Contents

Register Your

1 Go to **PrincetonReview.com/cracking**

2 You'll see a welcome page where you can register your book using the following ISBN: 9781101919880

3 After placing this free order, you'll either be asked to log in or to answer a few simple questions in order to set up a new Princeton Review account.

4 Finally, click on the "Student Tools" tab located at the top of the screen. It may take an hour or two for your registration to go through, but after that, you're good to go.

If you are experiencing book problems (potential content errors), please contact EditorialSupport@review.com with the full title of the book, its ISBN number (located above), and the page number of the error. Experiencing technical issues? Please e-mail TPRStudentTech@review.com with the following information:

- your full name
- e-mail address used to register the book
- full book title and ISBN
- your computer OS (Mac or PC) and Internet browser (Firefox, Safari, Chrome, etc.)
- description of technical issue

Book Online!

Once you've registered, you can...

- Find any late-breaking information released about the AP Computer Science A Exam

- Take a full-length practice PSAT, SAT, and ACT

- Get valuable advice about the college application process, including tips for writing a great essay and where to apply for financial aid

- Sort colleges by whatever you're looking for (such as Best Theater or Dorm), learn more about your top choices, and see how they all rank according to *The Best 380 Colleges*

- Check to see if there have been any corrections or updates to this edition

Look For These Icons Throughout The Book

- Online Articles
- Study Break
- Proven Techniques
- More Great Books
- Applied Strategies

The **Princeton** Review®

Part I
Using This
Book to Improve
Your AP Score

- Preview: Your Knowledge, Your Expectations
- Your Guide to Using This Book
- How to Begin

PREVIEW: YOUR KNOWLEDGE, YOUR EXPECTATIONS

Your route to a high score on the AP Computer Science A Exam depends a lot how you plan to use this book. Start thinking about your plan by responding to the following questions.

1. Rate your level of confidence about your knowledge of the content tested by the AP Computer Science A Exam:

    A. Very confident—I know it all
    B. I'm pretty confident, but there are topics for which I could use help
    C. Not confident—I need quite a bit of support
    D. I'm not sure

2. If you have a goal score in mind, circle your goal score for the AP Computer Science A Exam:

    5   4   3   2   1   I'm not sure yet

3. What do you expect to learn from this book? Circle all that apply to you.

    A. A general overview of the test and what to expect
    B. Strategies for how to approach the test
    C. The content tested by this exam
    D. I'm not sure yet

YOUR GUIDE TO USING THIS BOOK

This book is organized to provide as much—or as little—support as you need, so you can use this book in whatever way will be most helpful to improving your score on the AP Computer Science A Exam.

*   The remainder of **Part I** will provide guidance on how to use this book and help you determine your strengths and weaknesses

*   **Part II** of this book contains Practice Test 1, its answers and explanations, and a scoring guide. (Bubble sheets can be found in the very back of the book for easy tear-out.) We recommend that you take this test before going any further in order to realistically determine:
    o   your starting point right now
    o   which question types you're ready for and which you might need to practice on
    o   which content topics you are familiar with and which you will want to carefully review

Once you have nailed down your strengths and weaknesses with regard to this exam, you can focus your test preparation, build a study plan, and be efficient with your time.

- **Part III** of this book will:
  o provide information about the structure, scoring, and content of the AP Computer Science A Exam
  o help you to make a study plan
  o point you towards additional resources

- **Part IV** of this book will explore various strategies:
  o how to attack multiple-choice questions
  o how to write effective essays
  o how to manage your time to maximize the number of points available to you

- **Part V** of this book covers the content you need for the AP Computer Science A Exam.

- **Part VI** of this book contains Practice Test 2, its answers and explanations, and a scoring guide. (Again, bubble sheets can be found in the very back of the book for easy tear-out.) If you skipped Practice Test 1, we recommend that you do both (with at least a day or two between them) so that you can compare your progress between the two. Additionally, this will help to identify any external issues: if you get a certain type of question wrong both times, you probably need to review it. If you only got it wrong once, you may have run out of time or been distracted by something. In either case, this will allow you to focus on the factors that caused the discrepancy in scores and to be as prepared as possible on the day of the test.

You may choose to use some parts of this book over others, or you may work through the entire book. This will depend on your needs and how much time you have. Now let's look at how to make this determination.

HOW TO BEGIN

1. **Take Practice Test 1**

   Before you can decide how to use this book, you need to take a practice test. Doing so will give you insight into your strengths and weaknesses, and the test will also help you make an effective study plan. If you're feeling test-phobic, remind yourself that a practice test is a tool for diagnosing yourself—it's not how well you do that matters but how you use information gleaned from your performance to guide your preparation.

So, before you read further, take Practice Test 1 starting on page 9 of this book. Be sure to finish it in one sitting, following the instructions that appear before the test.

2. **Check Your Answers**

    Using the answer key on page 53, count how many multiple-choice questions you got right and how many you missed. Don't worry about the explanations for now, and don't worry about why you missed questions. We'll get to that soon.

3. **Reflect on the Test**

    After you take your first test, respond to the following questions:

    •   How much time did you spend on the multiple-choice questions?

    •   How much time did you spend on each free-response question?

    •   How many multiple-choice questions did you miss?

    •   Do you feel you had the knowledge to address the subject matter of the free-response questions?

    •   Circle the content areas that were most challenging for you and draw a line through the ones in which you felt confident and/or did well.

4. **Read Part III of this Book and Complete the Self-Evaluation**

    Part III will provide information on how the test is structured and scored. It will also set out areas of content that are tested.

    As you read Part III, re-evaluate your answers to the questions above. At the end of Part III, you will revisit and refine the questions you answer above. You will then be able to make a study plan, based on your needs and available time, that will allow you to use this book most effectively.

5. **Engage with Parts IV and V as Needed**

Notice the word *engage*. You'll get more out of this book if you use it intentionally than if you read it passively, hoping for an improved score through osmosis.

Strategy chapters will help you think about your approach to the question types on this exam. Part IV will open with a reminder to think about how you approach questions now and then close with a reflection section asking you to think about how or whether you will change your approach in the future.

Content chapters are designed to provide a review of the content tested on the AP Computer Science A Exam, including the level of detail you need to know and how the content is tested. You will have the opportunity to assess your mastery of the content of each chapter through test-appropriate questions and a reflection section.

6. **Take Practice Test 2 and Assess Your Performance**

Once you feel you have developed the strategies you need and gained the knowledge you lacked, you should take Practice Test 2, which starts on page 249 of this book. You should do so in one sitting, following the instructions at the beginning of the test.

When you are done, check your answers to the multiple-choice sections. See if a teacher will read your essays and provide feedback.

Once you have taken the test, reflect on the areas where you still need to work, and revisit the chapters in this book that address those deficiencies. Through this type of reflection and engagement, you will continue to improve.

7. **Keep Working**

As mentioned earlier, there are other resources available to you, including a wealth of information on AP Students. On this site, you can continue to explore areas that you could improve upon and engage in those areas right up until the day of the test. You should use a mix of web resources and book review to solidify your understanding of any question subjects that you keep getting wrong. Visit AP Students here: **https://apstudent. collegeboard.org/apcourse/ap-computer-science-a**.

Need Some Guidance?
If you're looking for a way to get the most out of your studying, check out our free study guide for this exam, which you can access via our online portal, AP Connect. See the "Register Your Book Online!" page for details on accessing this great resource and more.

Part II
Practice Test 1

- Practice Test 1
- Practice Test 1: Answers and Explanations

Practice Test 1

AP® Computer Science A Exam

SECTION I: Multiple-Choice Questions

DO NOT OPEN THIS BOOKLET UNTIL YOU ARE TOLD TO DO SO.

At a Glance
Total Time 1 hour 30 minutes **Number of Questions** 40 **Percent of Total Score** 50% **Writing Instrument** Pencil required

Instructions

Section I of this examination contains 40 multiple-choice questions. Fill in only the ovals for numbers 1 through 40 on your answer sheet.

Indicate all of your answers to the multiple-choice questions on the answer sheet. No credit will be given for anything written in this exam booklet, but you may use the booklet for notes or scratch work. After you have decided which of the suggested answers is best, completely fill in the corresponding oval on the answer sheet. Give only one answer to each question. If you change an answer, be sure that the previous mark is erased completely. Here is a sample question and answer.

Sample Question   Sample Answer

Chicago is a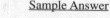
(A) state
(B) city
(C) country
(D) continent
(E) county

Use your time effectively, working as quickly as you can without losing accuracy. Do not spend too much time on any one question. Go on to other questions and come back to the ones you have not answered if you have time. It is not expected that everyone will know the answers to all the multiple-choice questions.

About Guessing

Many candidates wonder whether or not to guess the answers to questions about which they are not certain. Multiple-choice scores are based on the number of questions answered correctly. Points are not deducted for incorrect answers, and no points are awarded for unanswered questions. Because points are not deducted for incorrect answers, you are encouraged to answer all multiple-choice questions. On any questions you do not know the answer to, you should eliminate as many choices as you can, and then select the best answer among the remaining choices.

GO ON TO THE NEXT PAGE.

Quick Reference

class java.lang.Object
- boolean equals(Object other)
- String toString()

class java.lang.Integer
- Integer(int value)
- int intValue()
- Integer.MIN_VALUE   // minimum value represented by an int or Integer
- Integer.MAX_VALUE   // maximum value represented by an int or Integer

class java.lang.Double
- Double(double value)
- double doubleValue()

class java.lang.String
- int length()
- String substring(int from, int to)   // returns the substring beginning at from
                                        // and ending at to-1
- String substring(int from)   // returns substring(from, length())
- int indexOf(String str)   // returns the index of the first occurrence of str;
                                        // returns -1 if not found
- int compareTo(String other)   // returns a value < 0 if this is less than other
                                        // returns a value = 0 if this is equal to other
                                        // returns a value > 0 if this is greater than other

class java.lang.Math
- static int abs(int x)
- static double abs(double x)
- static double pow(double base, double exponent)
- static double sqrt(double x)
- static double random()   // returns a double in the range [0.0, 1.0)

interface java.util.List<E>
- int size()
- boolean add(E obj)   // appends obj to end of list; returns true
- void add(int index, E obj)   // inserts obj at position index (0 ≤ index ≤ size),
                                        // moving elements at position index and higher
                                        // to the right (adds 1 to their indices) and adjusts size
- E get(int index)
- E set(int index, E obj)   // replaces the element at position index with obj
                                        // returns the element formerly at the specified position
- E remove(int index)   // removes element from position index, moving elements
                                        // at position index + 1 and higher to the left
                                        // (subtracts 1 from their indices) and adjusts size
                                        // returns the element formerly at the specified position

class java.util.ArrayList<E> implements java.util.List<E>

GO ON TO THE NEXT PAGE.

COMPUTER SCIENCE A

SECTION I

Time—1 hour and 30 minutes

Number of Questions—40

Percent of total exam grade—50%

Directions: Determine the answer to each of the following questions or incomplete statements, using the available space for any necessary scratchwork. Then decide which is the best of the choices given and fill in the corresponding oval on the answer sheet. No credit will be given for anything written in the examination booklet. Do not spend too much time on any one problem.

Notes:
- Assume that the classes listed in the Quick Reference have been imported where appropriate.
- Assume that declarations of variables and methods appear within the context of an enclosing class.
- Assume that method calls that are not prefixed with an object or class name and are not shown within a complete class definition appear within the context of an enclosing class.
- Unless otherwise noted in the question, assume that parameters in the method calls are not `null` and that methods are called only when their preconditions are satisfied.

MULTIPLE CHOICE QUESTIONS

USE THIS SPACE FOR SCRATCHWORK

1. Consider the following methods.

```
public void trial()
{
    int a = 10;
        int b = 5;
        doublevalues(a,b);
        System.out.print(b);
    System.out.print(a);
}

public void doublevalues(int c, int d)
{
        c = c * 2;
        d = d * 2;
    System.out.print(c);
    System.out.print(d);
}
```

What is printed as the result of the call `trial()`?

(A) 2010

(B) 2010105

(C) 2010510

(D) 20102010

(E) 20101020

GO ON TO THE NEXT PAGE.

2. Consider the following method.

```
/**
 * Precondition: a > b > 0
 */
public static int mystery(int a, int b)
{
    int d = 0;
    for (int c = a; c > b; c--)
    {
        d=d+c;
    }
    return d;
}
```

What is returned by the call `mystery(x,y)`?

(A) The sum of all the integers greater than y but less than or equal to x
(B) The sum of all the integers greater than or equal to y but less than or equal to x
(C) The sum of all the integers greater than y but less than x
(D) The sum of all the integers greater than y but less than or equal to x
(E) The sum of all the integers less than y but greater than or equal to x

3. Consider the following method.

```
public void mystery (int  n)
{
    int k;
    for (k = 0 ; k < n ; k++)
    {
        mystery(k);
        System.out.print (n) ;
    }
}
```

What value is returned by the call `mystery(3)`?

(A) 0123
(B) 00123
(C) 0010012
(D) 00100123
(E) 001001200100123

4. Consider an array of integers.

| 4 | 10 | 1 | 2 | 6 | 7 | 3 | 5 |

If selection sort is used to order the array from smallest to largest values, which of the following represents a possible state of the array at some point during the selection sort process?

(A)	1	4	10	2	3	6	7	5
(B)	1	2	4	6	10	7	3	5
(C)	1	2	3	10	6	7	4	5
(D)	4	3	1	2	6	7	10	5
(E)	5	3	7	6	2	1	10	4

GO ON TO THE NEXT PAGE.

5. Consider the following code segment:

```
int  k;
int  A[];
A = new int [7];
for (k = 0; k < A.length; k++)
{
    A[k] = A.length - k;
}
for (k = 0; k < A.length - 1; k++)
{
    A[k+1] = A[k];
}
```

What values will A contain after the code segment is executed?

(A) 1   1   2   3   4   5   6
(B) 1   2   3   4   5   6   7
(C) 6   6   5   4   3   2   1
(D) 7   7   6   5   4   3   2
(E) 7   7   7   7   7   7   7

GO ON TO THE NEXT PAGE.

Questions 6–7 refer to the following two classes.

```
public class PostOffice
{
    // constructor initializes boxes
    // to length 100
    public PostOffice( )
    {   /* implementation not shown   */}

    // returns the given p.o. box
    //   0 <= theBox  <  getNumBoxes ()
    public Box getBox (int theBox)
    {   /* implementation not shown   */}
    // returns the number of p.o. boxes
    public int getNumBoxes ()
    {   /* implementation not shown   */}


    // private data members and
    // other methods not shown
}


public class Box
{
    // constructor
    public Box ( )
    {   /* implementation not shown  */}

    // returns the number of this box
    public int getBoxNumber ( )
    {   /* implementation not shown   */}

    // returns the number of pieces
    // of mail in this box
    public int getMailCount ( )
    {   /* implementation not shown  */}
    // returns the given piece of mail
    // 0 <= thePiece < getMailCount ( )
    public Mail getMail (int thePiece)
    {   /* implementation not shown  */}
    // true if the box has been assigned
    // to a customer
    public boolean isAssigned ( )
    {   /* implementation not shown  */}
    // true if the box contains mail
    public boolean hasMail ( )
    {   /* implementation not shown  */}
    // private data members and
    // other methods not shown
}
public class Mail
{
    // private members,  constructors, and
    // other methods not shown
}
```

GO ON TO THE NEXT PAGE.

6. Consider the following code segment:

```
PostOffice p[ ]
p = new PostOffice[10];
```

Assuming that the box has been assigned and that it has at least four pieces of mail waiting in it, what is the correct way of getting the fourth piece of mail from the 57th box of the tenth post office of p?

(A) `Mail m = p[10].getBox(57).getmail(4);`
(B) `Mail m = p[9].getBox(56).getMail (3);`
(C) `Mail m = p.getMail(57).getMail (4) [10];`
(D) `Mail m = getMail(getBox(p[9], 560, 3);`
(E) `Mail m = new Mail(10, 57, 4);`

GO ON TO THE NEXT PAGE.

7. Consider the incomplete function `printEmptyBoxes` given below. `printEmptyBoxes` should print the box numbers of all of the boxes that do not contain mail.

```
public void printEmptyBoxes (PostOffice p [ ])
{
    for (int k = 0; k < p.length - 1 ; k++)
    {
        for (int x = 0; x < p[k].getNumBoxes( ) - 1 ; x++)
        {
            //  missing expression
        }
    }
}
```

Which of the following could be used to replace

```
// missing expression
```

body so that `printBoxesWithoutMail` works as intended?

(A)
```
if (p[k].getBox(x).isAssigned( ) &&
!p[k].getBox(x).hasMail( ) )
{
    System.out.println(P[k].getBox(x).getBoxNumber( )) ;
}
```

(B)
```
if (p[x].getBox(k).isAssigned ( ) &&
!p[x].getBox(k).hasMail( ))
{
  System.out.println(p[x].getBox(k).getBoxNumber( ));
}
```

(C)
```
if (p[k].getBox(x).isAssigned( ) &&
!p[k].getBox(x).hasMail( ))
{
    System.out.println (p[k].getBoxNumber (x));
}
```

(D)
```
if (p[x].getBox(k).isAssigned( ) &&
!p[x].getBox (k).hasMail( ))
{
    System.out.println(p[x].getBoxNumber(k));
 }
```

(E)
```
if (p[x].getBox(k).isAssigned( ) &&
p[x].getBox(k).getMail( )   ==   0)
{
    System.out.println(k);
}
```

GO ON TO THE NEXT PAGE.

8. Assume that a and b are Boolean variables that have been initialized. Consider the following code segment.

```
a = a && b;
b = a || b;
```

Which of the following statements is true?

    I.   The final value of a is the same as the initial value of a.

    II.   The final value of b is the same as the initial value of b.

    III.   The final value of a is the same as the initial value of b.

(A) I only

(B) II only

(C) III only

(D) I and II only

(E) II and III only

9. Consider the following code segment.

```
int x;
x = 53;
if (x > 10)
{
    System.out.print("A") ;
}
if (x > 30)
{
    System.out.print("B") ;
}
else if (x > 40)
{
    System.out.print("C") ;
}
if (x > 50)
{
    System.out.print ("D") ;
}
if (x > 70)
{
    System.out.print ("E") ;
}
```

What is output when the code is executed?

(A) A

(B) D

(C) ABD

(D) ABCD

(E) ABCDE

GO ON TO THE NEXT PAGE.

10. Consider the following code segment:

```
int j;
int k;
for (j = -2; j <= 2; j = j + 2)
{
    for (k = j; k < j + 3; k++)
    {
        System.out.print(k + " " ) ;
    }
}
```

What is the output when the code is executed?

(A) -2 -1   0

(B) -2 -1   0   1   2

(C) 0   1   2   0   1   2   0   1   2

(D) -2   0   2

(E) -2 -1   0   0   1   2   2   3   4

11. Consider the following method.

```
public void mystery (int  count, String s)
{
    if  (count  <=  0)
    {
        return;
    }
    if  (count % 3 == 0)
    {
        System.out.print(s + "--" + s)
    }
    else if (count %  3 == 1)
    {
        System.out.print(s + "-" + s)
    }
    else
    {
        System.out.print (s) ;
    }
    mystery(count - 1, s) ;
}
```

What is output by the call mystery(5, "X");?

(A) XX - XX - - XXX - X

(B) XX - XX - XX - XX

(C) XXX - - XX - X - XX - - XXX

(D) XX - XXX - - XXX - XX

(E) XXXXX

GO ON TO THE NEXT PAGE.

Questions 12–13 refer to the following classes and method descriptions.

Class Table has a method, getPrice, which takes no parameters and returns the price of the table.

Class Chair also has a method, getPrice, which takes no parameters and returns the price of the chair.

Class DiningRoomSet has a constructor which is passed a Table object and an ArrayList of Chair objects. It stores these parameters in its private data fields myTable and myChairs.

Class DiningRoomSet has a method, getPrice, which takes no parameters and returns the price of the dining room set. The price of a dining room set is calculated as the sum of the price of its table and all of its chairs.

12. What is the correct way to define the signature of the constructor for the DiningRoomSet class?

(A) `public void DiningRoomSet (Table t, ArrayList, chairs)`
(B) `public DiningRoomSet (Table t, ArrayList chairs)`
(C) `public void DiningRoomSet (Table t, ArrayList Chair Chairs)`
(D) `public DiningRoomSet (Table t, ArrayList Chair Chairs)`
(E) `public DiningRoomSet (Table t, Chair Chairs)`

13. What is the correct way to implement the getPrice method of the DiningRoomSet class?

(A)
```
public double getPrice(Table t, ArrayList chairs)
{
        return t.getPrice() + chairs.getPrice() ;
}
```
(B)
```
public double getPrice(Table t, ArrayList chairs)
{
        return myTable.getPrice() + myChairs.getPrice();
}
```
(C)
```
public double getPrice()
{
        return myTable.getPrice() + myChairs.getPrice();
}
```
(D)
```
public double getPrice()
{
        double result  = myTable.getPrice();
        for (int k = 0; k < myChairs.size() - 1; k++)
        {
                result += ((Chair)myChairs.get(k)).getPrice();
        }
        return result;
}
```
(E)
```
public double getPrice()
{
        double result = myTable.getPrice() ;
        for (int k = 0; k  <  myChairs.length - 1; k++)
        {
                result += ((Chair)myChairs[k]).getPrice( );
        }
        return result ;
}
```

GO ON TO THE NEXT PAGE.

14. Consider the following output:

```
6   5   4   3   2   1
5   4   3   2   1
4   3   2   1
3   2   1
2   1
1
```

Which of the following code segments produces the above output when executed?

(A)
```
for  (int j = 6;  j  <  0;  j--)
{
    for (int k = j; k > 0 ; k --)
    {
        System.out.print (k  +  "    ") ;
    }
    System.out.println("") ;
}
```

(B)
```
for (int j = 6; j >= 0; j--)
{
    for (int k = j; k >= 0; k--)
    {
        System.out.print(k + " ");
    }
    System.out.println (" ") ;
}
```

(C)
```
for (int j = 0; j < 6; j++)
{
    for (int k = 6 - j; k > 0; k--)
    {
        System.out.print (k + "    ") ;
    }
    system.out.println (" ") ;
}
```

(D)
```
for (int j = 0; j < 6; j++)
{
    for (int k = 7 - j ; k > 0 ; k --)
    {
        System.out.print(k + " ");
    }
    System.out.println (" ") ;
}
```

(E)
```
for (int j = 0; j < 6; j++)
{
    for (int k = 6  -  j ; k >= 0; k--)
    {
        System.out.print(k + " ");
    }
    System.out.println (" ") ;
}
```

GO ON TO THE NEXT PAGE.

15. Consider the following code segment.

```
List<Integer> list = new ArrayList<Integer>();
list.add(new Integer (7));
list.add (new Integer (6));
list.add (1, new Integer (5));
list.add (1, new Integer (4));
list.add (new Integer (3));
list.set (2, new Integer (2));
list.add (1, new Integer (1));
System.out.prinln (list);
```

What is printed as a result of executing this code segment?

(A) [1, 4, 2, 7, 6, 3]
(B) [7, 1, 4, 2, 6, 3]
(C) [7, 2, 5, 4, 3, 1]
(D) [7, 6, 2, 4, 3, 1]
(E) [7, 1, 2]

16. Consider the following declarations.

```
public interface Animal
{
    String makeSound();
    String animalType();
}

    public static class Dog implements Animal
{
    public String makeSound(Animal a)
    {
        // Implementation not shown
    }
}
```

Which of the following methods must be included in the declaration of the Dog class in order for the class to successfully compile?

I. `public String makeSound()`
II. `public String animalType()`
III. `public String animalType(animal b)`

(A) I only
(B) II only
(C) I and II only
(D) II and III only
(E) I, II, and III

GO ON TO THE NEXT PAGE.

17. Consider the following two classes.

```
public static class Fish
{
  public String endoskeleton = "bone";

  public void action()
  {
      System.out.println("splash splash");
  }
}

public static class Shark extends Fish
{
  public void action()
  {
      System.out.println("chomp chomp");
  }

  public String endoskeleton="cartilage";
}
```

Which of the following is the correct output after the following code segment is executed?

```
Fish Bob = new Shark();
System.out.println(Bob.endoskeleton);
Bob.action();
```

(A) bone
    chomp chomp
(B) bone
    splash splash
(C) cartilage
    splash splash
(D) cartilage
    chomp chomp
(E) cartilage
    splash splash
    chomp chomp

GO ON TO THE NEXT PAGE.

Questions 18–19 refer to the following incomplete method.

18. The following insertSort method sorts the values in an integer array, sort, in ascending order.

```
Line 1:    public static void insertSort(int[] sort)
Line 2:        {
Line 3:            for (int index=1;index<sort.length;index++)
Line 4:            {
Line 5:        int temp=sort[index];
Line 6:        while (index > 0 && sort[index-1]>temp)
Line 7:                {
Line 8:            // Missing code
Line 9:                }
Line 10:       sort[index]=temp;
Line 11:           }
Line 12:       }
```

Which of the following can be used to replace "// Missing code" so that the insertSort method will execute properly?

(A) sort[index]=sort[index-1];
    index++;
(B) sort[index-1]=sort[index];
    index--;
(C) sort[index]=sort[index+1];
    index++;
(D) sort[index]=sort[index-1];
    index--;
(E) sort[index]=sort[index+1];
    index--;

19. Assuming that the "// Missing code" is implemented properly, what change can be made to the code in order for the array to be sorted in descending order?

(A) Replace Line 6 with: while (index < 0 && sort[index-1]<temp)
(B) Replace Line 6 with: while (index < 0 && sort[index-1]<temp)
(C) Replace Line 6 with: while (index > 0 && sort[index-1]<temp)
(D) Replace Line 3 with: for (int index=sort.length-1;index>0;index--)
(E) Replace Line 3 with: for (int index=1;index>0;index--)

20. Which of the following arrays would be sorted the slowest using insertion sort?

(A) [3 4 6 2 7 3 9]
(B) [3 2 5 4 6 7 9]
(C) [9 7 6 5 4 3 2]
(D) [2 3 4 5 6 7 9]
(E) [9 3 2 4 5 7 6]

GO ON TO THE NEXT PAGE.

Questions 21–23 refer to the following incomplete class declaration used to represent fractions with integral numerators and denominators.

```java
public class Fraction
{
  private int numerator ;
  private int denominator ;

  public Fraction ( )
  {
      numerator = 0 ;
      denominator = 1 ;
  }

  public Fraction (int n, int d)
  {
      numerator = n;
      denominator = d;
  }

  // postcondition: returns the
  //  numerator
  public int getNumerator ( )
  {   /* implementation not shown */  }

  // postcondition: returns the
  //  denominator
  public int getDenominator ( )
  {   /* implementation not shown*/   }

  // postcondition: returns the greatest
  // common divisor of x and y
  public int gcd (int x, int y)
  {   /* implementation not shown*/   }

  // postcondition: returns the Fraction
  //  that is the result of multiplying
  //  this Fraction and f

  public Fraction multiply (Fraction f)
  {   /* implementation not shown */  }
  // . . . other methods not shown
}
```

GO ON TO THE NEXT PAGE.

21. Consider the method multiply of the Fraction class.

```
// postcondition: returns the Fraction
//    that is the result of multiplying
//    this Fraction and f
public Fraction multiply (Fraction f)
{   /* missing code*/     }
```

Which of the following statements can be used to replace /* missing code */ so that the muliply method is corretly implemented?

```
I.   return Fraction (
        numerator * f.getNumerator ( ) ,
        denominator * f.getDenominator ( ) );
II.  return new Fraction (
        numerator * f.numerator ,
        denominator * f.denominator ( ) );
III. return new Fraction (
        numerator * f.getNumerator ( ) ,
        denominator * f.getDenominator ( ) );
```

(A) I only
(B) II only
(C) III only
(D) I and III
(E) II and III

22. Consider the use of the Fraction class to muliply the fractions $\dfrac{3}{4}$ and $\dfrac{7}{19}$. Consider the following code:

```
Fraction fractionOne;
Fraction fractionTwo;
Fraction answer;
fractionOne = new Fraction (3, 4) ;
fractionTwo = new Fraction (7, 19) ;
/* missing code */
```

Which of the following could be used to replace /* missing code */ so that answer contains the result of muliplying fractionOne by fractionTwo?

(A) `answer = fractionOne * fractionTwo`
(B) `answer = multiply (fractionOne,fractionTwo) ;`
(C) `answer = fractionOne.multiply (fractionTwo) ;`
(D) `answer = new Fraction (fractionOne,fractionTwo) ;`
(E) `answer = (fractionOne .getNumerator ( ) * fractionTwo .getNumerator ( ) ) /`
    `        (fractionOne .getDenominator ( ) * fractionTwo .getDenominator ( ) ) ;`

GO ON TO THE NEXT PAGE.

23. The following incomplete class declaration is intended to extend the `Fraction` class so that fractions can be manipulated in reduced form (lowest terms).

Note that a fraction can be reduced to lowest terms by dividing both the numerator and denominator by the greatest common divisor (gcd) of the numerator and denominator.

```
public class ReducedFraction extends Fraction
{
    private int reducedNumerator ;
    private int reducedDenominator ;
    // . . . constructors and other methods not shown
}
```

Consider the following proposed constructors for the `ReducedFraction` class:

```
I.   public ReducedFraction ( )
     {
       reducedNumerator = 0;
       reducedDenominator = 1;
     }
II.  public reducedFraction (int n, int d)
     {
       numerator = n;
       denominator = d;
       reducedNumerator = n / gcd (n, d);
       reducedDenominator = d / gcd (n, d);
     }
III. public ReducedFraction (int n, int d)
     {
       super (n, d) ;
       reducedNumerator = n / gcd (n, d) ;
       reducedDenominator = d / gcd (n, d) ;
     }
```

Which of these constructor(s) would be legal for the `ReducedFraction` class?

(A) I only
(B) II only
(C) III only
(D) I and III
(E) II and III

GO ON TO THE NEXT PAGE.

24. Consider s1 and s2 defined as follows.

    ```
    String s1 = new String("hello") ;
    String s2 = new String("hello") ;
    ```

    Which of the following is/are correct ways to see if s1 and s2 hold identical strings?

    ```
    I.   if (s1 == s2)
             /* s1 and s2 are identical */
    II.  if (s1 .compareTo (s2) == 0 )
             /* s1 and s2 are identical */
    III. if (s1 .equals (s2) )
             /* s1 and s2 are identical */
    ```

    (A) I only
    (B) III only
    (C) I and III only
    (D) II and III only
    (E) I, II, and III

25. Consider the following variable and method declarations:

    ```
    String s ;
    String t ;
    public void mystery (String a, String b)
    {
        a = a + b ;
        b = b + a ;
    }
    ```

    Assume that s has the value "Elizabeth" and t has the value "Andrew" and mystery (s, t) is called. What are the values of s and t after the call to mystery?

	a	b
(A)	Elizabeth	Andrew
(B)	ElizabethAndrew	AndrewElizabeth
(C)	ElizabethAndrew	AndrewElizabethAndrew
(D)	ElizabethAndrew	ElizabethAndrewAndrew
(E)	ElizabethAndrewElizabeth	AndrewElizabethAndrew

GO ON TO THE NEXT PAGE.

26. Consider the following incomplete and *incorrect* class declaration:

```
public class Point implements Comparable
{
    private int x;
    private int y;
    public boolean compareTo (Point other)
    {
        return (x == other.x &&
                y == other.y);
    }
    // . . . constructors and other methods
    // not shown
}
```

For which of the following reasons is the above class declaration incorrect?

    I.   Objects may not access private data fields of other objects in the same class.

    II.   The `Comparable` interface requires that `compareTo` be passed an `Object` rather than a `Point`.

    III.   The `Comparable` interface requires that `compareTo` return an `int` rather than a `boolean`.

(A) I only

(B) III only

(C) I and III

(D) II and III

(E) I, II, and III

GO ON TO THE NEXT PAGE.

27. Consider the following abstraction of a `for` loop where `<1>`, `<2>`, `<3>`, and `<4>` represent legal code in the indicated locations:

```
for (<1>; <2>; <3>)
{
    <4>
}
```

Which of the following `while` loops has the same functionality as the above `for` loop?

(A)
```
<1> ;
while (<2>)
{
    <3>;
    <4>
}
```

(B)
```
<1> ;
while ( <2>)
{
    <4>
    <3> ;
}
```

(C)
```
<1> ;
    while ( !<2>)
{
    <3> ;
    <4>
}
```

(D)
```
<1> ;
while ( !<2>)
{
    <4>
    <3>;
}
```

(E)
```
<1> ;
<3> ;
while ( <2>)
{
    <4>
    <3> ;
}
```

28. Consider the following expression:

```
a / b + c - d % e * f
```

Which of the expressions given below is equivalent to the one given above?

(A) `( (a / b) + (c - d) ) % (e *f)`
(B) `( ( ( ( a / b) + c) - d) % e) * f`
(C) `( (a / b) + c) - (d % (e * f)`
(D) `(a / ( (b + c) - d)  % e) * f`
(E) `( (a / b) + c) - ( (d % e) * f)`

GO ON TO THE NEXT PAGE.

29. Assume that a program declares and initializes x as follows:

```
String [] x ;
x = new String[10] ;
initialize(x);            // Fills the array x with
                          // valid strings each of
                          // length 5
```

Which of the following code segments correctly traverses the array and prints out the first character of all ten strings followed by the second character of all ten strings, and so on?

```
I. int i;
   int j;
   for (i = 0 ; i < 10 ; i++)
        for (j = 0 ; j < 5 ; j++)
             System.out.print (x[i].substring (j, j+1));
II. int i;
    int j;
    for (i = 0 ; i < 5 ; i++)
       for (j = 0 ; j < 10 ; j++)
            System.out.print (x[j].substring (i, i+1));
III. int i ;
     int j ;
     for (i = 0 ; i < 5 ; i++)
         for (j = 0 ; j < 10 ; j++)
             System.out.print (x[i].substring (j, j+1));
```

(A) I only

(B) II only

(C) I and II

(D) II and III

(E) I, II, and III

30. Consider the following declaration and assignment statements:

```
int a = 7 ;
int b = 4 ;
double c ;
c = a / b ;
```

After the assignment statement is executed, what's the value of c?

(A) 1.0

(B) 1.75

(C) 2.0

(D) An error occurs because c was not initialized.

(E) An error occurs because because a and b are integers and c is a double.

GO ON TO THE NEXT PAGE.

31. Consider the following code segment:

```
int x ;
x = /* initialized to an integer */
if (x % 2 == 0 && x / 3 == 1)
    System.out.print("Yes") ;
```

For what values of x will the word "Yes" be printed when the code segment is executed?

(A) 0

(B) 4

(C) Whenever x is even and x is not divisible by 3

(D) Whenever x is odd and x is divisible by 3

(E) Whenever x is even and x is divisible by 3

32. Consider the following incomplete class definition:

```
public class SomeClass
{
    private String myName ;
    // postcondition: returns myName
    public String getName ( )
    { /* implmentation not shown */ }
    // postcondition: myName == name
    public void setName (String name)
    { /* implmentation not shown */ }
    // . . . constructors, other methods
    // and private data not shown
}
```

Now consider the method swap, not part of the SomeClass class.

```
// precondition: x and y are correctly
// constructed
// postcondition: the names of objects
// x and y are swapped
public void swap (SomeClass x, SomeClass y)
{
    <missing code>
}
```

GO ON TO THE NEXT PAGE.

Which of the following code segments can replace `<missing code>` so that the method swap works as intended?

```
I.   SomeClass temp ;
     temp = x;
     x = y ;
     y = temp ;
II.  String temp ;
     temp = x.myName ;
     x .myName = y .myName
     y .myName = temp ;
III. String temp ;
     temp = x .getName ( ) ;
     x .setName (y .getName ( ) ) ;
     y .setName (temp) ;
```

(A) I only

(B) III only

(C) I and III

(D) II and III

(E) I, II, and III

33. A bookstore wants to store information about the different types of books it sells.

For each book, it wants to keep track of the title of the book, the author of the book, and whether the book is a work of fiction or nonfiction.

If the book is a work of fiction, then the bookstore wants to keep track of whether it is a romance novel, a mystery novel, or science fiction.

If the book is a work of nonfiction, then the bookstore wants to keep track of whether it is a biography, a cookbook, or a self-help book.

Which of the following is the best design?

(A) Use one class, `Book`, which has three data fields: `String title`, `String author`, and `int bookType`.

(B) Use four unrelated classes: Book, Title, Author, and BookType.

(C) Use a class `Book` which has two data fields: `String title`, `String author`, and a subclass: `BookType`.

(D) Use a class `Book` which has two data fields: `String title`, `String author`, and two subclasses: `RomanceNovel`, `Mystery`, `ScienceFiction`, `Biography`, `Cookbook`, and `SelfHelpBook`.

(E) Use a class `Book` which has two data fields: `String title`, `String author`, and two subclasses: `FictionWork` and `NonFictionWork`. The class `FictionWork` has three subclasses, `RomanceNovel`, `Mystery`, and `ScienceFiction`. The class `NonFictionWork` has three subclasses: `Biography`, `Cookbook`, and `SelfHelpBook`.

GO ON TO THE NEXT PAGE.

34. Consider the following code:

```
public int mystery (int x)
{
    if (x == 1)
        return <missing value> ;
    else
        return (2 * mystery (x-1) ) + x ;
}
```

Which of the following can be used to replace <missing value> so that mystery (4) returns 34?

(A) 0
(B) 1
(C) 2
(D) 3
(E) 4

35. Consider the following code segment:

```
int [ ] X;
int [ ] Y;
X = initializeX ( ) ;     // returns a valid
                          // initialized int [ ]
Y = initializeY ( ) ;     // returns a valid
                          // initialized int [ ]
for (int k = 0 ;
    k < X.length && X[k] = = Y[k];
    k++)
{
    /* some code */
}
```

Assuming that after X and Y are initialized, X.length == Y.length, which of the following must be true after executing this code segment?

(A) k < X.length
(B) k < X.length && X[k] == Y[k]
(C) k < X.length && X[k] ! = Y[k]
(D) k >= X.length | | X[k] == Y[k]
(E) k >= X.length | | X[k] ! = Y[k]

36. Which of the following would *not* cause a run-time exception?

(A) Dividing an integer by zero
(B) Using an object that has been declared but not instantiated
(C) Accessing an array element with an array index that is equal to the length of the array
(D) Attempting to cast an object to a subclass of which it is not an instance
(E) Attempting to call a method with the wrong number of arguments

GO ON TO THE NEXT PAGE.

37. Assume that a and b are properly initialized variables of type `Double`.

Which of the following is an equivalent expression to:

```
a.doubleValue ( ) ! = b.doubleValue ( )
```

(A) `a ! = b`

(B) `a.notEquals (b)`

(C) `! (a.doubleValue ( ) .equals(b.doubleValue ( ) ) )`

(D) `! (a.compareTo(b) )`

(E) `a.compareTo(b) ! = 0`

38. Which of the following would be the least effective way of ensuring reliability in a program?

(A) Encapsulating functionality in a class by declaring all data fields to be public

(B) Defining and following preconditions and postconditions for every method

(C) Including assertions at key places in the code

(D) Using descriptive variable names

(E) Indenting code in a consistent and logical manner

39. Consider a dictionary that has 1,000 pages with 50 words on each page.

In order to look up a given target word, a student is considering using one of the following three methods:

Method 1

Use a binary search technique to find the correct page (comparing the target word with the first word on a given page). When the correct page is found, use a sequential search technique to find the target word on the page.

Method 2

Use a sequential search technique to find the correct page (comparing the target word with the first word on a given page). When the correct page is found, use another sequential search technique to find the target word on the page.

Method 3

Use a sequential search technique on all of the words in the dictionary to find the target word.

Which of the following best characterizes the greatest number of words that will be examined using each method?

	Method 1	Method 2	Method 3
(A)	10	50	1,000
(B)	55	500	2,500
(C)	55	525	25,000
(D)	60	1,050	1,050
(E)	60	1,050	50,000

GO ON TO THE NEXT PAGE.

40. Which of the following is *not* a peripheral?

    (A) A color laser printer
    (B) A monitor
    (C) A word processing application
    (D) A mouse
    (E) An external CD-ROM drive

END OF SECTION I

**IF YOU FINISH BEFORE TIME IS CALLED,
YOU MAY CHECK YOUR WORK ON THIS SECTION.**

DO NOT GO ON TO SECTION II UNTIL YOU ARE TOLD TO DO SO.

COMPUTER SCIENCE A

SECTION II

Time—1 hour and 30 minutes

Number of Questions—4

Percent of Total Grade—50%

<u>**Directions:**</u> SHOW ALL YOUR WORK. REMEMBER THAT PROGRAM SEGMENTS ARE TO BE WRITTEN IN JAVA™.

<u>**Notes:**</u>

- Assume that the classes listed in the Java Quick Reference have been imported where appropriate.

- Unless otherwise noted in the question, assume that parameters in method calls are not null and that methods are called only when their preconditions are satisfied.

- In writing solutions for each question, you may use any of the accessible methods that are listed in classes defined in that question. Writing significant amounts of code that can be replaced by a call to one of these methods will not receive full credit.

FREE RESPONSE QUESTIONS

1. In a certain school, students are permitted to enroll in one elective class from a list of electives offered. Because there are a limited number of spaces in each class for students, and because some electives are more popular than others, a lottery system was devised by the school to assign students to electives.

Each student lists three choices for electives. The school orders the students randomly and assigns each student to the first available elective in the student's list of three choices. If none of the three choices is available (because those electives are fully enrolled), the school does not assign the student to an elective.

After the school attempts to assign all of the students to electives, it produces a list of students it was unable to assign.

For example, suppose there are six electives available to students: Astronomy, Ballroom Dance, Basketweaving, Constitutional Law, Marine Biology, and Programming.

The following table shows the name, maximum enrollment, and current enrollment for six electives after 64 students have been successfully assigned to electives:

Elective Name	Maximum Enrollment	Current Enrollment
Astronomy	12	12
Ballroom Dance	20	3
Basketweaving	15	14
Constitutional Law	10	7
Marine Biology	10	10
Programming	30	30

GO ON TO THE NEXT PAGE.

Note that three elctives, Astronomy, Programming, and Marine Biology, are fully enrolled and are no longer options for students.

Now suppose that the following students need to be assigned to electives:

Student	First Choice getChoice (0)	Second Choice getChoice (1)	Third Choice getChoice (2)
Andrew	Programming	Marine Biology	Ballroom Dance
David	Constitutional Law	Basketweaving	Programming
Elizabeth	Marine Biology	Programming	Astronomy
Ethan	Basketweaving	Marine Biology	Astronomy
Katharine	Programming	Basketweaving	Marine Biology

Andrew's first and second choices are fully enrolled, but his third choice has openings. Andrew will be enrolled in Ballroom Dance.

David's first choice has openings. David will be enrolled in Constitutional Law.

All three of Elizabeth's choices are fully enrolled. Elizabeth will remain unassigned to an elective.

Ethan's first choice has one opening left. Ethan will be enrolled in Basketweaving. Note that Basketweaving is now fully enrolled.

All three of Katharine's choices are now fully enrolled. Katharine will remain unassigned to an elective.

In this problem, the school is modeled by the class School. Students and electives are modeled by the classes Student and Elective respectively.

The School class includes the following methods and private data:

- studentList—This ArrayList holds the list of students in the order in which the students should be scheduled.

- electiveList—This ArrayList holds the electives that students may choose.

- getElectiveByName—This method returns the Elective in electiveList with the given name.

- assignElectivesToStudents—This method encapsulates the functionality of assigning students (if possible) their first, second, or third elective choice.

- studentsWithoutElectives—This method returns an ArrayList containing students that have not been assigned an elective.

GO ON TO THE NEXT PAGE.

```
public class School
{
    private ArrayList<Student> studentList;
    // each entry is an instance of a
    // Student representing one student
    // at the school; students are in
    // the order they should be scheduled

    private ArrayList<Elective> electiveList;
    // each entry is an instance of an
    // Elective representing one elective
    // offered at the school

    // precondition: name is the name of an
    //     Elective in electiveList
    // postcondition: returns the Elective
    //     in electiveList with the given
    //     name
    private Elective getElectiveByName (String name)
    { /* to be implemented in part (a) */ }
        // postcondition: returns the size
    // of electiveList
    private int getElectiveListSize()
{

    return electiveList.size();

}
    private int getStudentListSize()
{

    return studentList.size();

}

    // postcondition: All Students in
    //     studentList have been either
    //     assigned their first available
    //     elective choice or not assigned;
    //     All Electives in electiveList have
    //     been updated appropriately as
    //     Students are assigned to them
    public void assignElectivesToStudents ( )
    { /* to be implemented in part (b) */ }

    // postcondition: returns a list of
    //     those Students who have not been
    //     assigned an Elective
    public ArrayList<Student>
        studentsWithoutElectives ( )
    { /* to be implemented in part (c) */}

    // ... constructors, other methods,
    //     and other private data not shown
}
```

GO ON TO THE NEXT PAGE.

The Student class includes the following methods and private data:

- getChoice—This method returns the name of the given elective choice of the student. The first elective choice has index 0, the second has index 1, and the third has index 2.

- hasElective—This method returns true if the student has been assigned an elective; it returns false otherwise.

- assignElective—This method assigns the given elective to this student.

```
public class Student
{
    // precondition: 0 <= index < 3
    // postcondition: returns the name
    //     of the given elective choice
    public String getChoice (int index)
    { /* code not shown */}

    // postcondition: returns true if
    //     an Elective has been assigned
    //     to this Student
    public boolean hasElective ( )
    { /* code not shown */ }

    // precondition: e is not null
    // postcondition: e has been assigned
    //     to this Student; e has not been
    //     modified
    public void assignElective (Elective e)
    { /* code not shown */ }

    // ... constructors, other methods,
    // and other private data not shown
}
```

The Elective class includes the following methods:

- getName—This method returns the name of this elective.

- getMaxClassSize—This method returns the maximum number of students that can be assigned to this elective.

- getClassSize—This method returns the number of students that have been assigned to this elective.

- addStudent—This method assigns the given student to this elective.

GO ON TO THE NEXT PAGE.

```
public class Elective
{
    // postcondition: returns the name
    //     of this Elective
    public String getName ( )
    { /* code not shown */ }

    // postcondition: returns the
    //     maximum number of Students
    //     that can be added to this
    //     Elective
    public int getMaxClassSize ( )
    { /* code not shown */ }

    // postcondition: returns the
    //     number of Students that have
    //     been added to this Elective;
    //     0 < = getClassSize ( ) < =
    //     getMaxClassSize ( )
    public int getClassSize ( )
    { /* code not shown */ }

    // precondition: getClassSize ( ) <
    //     getMaxClassSize ( ); s is not null
    // postcondition: s has been added to
    //     this Elective; getClassSize ( ) has
    //     been increased by 1
    public void addStudent (Student s)
    { /* code not shown */ }

    // ... constructors, other methods,
    //     and other private data not shown
}
```

(a) Write the `School` method `getElectiveByName`. Method `getElectiveByName` should return the `Elective` in `electiveList` that has the given name.

Complete method `getElectiveByName` below.

```
    // precondition: name is the name of an
    //         Elective in electiveList
    // postcondition: returns the Elective in
    //         electiveList with the given name
    private Elective getElectiveByName (String name)
```

GO ON TO THE NEXT PAGE.

(b) Write the `School` method `assignElectivesToStudents`. Method `assignElectivesToStudents` should assign electives to students as described at the beginning of this question.

In writing method `assignElectivesToStudents` you may use the `private` helper method `getElectiveBy-Name` specified in part (a). Assume that `getElectiveByName` works as specified, regardless of what you wrote in part (a). Solutions that reimplement functionality provided by this method, rather than invoking itt, will not receive full credit.

Complete method `assignElectivesToStudents` below

```
// postcondition: All Students in
//        studentList have been either
//        assigned their first available
//        elective choice or not assigned;
//        All electives in electiveList have
//        been updated appropriately as
//        Students are assigned to them
public void assignElectivesToStudents ( )
```

GO ON TO THE NEXT PAGE.

(c) Write the `School` method `studentsWithoutElectives`. Method `studentsWithoutElectives` should return `ArrayList` of all Students in `studentList` who do not have an `Elective` assigned to them.

Complete method `studentsWithoutElectives` below

```
// postcondition: returns a list of those
//        Students who have not been assigned
//        an Elective
public ArrayList studentsWithoutElectives ( )
```

GO ON TO THE NEXT PAGE.

2. Consider a deck of n cards where n is even and each card is uniquely labeled from 1 to n.

A *shuffle* is performed when the deck is divided into two stacks and the stacks are interlaced so that a new stack is formed by alternately taking cards from each stack.

For instance, a deck of ten cards is in order when the card labeled 0 is on the top of the deck and the card labeled 9 is on the bottom of the deck.

Dividing the deck in half produces two stacks of cards – one stack with cards 0 through 4, the other with cards 5 through 9. Interlacing the stacks produces a deck in the following order:

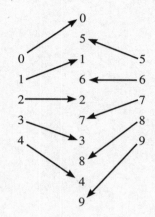

The number of times needed to shuffle the deck until it returns to its original order is called the *reorder count*. Note that the reorder count for a deck of ten cards is six:

Shuffle number

Original	1	2	3	4	5	6
0	0	0	0	0	0	0
1	5	7	8	4	2	1
2	1	5	7	8	4	2
3	6	3	6	3	6	3
4	2	1	5	7	8	4
5	7	8	4	2	1	5
6	3	6	3	6	3	6
7	8	4	2	1	5	7
8	4	2	1	5	7	8
9	9	9	9	9	9	9

GO ON TO THE NEXT PAGE.

A deck is modeled by the following incomplete declaration of the **Deck** class:

```
public class Deck
{
    private int [ ] cards;

    public Deck (int numCards)
    { /* code not shown */ }

    public boolean inOrder ( )
    { /* to be implemented in part (a) */ }

    public void shuffle ( )
    { /* to be implemented in part (b) */ }

    public int reorderingCount ( )
    { /* to be implemented in part (c) */ }
}
```

(a) Write the Deck method inOrder. Method inOrder should return true if the cards in the deck are in numerical order from 0 to cards.length – 1 and should return false otherwise. Cards are in numerical order if cards [k] = = k for all 0 < = k < cards.length.

Complete method inOrder below.

```
// precondition: For all k such that
//      0 < = k < cards.length,
//      0 < = cards [k] < cards.length and
//      each cards [k] is unique
// postcondition: returns true if
//      cards [k] = = k for all
//      0 < = k < cards.length; returns
//      false otherwise
public boolean inOrder ( )
```

GO ON TO THE NEXT PAGE.

(b) Write the Deck method shuffle. Method shuffle should divide the deck into two equal stacks and interlace them evenly as described at the beginning of this question.

Complete method shuffle below.

```
// postcondition: the deck is shuffled by
//        dividing the deck into two equal stacks
//        that are evenly interlaced
public void shuffle ( )
```

GO ON TO THE NEXT PAGE.

(c) Write the Deck method reorderCount. Method reorderCount should return the number of shuffles necessary to return the deck to its original order.

In writing method reorderCount you may use the methods inOrder and shuffle as specified in parts (a) and (b). Assume that inOrder and shuffle work as specified, regardless of what you wrote in parts (a) and (b). Solutions that reimplement functionality provided by these methods, rather than invoking them, will not receive full credit.

Complete method reorderCount below.

```
// postcondition: returns the number of
//        shuffles necessary to return the cards
//        in the deck to their original numerical
//        order such that inOrder ( ) = = true; the
//        cards in the deck are in their original
//        numerical order
public int reorderCount ( )
```

GO ON TO THE NEXT PAGE.

3. Consider the design of an electronic cookbook modeled with the following class declarations:

```
public class Cookbook
{
    private ArrayList recipeList;
    // each entry is an instance of a
    // Recipe representing one recipe
    // in the cookbook
    // precondition: numPeople > 0
    // postcondition: All recipes in
    //     recipeList have been converted to
    //     serve numPeople number of people

    public void standardize (int numPeople)
    { /* code not shown */ }

    // ... constructors, other methods,
    //     and other private data not shown
}


public class Ingredient
{
    private String name;
    // the name of this ingredient

    private double amount;
    // the amount of this ingredient needed
    // in the recipe
    // postcondition: returns the amount of
    //     this ingredient needed in the
    //     recipe

    public double getAmount ( )
    { /* code not shown */ }
    // precondition: amt > 0.0
    // postcondition: amount has been set
    //     to amt

    public void setAmount (double amt)
    { /* code not shown */ }
    // precondition: newNumber > 0
    // postcondition: numberServed has
    // been set to newNumber

    public void setNumberServed(int newNumber)
    { /* code not shown */ }
    // ... constructors and other methods
    //     not shown
}
```

GO ON TO THE NEXT PAGE.

(a) A recipe in the cookbook is modeled by the class Recipe with the following data and operations:

Data

- return the list of ingredients
- the name of the recipe
- the list of ingredients used in the recipe
- the description of the preparation process for the recipe
- the number of people served by the recipe

Operations

- create a recipe with a given name and number of people served
- add an ingredient to the recipe
- set the description of the preparation process for the recipe
- return the name of the recipe
- return the number of people served by the recipe
- scale the recipe to serve a given new number of people by changing the amount of each ingredient appropriately

Write the definition of the class Recipe, showing the appropriate data definitions and constructor and method signatures. You should *not* write the implementations of the constructor or methods for the Recipe class.

(b) Using the signature you wrote in part (a), write the implementation for the method that scales the recipe to serve a given new number of people.

In writing this method, you may call any of the methods in the Recipe class (as you defined it in part (a)) or in the Ingredient class. Assume that these methods work as specified.

(c) Write the Cookbook method standardize as described at the beginning of the question.

In writing this method, you may call any of the methods in the Recipe class (as you defined it in part (a)). Assume that these methods work as specified.

Complete method standardize below.

```
// precondition: numPeople > 0
// postcondition: All recipes in
//        recipeList have been scaled to
//        serve numPeople number of people
public void standardize (int numPeople)
```

GO ON TO THE NEXT PAGE.

4. Consider a school that contains x number of students that all start their first period class in one of n classrooms. This scenario can be represented using three classes. The School class contains an array of all the Classrooms in the school. The Classroom class has fields for the teacher in charge of the room teacherName and an array of all the Students in the classroom Students. The Student class has a field for the name of the student studentName and the ID number of the student studentID.

The School class contains a method findStudent that takes a teacher's name and a student ID as arguments and returns the name of the student. The method utilizes a sequential search algorithm to find the correct classroom and a binary search algorithm to find the correct student. If the student is not found in the school, the method returns "Student Not Found."

Write the complete School, Classroom, and Student classes, including any instance variables, constructors, and necessary methods. You may assume that the student ID numbers in each classroom are sorted in ascending order.

STOP

END OF EXAM

Practice Test 1:
Answers and
Explanations

PRACTICE TEST 1 ANSWER KEY

1. C
2. A
3. D
4. C
5. E
6. B
7. A
8. B
9. C
10. E
11. A
12. B
13. D
14. C
15. B
16. C
17. A
18. D
19. C
20. C

21. E
22. C
23. D
24. D
25. A
26. E
27. B
28. E
29. B
30. A
31. B
32. B
33. E
34. C
35. E
36. E
37. E
38. A
39. E
40. C

PRACTICE TEST 1 EXPLANATIONS

Section I: Multiple Choice

1. **C** This question tests how well you understand assigning values to variables and following the steps of the code.

    When `trial()` is called, a is assigned to the integer value of 10 and b is assigned to the integer value of 5. Next `doublevalues()` is called with a and b as inputs c and d. The method `doublevalues()` multiplies the input values c and d by 2 and prints them out, printing "2010." While c and d have been reassigned new values, the values of a and b are unchanged. After the `doublevalues()` method is completed, the `trial()` method then prints the values of b and then a, printing "510." Combined together, what is printed from calling `trial()` is "2010510."

2. **A** The method `mystery(int a, int b)` takes as input integers a and b with the precondition that a > b > 0. In the `for` loop, the value of a is incrementally decreased until the value is no longer greater than b. Each value that is greater than b is summed. The returned value is then the sum of all the integers greater than b but less than or equal to a. With the call `mystery(x,y)`, this translates as the sum of all the integers greater than y but less than or equal to x.

3. **D** In questions involving recursion, it is often best to start with either the base case or the smallest value used as an argument to the recursive function.

    In this problem, the function mystery is called with values 0, 1, 2, and 3.

    `mystery(0)` does not execute the recursive call in the for loop and does not print anything.

    `mystery(1)` calls `mystery(0)` and then prints the value 0. Since `mystery(0)` does not print anything, `mystery(1)` prints 0.

    `mystery(2)` calls `mystery(0)`, then prints the value 0, then calls `mystery(1)`, and then prints the value 1. Using the output from `mystery(0)` and `mystery(1)` as calculated above, `mystery(2)` prints 001.

    Finally, `mystery(3)` calls `mystery(0)`, then prints the value 0, then calls `mystery(1)`, then prints the value 1, then calls `mystery(2)`, and then prints 2 to result in 0010012.

In other words, the calling sequence looks like this

Function Call   Prints

```
mystery(3)
    mystery(0)
            System.out.print(0)                                      0
    mystery(1)
        mystery(0)
                System.out.print(0)                                  0
        System.out.print(1)                                          1
    mystery(2)
        mystery(0)
                System.out.print(0)                                  0
        mystery(1)
            mystery(0)
                    System.out.print(0)                              0
            System.out.print(1)                                      1
        System.out.print(2)                                          2
```

4. **C** Selection sort walks through the array to find the smallest element in the part of the array not yet sorted. It then swaps that smallest element with the first unsorted element.

Start with the original array of values.

4   10   1   2   6   7   3   5

The smallest element is 1. We swap that with the first unsorted element, 4. The array now looks like this.

1   10   4   2   6   7   3   5

The smallest element in the unsorted part of the array (from 10 to 5) is 2. We swap that with the first unsorted element, 10.

1   2   4   10   6   7   3   5

Continuing this process, the smallest element in the unsorted part of the array (from 4 to 5) is 3. We swap that with the first unsorted element, 4.

1   2   3   10   6   7   4   5

At this point, we match answer (C) and are finished.

For good measure, we'll complete the moves for selection sort, giving us

1	2	3	4	6	7	10	5
1	2	3	4	5	7	10	6
1	2	3	4	5	6	10	7
1	2	3	4	5	6	7	10

5. **E** The array, A, has seven elements with indices from 0 to 6. The first for loop sets each element in the array to the length of the array, 7, minus the index value:

7	6	5	4	3	2	1

The second for loop puts the value of the kth element of the array into the $(k + 1)^{st}$ element. Be careful! A quick glance might lead you to believe that each value is shifted in the array one spot to the right giving an answer of (D).

However, a step-by-step analysis demonstrates that the first value in the array is copied into every array element.

K	Assignment	A[]						
0	A[1] = A[0]	7	7	5	4	3	2	1
1	A[2] = A[1]	7	7	7	4	3	2	1
2	A[3] = A[2]	7	7	7	7	3	2	1
3	A[4] = A[3]	7	7	7	7	7	2	1
4	A[5] = A[4]	7	7	7	7	7	7	1
5	A[6] = A[5]	7	7	7	7	7	7	7

6. **B** Choices (C), (D), and (E) are syntactically invalid according to the given class definitions.

In (C), p is used as a PostOffice object rather than an array of PostOffice objects.

Choice (D) treats getMail and getBox as static methods without invoking them from an object.

Choice (E) creates a new Mail object attempting to use a Mail constructor. Even if such a constructor were available, there would be no way for the constructor to know about p, the array of PostOffices.

Choices (A) and (B) differ only in the indices of the array and methods. There are two clues in the question that indicate that (B) is the correct answer.

First, p is declared as an array of ten PostOffices. This means that p[10] would raise an Array-ListOutOfBoundsException. Remember that p[9] actually refers to the tenth post office.

Second, the comments in the class definitions for the `getBox` and `getMail` methods indicate that the parameter they take is zero-based. Therefore, they should be passed an integer one less than the number of the box or piece of mail needed.

7. **A**   In the method `printEmptyBoxes`, the loop variable `k` refers to the index of the post office and the loop variable `x` refers to the index of the box within the post office.

Choice (A) is correct. It checks to see if the box is assigned and if it does not have mail using the appropriate methods of the `Box` class. It then prints out the box number of the box.

Choice (B) is similar to (A) but incorrectly interchanges `x` and `k`.

Choice (C) attempts to print the box number of a post office by omitting the call to the method `getBox`.

Choice (D) is similar to (C) but interchanges `x` and `k`.

Choice (E) prints the index of the post office rather than the index of the box.

8. **B**   There are four possibilities for the values of `a` and `b`. Either both `a` and `b` are true, both `a` and `b` are false, `a` is true and `b` is false, or `a` is false and `b` is true.

Analyzing the possibilities in a table, we see that in all four cases, the final value of `b` is the same as the initial value of `b`.

a (initial value)	b (initial value)	a = a && b (final value)	b = a || b (final value)
true	true	true	true
false	false	false	false
true	false	false	false
false	true	false	true

Remember when calculating `b = a || b` that `a` has already been modified. Therefore, use the final, rather than the initial value of `a` when calculating the final value of `b`.

9. **C** The best way to solve this problem is to look at each if statement individually.

```
int x;
x = 53;
if (x   >   10)
{
    System.out.print("A") ;
} // Because the value of x is 53, it is greater than 10 and the letter
"A" is printed.
if (x   >   30)
{
    System.out.print("B") ;
} // Again, the value of x is greater than 30, so the letter "B" is
printed. Note that the second conditional (if x > 40) is not tested
because it is part of the else clause.
else   if   (x   >   40)
{
    System.out.print("C") ;
}
if (x   >   50)
{
    System.out.print ("D") ;
} // The letter "D" is printed because the value of x is also greater than
50.
if (x > 70)
{
    System.out.print ("E") ;
} //
```

However, the value of x is not greater than 70, so the letter "E" is not printed.

10. **E** This problem tests your ability to work with nested for loops. Although it appears complicated at first glance, it can easily be solved by systematically walking through the code.

Be sure to write the values of the variables j and k down on paper; don't try to keep track of j and k in your head. Use the empty space in the question booklet for this purpose.

Code	j	k	Output
Initialize j to the value −2.	−2		
Test the condition: j <= 2? Yes.	−2		
Initialize k to the value that j has.	−2	−2	
Test the condition: k < j + 3? Yes.	−2	−2	
Output k.	−2	−2	−2
Update k: k++	−2	−1	−2
Test the condition: k < j + 3? Yes.	−2	−1	−2
Output k.	−2	−1	−2 −1
Update k: k++	−2	0	−2 −1
Test the condition: k < j + 3? Yes.	−2	0	−2 −1
Output k.	−2	0	−2 −1 0
Update k: k++	−2	1	−2 −1 0

Test the condition: `k < j + 3`? No.	−2	1	−2 −1 0
Update `j`: `j = j + 2`	0	1	−2 −1 0
Test the condition: `j <= 2`. Yes	0	1	−2 −1 0
Initialize `k` to the value that `j` has.	0	0	−2 −1 0
Test the condition: `k < j + 3`? Yes.	0	0	−2 −1 0
Output `k`.	0	0	−2 −1 0 0

At this point we can stop because (E) is the only choice that starts −2 −1 0 0. However, repeating this process will result in the correct output of −2 −1 0 0 1 2 2 3 4.

11. **A** To solve this problem, first note that count % 3 is equal to the remainder when count is divided by 3.

Because 5 % 3 = 2, calling mystery(5, "X") will print X, call mystery(4, "X"), and return.

Because 4 % 3 = 1, calling mystery(4, "X") will print X-X, call mystery(3, "X"), and return. At this point, (C) and (E) have been eliminated.

Because 3 % 3 = 0, calling mystery(3, "X") will print X- - X, call mystery(2, "X"), and return. Note that you can stop at this point because (B) and (D) have also been eliminated from consideration.

To continue for the sake of completeness, because 2 % 3 = 2, calling mystery(2, "X") will print X, call mystery(1, "X"), and return.

Because 1 % 3 = 1, calling mystery(1, "X") will print X-X, call mystery(0, "X"), and return.

Finally, calling mystery(0, "X") will simply return because count is less than or equal to zero.

Putting it all together, mystery(5, "X") prints

XX-XX- -XXX-X

12. **B** The only information that we need to solve this problem is the first sentence in the description of the constructor.

Class `DiningroomSet` has a constructor, which is passed a Table object and an `ArrayList` of Chair objects.

Because we are writing a constructor, we can immediately eliminate (A) and (C), which are void methods. Constructors never return anything.

Choice (E) is incorrect because the constructor is passed a Table object and a Chair object; not a Table object and an `ArrayList` of Chair objects.

Choice (C) is incorrect because the second parameter has two types associated with it. It should have only one type: `ArrayList`.

Choice (B) is correct.

13. **D** The best way to solve this problem is to eliminate choices.

Choices (A) and (B) are incorrect because the class description states that the `getPrice` method of the `DiningRoomSet` class does not take any parameters.

Choice (C) can be eliminated because the private data field `myChairs` is not a Chair; it is an `ArrayList`. Therefore, it does not have a `getPrice` method.

This leaves (D) and (E). You need to know that `ArrayLists` are accessed using the get method while arrays are accessed using the [] notation.

`MyChairs` is an `ArrayList`, so the correct answer is (D).

14. **C** To solve this type of problem, use information about the output and the loops to eliminate incorrect choices. Then, if necessary, work through the code for any remaining choices to determine the correction answer.

There are six lines of output. By examining the outer loop of each of the choices, we can eliminate (B) because it will traverse the loop seven times, and during each traversal at least one number will be printed.

We can also eliminate (A) because the outer loop will never be executed. The initial value of j is 6, but the condition $j < 0$ causes the loop to terminate immediately.

Turning our attention to the inner loop, we can eliminate (D) because the first time through the loop, a 7 will be printed—clearly not the correct output.

Finally, we can eliminate (E) because the condition of the inner loop, $k >= 0$ will cause a 0 to be printed at the end of each line.

This leaves (C) which is indeed the correct answer.

15. **B**   This problem tests your knowledge of the methods of the ArrayList class.

The following table shows the contents of list after each line of code.

Code	Contents of list	Explanation
`list = new ArrayList();`	[]	A newly created ArrayList is empty.
`list.add(new Integer(7));`	[7]	Adds 7 to the end of list.
`list.add(new Integer(6));`	[7, 6]	Adds 6 to the end of list.
`list.add(1, new Integer(5));`	[7, 5, 6]	Inserts 5 into list as position 1 shifting elements to the right as necessary.
`list.add(1, new Integer(4));`	[7, 4, 5, 6]	Inserts 4 into list at position 1 shifting elements to the right as necessary.
`list.add(new Integer(3));`	[7, 4, 5, 6, 3]	Adds 3 to the end of list.
`list.set(2, new Integer(2);`	[7, 4, 2, 6, 3]	Replaces the number at position 2 in list with 2.
`list.add(1, new Integer(1));`	[7, 1, 4, 2, 6, 3]	Inserts 1 into list at position 1 shifting elements to the right as necessary.

16. **C**   Because the Dog class implements the interface Animal, all methods defined in the interface Animal must appear in the Dog class.

I. `public String makeSound()`

While the Dog class contains the method "public String makeSound(animal a)," this method does not match the one defined in the interface. As a result, the Dog class must include this method.

II. `public String animalType()`

This method is defined in the animal interaface so the Dog class must include this method.

III. `public String animalType(animal b)`

This method is not defined in the animal interaface so the Dog class does not have to include this method.

17. **A**   This question is testing your understanding of static and dynamic types.

`Fish Bob = new Shark();`

This line creates the Bob variable with the static type of Fish and the dynamic type of Shark.

`System.out.println(Bob.endoskeleton);`

This line prints the endoskeleton field of the variable Bob. When looking up a field, the static type is used so "bone" is printed.

```
Bob.action();
```

This line executes the method action(). When looking up a method, the dynamic type is used so "chomp chomp" is printed.

18. **D**   The insertion sort algorithm creates a sorted array by sorting elements one at a time.

The for loop of the code shows that the elements are being sorted from left to right. To determine the position of the new element to be sorted, the value of the new element must be compared with the values of the sorted elements from right to left. This requires "index--" in the while loop, not "index++." Choices (A) and (C) are wrong.

In order to place the new element to be sorted in its correct position, any sorted elements larger than the new element must be shifted to the right. This requires "sort[index]=sort[index-1]." Choices (B) and (E) are wrong.

19. **C**   In order for the array to be sorted in descending order, you will need to make a change. Plug each answer choice into the array to see which is correct.

In (A), as the index will never be less than 0, the contents of the while loop will never be executed.

In (B), as the index will never be less than 0, the contents of the while loop will never be executed.

In (C), this is the correct answer as it changes the condition of finding the position of the new element from being less than the compared element to greater.

In (D), altering the for loop this way would lead to the elements being sorted from right to left but still in ascending order.

In (E), setting index to sort.length would lead to an Array Index out of Bounds Exception as the indices or arrays start with 0 and end at length-1.

20. **C**   The rate at which insertion sort runs depends on the number of comparisons that are made. The number of comparisons is minimized with an array with elements that are already sorted in ascending order and maximized with an array with elements that are sorted in descending order. Choice (C), this array is sorted in reverse order and will require the most comparisons to sort, and will taken the longest to sort.

21. **E**   Although all three responses look very similar, statement I does not actually construct a new Fraction because it is missing the keyword new.

Note that because f is also a Fraction object, the current Fraction object can also access f's private data. Contrast this with the behavior of derived objects in question 23.

22. **C** Choice (C) correctly multiplies FractionOne by FractionTwo and returns the result as a Fraction. Furthermore, it is the only code that compiles!

Choice (A) is incorrect because the multiplication operator, *, is not defined to work on Fraction objects.

Choice (B) is incorrect because the multiply method only takes on parameter and it is not correctly invoked by a Fraction object.

Choice (D) attempts to create a new Fraction object but incorrectly constructs it by passing two Fraction objects rather than two integers.

Finally, while (E) calculates the value of the result of the multiplication, it incorrectly assigns that value to a Fraction object rather than an integer or double variable.

23. **D** Statement II is illegal because derived classes may not access the private data of their super classes. In other words, the constructor for a ReducedFraction may not directly access numerator and denominator in the Fraction class.

Statement I is legal. This default constructor of the ReductionFraction class will automatically call the default constructor of the Fraction class and the private data of both classes will beset appropriately.

Statement III is also legal. The call `super(n, d)` invokes the second constructor of the Fraction class which set the private data of the Fraction class appropriately. The private data of the Reduced-Fraction class is then set explicitly in the ReducedFraction constructor.

Note that if the call `super(n, d)` were not present, statement III would still be legal. However, it would create a logical error in the code as the default constructor of the Fraction class would be invoked and the private data of the Fraction class would not be set appropriately.

24. **D** Statement I is incorrect. "==" checks object references as opposed to their contents. This is an important distinction as two different objects may hold the same data.

Statement II is correct. The compareTo method of the String class returns 0 if the two String objects hold the same strings.

Statement III is also correct. The equals method of the String class returns true if the two String objects hold the same strings.

25. **A** The values of s and t are not changed in Java, all parameters to methods are passed by value and after a method returns to its caller, the value of the caller's parameters are not modified.

Contrast this with question 32, in which the private data of objects is modified by a function even though the objects themselves are not changed.

26. **E** Statement I, II, and III are correct. The proper method to parametrize Comparable is:

```
public class Point implements Comparable<Point>
```

The signature for the `compareTo` method of the Comparable interface is

Public int `compareTo`(Object other)

It requires that compareTo be passed an Object and return an int.

Statement III is also correct. The equals method of the String class returns true if the two String objects hold the same strings.

27. **B** An example will help clarify this question.

Consider the following for loop:

```
for (int k = 0; k < 5; k++)
{
  Systemout.printIn(k);
}
This prints out the integers 0 to 4; one number per line.
It is equivalent to the while loop.
int k = 0;
while (k , 5)
{
  System.out.printIn(k);
  k++;
}
```

Matching "`int k = 0`" to <1>; "`k < 5`" to <2>; "`k++`" to <3> and "`System.out.printIn(k);`" to <4>, we can see that (B) is correct.

28. **E** This question tests your knowledge of operator precedence.

In Java, multiplication, division, and modulus are performed before addition and subtraction. If more than one operator in an expression has the same precedence, the operations are performed left-to-right.

Parenthesizing the expression one step at a time

```
    a / b + c - d % e * f
→   (a / b) + c - d % e * f

→   (a / b) + c - (d % e) * f

→   (a / b) + c - ((d % e) * f)

→   ((a / b) + c) - ((d % e) * f)
```

29. **B** Only statement II correctly prints out the first character of all ten strings followed by the second character of all ten strings, and so on.

Statement I prints all of the characters of the first string followed by all of the characters of the second string, and so on.

Statement III attempts to print the first 10 characters of the first five strings but throws a `String-IndexOutOfBoundsException`.

30. **A** It is perfectly legal to assign a value of type int to a variable of type double in an expression. However, certain rules apply when evaluating the expression.

In the expression

```
C = a / b;
```

a and b are both integers. Therefore, the / operator represents integer division. The result of the division is truncated by discarding the fractional component.

In this example, 7 / 4 has the value 1—the result of truncating 1.75.

When assigning an integer to a variable of type double, the integer value is converted to its equivalent double value.

Note that the variable c is, in fact, initialized. Specifically, it is initialized to the value a / b.

31. **B** For the code to print the word "Yes" two conditions must be true.

The remainder must be zero when x is divided by 2. In other words, x must be even.

The value after truncating the result when x is divided by 3 must be 1. In other words, $1 \leq x / 3 < 2$.

The second condition is more narrow than the first. The only integers that fulfill the second condition are 3, 4, and 5.

Of those, only 4 is even and therefore also fulfills the first condition.

32. **B** Statement I is incorrect because all parameters in Java are passed by value. After a method returns to its caller, the value of the caller's parameters are not modified. The strings will not be swapped.

Statement II is incorrect because myName is a private data field of the SomeClass class and may not be accessed by the swap method. Note that the question specifically states that the swap method is not a method of the SomeClass class. Be sure to watch for statements that narrow the answer possibilities.

Statement III correctly swaps the names of the objects.

Contrast this with question 25, which also concerns parameter passing.

33. **E** The way to approach this type of design problem is to look for HAS-A and IS-A relationships among the distinct pieces of data.

A book HAS-A title and author. The title and author should be data fields of the Book class, either as Strings or as their own unrelated classes.

This information is not enough to answer the question though.

Looking for the IS-A relationships, a mystery IS-A work of fiction which IS-A book. Therefore, it makes good design sense for these three items to be separate classes. Specifically, Mystery should be a subclass of FictionWork, which should be a subclass of Book.

Similarly, RomanceNovel and ScienceFiction should be subclasses of FictionWork and Biography, Cookbook, and SelfHelpBook should be subclasses of NonFictionWork, which should be a subclass of Book.

Only (E) meets of these design criteria.

34. **C** In order to solve this recursive problem, work backward from the base case to the known value of mystery(4).

Let y represent the <missing value>. Note that mystery(1) = y.

Now calculate mystery(2), mystery(3), and mystery(4) in terms of y.

```
mystery(2)   = 2 * mystery(1) + 2
             = 2 * y + 2
mystery(3)   = 2 * mystery(2) + 3
             = 2 * (2 * y + 2) + 3
             = 4 * y + 4 + 3
             = 4 * y + 7
mystery(4)   = 2 * mystery(3) + 4
             = 2 * (4 * y + 7) + 4
             = 8 * y + 14 + 4
             = 8 * y + 18
```

Because mystery(4) also equals 34, set 8 * y + 18 = 34 and solve for y.

```
8 * y + 18 = 34
8 * y = 16
y = 2
```

35. **E** The for loop terminates when the condition is no longer true. This can happen either because k is no longer less than X.length or because X[k] odes not equal Y[k]. Choice (E) states this formally.

Another way to approach the problem is to use DeMorgan's law to negate the condition in the for loop.

Recall that DeMorgan's law states that

```
! (P && q) is equivalent to !p || !q
```

Negating the condition in the for loop gives us

```
! (k < X.length && X[k] == Y[k])
=>!(k < X.length) || !(X[k] == Y[k])
```
=>k >= X.length || X[k] != Y[k]

This method also gives (E) as the correct answer.

36. **E** Choices (A), (B), (C), and (D) are examples of an ArithmeticException, a `IllegalArgumentException`, an `ArrayIndexOutOfBoundsException`, and a `ClassCastException`.

Be careful! While (E) may appear to be an example of an `IllegalArgumentException`, it is actually an example of an error that is caught at compile time rather than at runtime.

An `IllegalArgumentException` occurs when a method is called with an argument that is either illegal or inappropriate—for instance, passing –1 to a method that expects to be passed only positive integers.

37. **E** First note that a and b are of type Double, not of type double. This distinction is important. The type double is a primitive type; the type Double is a subclass of the Object class that implements the Comparable interface. A Double is an object wrapper for a double value.

Choice (A) is incorrect. It compares a and b directly rather than the double values inside the objects. Even if a and b held the same value, they might be different objects.

Choice (B) is incorrect. The Double class does not have a notEquals method.

Choice (C) is incorrect. a.doubleValue() returns a double. Because double is a primitive type, it does not have any methods. Had this choice been

```
!(a.equals(b))
```
It would have been correct.

The expression a.compareTo(b) returns a value less than zero if a.doubleValue() is less than b.doubleValue(); a value equal to zero if a.doubleValue() is equal to b.doubleValue(), and a value greater than zero if a.doubleValue() is greater than b.doubleValue().

Choice (D) is incorrect because the compareTo method does not return a Boolean.

Choice (E) is correct.

38. **A**   While "encapsulating functionality in a class" sounds like (and is) a good thing, "declaring all data fields to be public" is the exact opposite of good programming practice. Data fields to a class should be declared to be private in order to hide the underlying representation of an object. This, in turn, helps increase system reliability. Choices (B), (C), (D), and (E) all describe effective ways to ensure reliability in a program.

39. **E**   Method 1 examines at most 10 words using a binary search technique on 1,000 pages to find the correct page. Remember, the maximum number of searches using binary search is 2^n where n is the max number of searches. It then searches sequentially on the page to find the correct word. If the target word is the last word on the page, this method will examine all 50 words on the page. Therefore, method 1 will examine at most 60 words.

Method 2 first uses a sequential search technique to find the correct page. If the target word is on the last page, this method will examine the first word on all 1,000 pages. Then, as with method 1, it may examine as many as all 50 words on the page to find the target word. Therefore, method 2 will examine at most 1,050 words.

Method 3 sequentially searches through all of the words in the dictionary. Because there are 50,000 words in the dictionary and the target word may be the last word in the dictionary, this method may have to examine all 50,000 words in order to find the target word.

40. **C**   A peripheral is a hardware device that you use with your computer. Printers, monitors, keyboards, mice, and external disk drives are all examples of peripherals.

Choice (C) is correct because a word-processing application is software, not hardware.

Section II: Free-Response Questions

1. (a)
```
    private Elective getElectiveByName (

    String name)

    {
        for (int eIndex = 0;
             eIndex < this.getElectiveListSize();<
             eIndex++)
        {
            Elective e = (Elective)
            electiveList.get(eIndex);
            String eName = e.getName();
            if (name.equals(eName))
                Return e;
        }
    }
```

(b)
```
    public void assignElectivesToStudents()

    {
        for (int sIndex = 0;
            sIndex < this.getStudentListSize();<
            sIndex++)
        {
            Student s = (Student)
            studentList.get(sIndex);
            int choice = 0;
            while (choice < 3 &&
                !s.hasElective())
            {
            String name =
            s.getChocie(choice);
            Elective e =
            getElectiveByName(name);
            if (e.getClassSize() <
                e.getMaxClassSize())
            {
                e.addStudent(s);
                s.assignElective(e);
            }
            choice += 1;
            }
        }
    }
```

(c)
```
    public ArrayList studentsWithoutElectives()

    {
        ArrayList<Student> result = new ArrayList<Student>();
        for (int sIndex = 0;
            sIndex < this.getStudentListSize();
            sIndex++)
        {
            Student s = (Student)
                studentList.get(sIndex);
            if (!s.hasElective())
                result.add(s);
        }
        return result;
    }
```

2. (a)
```java
public boolean inOrder()
{
    for (int k = 0;
        k < cards.length; k++)
    {
        if (cards[k] != k)
            return false;
    }
    return true;
}
```

(b)
```java
public void shuffle()
{
    int[] newCards = new int[cards.length];
    for(int k = 0; k < cards.length/2; k++)
    {
    newCards[k*2] = cards[k];
    newCards[k*2+1] = cards[cards.length/2+k];
    }
        cards = newCards;
}
```

(c)
```java
public int reorderingCount()
{
    Int count = 0;
    while (!inOrder() || count == 0)
    {
        shuffle();
        count += 1;
    }
    return count;
}
```

3.　(a)　```
public class Recipe
{

    private String name;
    private ArrayList<Ingredient> ingredientList;
    private String preparationProcess;
    private int numberServed;
    public ArrayList<Ingredient> getIngredientList()
    { /* implementation not needed */ }
    public Recipe(String recipeName,
            int numServed)
    { /* implementation not needed */ }
    public void addIngredient(Ingredient
            newIngredient)
    { /* implementation not needed */ }
    public void setPreparationProcess(
            String newPreparationProcess)
    { /* implementation not needed */ }
    public String getName()
    { /* implementation not needed */ }
    public int getNumberServed()
    { /* implementation not needed */ }
    publicvoid scale(int newNumberServed)
    { /* implementation no needed */ }
}
```

　(b)　```
public void scale(int newNumberServed)

{
    double OldAmount;
    double newAmount;
    for (int k = 0;
            k < ingredientList.size; k++)
    {
            ingredient ingred = (Ingredient)
                ingredientList.get(k);
            oldAmount = ingred.getAmount();
            newAmount =  newNumberServed *
                (oldAmount / numberServed);
            ingred.setAmount(newAmount);
    }
    numberServed = newNumberServed;
}
```

```
(c)  public void standardize(int numPeople )

    {
        double oldAmount;
        double newAmount;
        for (int j=0; j<recipeList.size(); j++)
        {
            for (int k = 0; k < recipeList.size(); k++)
            {
                Ingredient    ingred    =    (Ingredient)    recipeList.
                get(j).get
                IngredientList().get(k);
                oldAmount = ingred.getAmount();
                newAmount = numPeople / oldAmount;
                ingred.setAmount(newAmount);
            }
            recipeList.get(j).setNumberServed(numPeople);
        }}
```

```
4. public class School {
       private ArrayList<Classroom> classrooms;

       public School(ArrayList<Classroom> SchoolRooms) {
           classrooms = SchoolRooms;
       }

       public String findStudent(String teacher, int IDnumber) {
           for (int k = 0; k < classrooms.size(); k++) {
               if (classrooms.get(k).getTeacherName() == teacher) {
                   int low = 0;
                   int high = classrooms.get(k).getStudents().size();
                   while (low <= high) {
                       int middle = (low + high) / 2;
                       if (IDnumber <
classrooms.get(k).getStudents().get(middle).getStudentID()) {
                       high = middle - 1;
                   }
               else if (IDnumber >
classrooms.get(k).getStudents().get(middle).getStudentID()) {
                       low = middle + 1;
                   }
               else {
                   return
classrooms.get(k).getStudents().get(middle).getStudentName();
                       }
                   }
               }
           }
       return "Student Not Found";
       }
   }
   public class Classroom {

       private String teacherName;
       private ArrayList<Student> Students;

       public Classroom(String teacher, ArrayList<Student> theStudents) {
               teacherName = teacher;
               Students = theStudents;
       }

       public String getTeacherName() {
               return teacherName;
       }

       public ArrayList<Student> getStudents() {
               return Students;
       }
   }
```

```java
public class Student {

private String studentName;
private int studentID;

public Student(String name, int ID) {
    studentName = name;
    studentID = ID;
}

        public int getStudentID() {
    return studentID;
}

public String getStudentName() {
    return studentName;
);
```

Part III
About the
AP Computer
Science A Exam

- The Structure of the AP Computer Science A Exam
- How AP Exams Are Used
- Other Resources
- Designing Your Study Plan

THE STRUCTURE OF THE AP COMPUTER SCIENCE A EXAM

The AP Computer Science A Exam is a two-part test. The chart below illustrates the test's structure:

Section	Question Type	Number of Questions	Time Allowed	Percent of Final Grade
I	Multiple Choice	40	90 minutes	50%
II	Free Response	4	90 minutes	50%

The AP Computer Science A course and exam require that potential solutions of problems be written in the Java programming language. Students should be able to perform the following tasks:

- design, implement, and analyze solutions to problems.
- use and implement commonly used algorithms.
- use standard data structures.
- develop and select appropriate algorithms and data structures to solve new problems.
- write solutions fluently in an object-oriented paradigm.
- write, run, test, and debug solutions in the Java programming language, utilizing standard Java library classes and interfaces from the AP Java subset.
- read and understand programs consisting of several classes and interacting objects.
- read and understand a description of the design and development process leading to such a program. (Examples of such solutions can be found in the AP Computer Science Labs.)
- understand the ethical and social implications of computer use.

The table below shows the classification categories and how they are represented in the multiple-choice section of the exam. Because questions can be classified as being in more than one category, the total of the percentages is greater than 100%.

Classification Category	Percent of multiple-choice items
Programming Fundamentals	55–75%
Data Structures	20–40%
Logic	5–15%
Algorithms/Problem Solving	24–45%
Object-Oriented Programming	15–25%
Recursion	5–15%
Software Engineering	2–10%

Ch-Ch-Ch-Changes

Beginning with the 2016 exam, the Multiple Choice section will be 90 minutes and the Free Response section will also be 90 minutes. The sections used to be different lengths, so here is the updated information in case an older sibling or friend told you it was 75 minutes and 105 minutes the last time they took the exam. The exam you will take is 90 mins and 90 mins and you are going to rock it.

In addition to the multiple-choice questions, there are four mandatory free-response questions. You'll have a total of 90 minutes to answer all four of them. You should spend approximately 22 minutes per question, but be aware that you must manage your own time. Additional time spent on one question will reduce the time that you have left to answer another.

The multiple-choice questions are scored by machine while the free-response questions are scored by thousands of college faculty and expert AP teachers at the annual AP Reading.   Scores on the free-response questions are weighted and combined with the weighted results of the multiple-choice questions. These composite, weighted raw scores are then converted into the reported AP Exam scores of 5, 4, 3, 2, and 1.

Score (Meaning)	Percentage of test takers receiving this score	Equivalent grade in a first-year college course	Credit granted for this score?
5 (Extremely well qualified)	24.4%	A	Most schools
4 (well qualified)	24.6%	A-, B+, B	Most schools
3 (qualified)	15.3%	B-, C+, C	Some do, but some don't
2 (possibly qualified)	7.1%	C-	Very few do
1 (no recommendation)	28.6%	D	No

The data above is about the May 2015 administration of the AP Exams. Information is from College Board data found here: **https://secure-media.collegeboard. org/digitalServices/pdf/ap/ap15-computer-science-a-score-dist.pdf.**

To score your multiple-choice questions, award yourself one point for every correct answer and credit 0 points to your score for every question that you left blank.

How Will I Know?
Your dream college's website may list such information or you can contact the school's admission's department to verify AP exam score acceptance information.

Free Response Questions

Section II of the AP Computer Science A Exam is the free response section. Free response questions are scored from 0 to 9.

Unfortunately, we can't give you a ton of black and white rules about free response question scoring—the actual scoring for each question is all based on the questions themselves. There is no one-fits-all way to score a Computer Science A free response question. The College Board does map out some penalties, though, and they're in this handy list.

1-Point Penalty
- Extraneous code that causes a side effect or prevents earning points in the rubric (e.g., *information written to output*)
- Local variables used but none declared
- Destruction of persistent data (e.g., *changing value referenced by parameter*)
- Void method or constructor that returns a value

No Penalty
- Extraneous code that causes no side effect
- Extraneous code that is unreachable and would not have earned points in rubric
- Spelling/case discrepancies where there is no ambiguity*
- Local variable not declared, provided that other variables are declared in some part
- `private` qualifier on local variable
- Missing `public` qualifier on class or constructor header
- Keyword used as an identifier
- Common mathematical symbols used for operators ($\times \bullet \div \leq \geq < > \neq$)
- [] vs. () vs. <>
- = instead of == (and vice versa)
- Array/collection element access confusion ([] vs. get for r-values)
- Array/collection element modification confusion ([] vs. set for l-values)
- length/size confusion for array, `String`, and `ArrayList`, with or without ()
- Extraneous [] when referencing entire array
- [i,j] instead of [i][j]
- Extraneous size in array declaration, (e.g., `int[size] nums = new int[size];`)
- Missing ; provided that line breaks and indentation clearly convey intent
- Missing { } where indentation clearly conveys intent and { } are used elsewhere
- Missing ( ) on parameter-less method or constructor invocations
- Missing ( ) around `if`/`while` conditions
- Use of local variable outside declared scope (must be within same method body)
- Failure to cast object retrieved from nongeneric collection

HOW AP EXAMS ARE USED

Different colleges use AP Exams in different ways, so it is important that you visit a particular college's website in order to determine how it accepts AP Exam scores. The three items below represent the main ways in which AP Exam scores can be used.

- **College Credit.** Some colleges will give you college credit if you receive a high score on an AP Exam. These credits count toward your graduation requirements, meaning that you can take fewer courses while in college. Given the cost of college, this could be quite a benefit, indeed.

- **Satisfy Requirements.** Some colleges will allow you to "place out" of certain requirements if you do well on an AP Exam, even if they do not give you actual college credits. For example, you might not need to take an introductory-level course, or perhaps you might not need to take a class in a certain discipline at all.

- **Admissions Plus.** Even if your AP Exam will not result in college credit or even allow you to place out of certain courses, most colleges will respect your decision to push yourself by taking an AP Course. In addition, if you take an AP Exam outside of an AP Course, they will likely respect that drive, too. A high score on an AP Exam shows mastery of more difficult content than is typically taught in high school courses, and colleges may take that into account during the admissions process.

Some people think that AP Courses are reserved for high school seniors, but that is not the case. Don't be afraid to see about being placed into an AP course during your junior or even sophomore year. A good AP Exam score looks fantastic on a college application and can set you apart from other candidates.

OTHER RESOURCES

There are many resources available to help you improve your score on the AP Computer Science A Exam, not the least of which are your teachers. If you are taking an AP course, you may be able to get extra attention from your teacher, such as feedback on your essays. If you are not in an AP course, you can reach out to a teacher who teaches AP Computer Science A and ask if he or she will review your free response questions or otherwise help you master the content.

Another wonderful resource is AP Students, the official website of the AP Exams (part of The College Board's website). The scope of information available on AP Central is quite broad and includes the following:

- course descriptions, which include further details on what content is covered by the exam
- sample questions from the AP Computer Science A Exam
- free-response question prompts and multiple-choice questions from previous years

The AP Students home page address is: **https://apstudent.collegeboard.org/exploreap**

For up-to-date information about the AP Computer Science A Exam, please visit: **https://apstudent.collegeboard.org/apcourse/ap-computer-science-a**

Finally, The Princeton Review offers tutoring and small group instruction. Our expert instructors can help you refine your strategic approach and enhance your content knowledge. For more information, call 1-800-2REVIEW.

DESIGNING YOUR STUDY PLAN

In Part I, you identified some areas of potential improvement. Let's now delve further into your performance on Practice Test 1, with the goal of developing a study plan appropriate to your needs and time commitment.

Read the answers and explanations associated with the multiple-choice questions (starting on page 54.) After you have done so, respond to the following questions:

- Review the topic chart on page 76. Next to each topic, indicate your rank of the topic as follows: "1" means "I need a lot of work on this," "2" means "I need to beef up my knowledge," and "3" means "I know this topic well."

- How many days/weeks/months away is your exam?

- What time of day is your best, most focused study time?

- How much time per day/week/month will you devote to preparing for your exam?

- When will you do this preparation? (Be as specific as possible: Mondays and Wednesdays from 3:00 to 4:00 P.M., for example)

- Based on the answers above, will you focus on strategy (Part IV) or content (Part V) or both?

- What are your overall goals for using this book?

Part IV
Test-Taking Strategies for the AP Computer Science A Exam

PREVIEW

Review your Practice Test 1 results and then respond to the following questions:

- How many multiple-choice questions did you miss even though you knew the answer?

- On how many multiple-choice questions did you guess blindly?

- How many multiple-choice questions did you miss after eliminating some answers and guessing based on the remaining answers?

- Did you find any of the free-response questions easier or harder than others—and, if so, why?

HOW TO USE THE CHAPTERS IN THIS PART

Before reading the following strategy chapters, think about what you are doing now. As you read and engage in the directed practice, be sure to think critically about the ways you can change your approach.

Chapter 1
How to Approach
Multiple-Choice
Questions

THE BASICS

The directions for the multiple-choice section of the AP Computer Science A Exam are pretty simple. They read as follows:

Directions: Determine the answer to each of the following questions or incomplete statements, using the available space for any necessary scratchwork. Then decide which is the best of the choices given and fill in the corresponding oval on the answer sheet. No credit will be given for anything written in the examination booklet. Do not spend too much time on any one problem.

In short, you're being asked to do what you've done on many other multiple-choice exams: Pick the best answer and then fill in the corresponding bubble on a separate sheet of paper. You will not be given credit for answers you record in your test booklet (by circling them, for example) but do not fill in on your answer sheet. The section consists of 40 questions and you will be given 90 minutes to complete it.

The College Board also provides a breakdown of the general subject matter covered on the exam. This breakdown will not appear in your test booklet; it comes from the preparatory material that the College Board publishes. Here again is the chart we showed you in Part III:

Classification Category	Percent of multiple-choice items
Programming Fundamentals	55–75%
Data Structures	20–40%
Logic	5–15%
Algorithms/Problem Solving	24–45%
Object-Oriented Programming	15–25%
Recursion	5–15%
Software Engineering	2–10%

A few important notes about the AP Computer Science A Exam directly from the College Board:

- Assume that the classes listed in the Java Quick Reference have been imported where appropriate.
- Assume that declarations of variables and methods appear within the context of an enclosing class.
- Assume that method calls that are not prefixed with an object or class name and are not shown within a complete class definition appear within the context of an enclosing class.
- Unless otherwise noted in the question, assume that parameters in method calls are not null and that methods are called only when their preconditions are satisfied.

MULTIPLE-CHOICE STRATEGIES

Process of Elimination (POE)

As you work through the multiple-choice section, always keep in mind that you are not graded on your thinking process or scratchwork. All that ultimately matters is that you indicate the correct answer. Even if you aren't sure how to answer a question in a methodically "correct" way, see if you can eliminate any answers based on common sense and then take a guess.

Throughout the book, we will point out areas where you can use common sense to eliminate answers.

Although we all like to be able to solve problems the "correct" way, using a Process of Elimination (POE) and guessing aggressively can help earn you a few more points. And if may be these points that make the difference between a 3 and a 4 or push you from a 4 to a 5.

Don't Be Afraid Of Guessing

If you don't know the answer but can eliminate an answer choice, guess! Eliminating just one of the answer choices from consideration means that it is worth your while to guess if you don't know the answer to any given problem. Obviously, the more incorrect answers you can eliminate, the better your odds of guessing the correct answer.

Be Strategic About Long Questions

Some multiple-choice questions require a page or two of reading to answer the question. Skip any questions that will either take a long time to read or a long time to calculate. Circle the questions and come back to them after you've completed the rest of the section.

Don't Turn a Question into a Crusade!

Most people don't run out of time on standardized tests because they work too slowly. Instead, they run out of time because they spend half of the test wrestling with two or three particular questions.

You should never spend more than a minute or two on any question. If a question doesn't involve calculation, then you know the answer, you can take an educated guess at the answer, or you don't know the answer. Figure out where you stand on a question, make a decision, and move on.

Any question that requires more than two minutes worth of calculations probably isn't worth doing. Remember, skipping a question early in the section is a good thing if it means that you'll have time to get two right later on.

Watch for Special Cases in Algorithm Descriptions

On the exam, you may know that the average runtime for finding an element in a binary search tree is $O(n \log n)$. Watch out if the question casually mentions that the data is inserted in the tree in sorted order. Now the runtime deteriorates into the worst case, $O(n)$. These special occasions may pop up on the AP Computer Science A exam, so watch out.

Remember the Base Case in Recursive Algorithms

Recursive methods without a base case run forever. Be sure that a base case exists and is the correct base case. For example, a factorial function whose base case is

```
if (n == 1)
    return 0;
```

is incorrect because 1! = 1.

Watch for < vs. <= and > vs. >=

The difference between < and <= or between > and >= can be huge, especially in loops. You can bet that this discrepancy will appear in multiple-choice questions!

Know How to Use the Java Library Classes

This chapter offers strategies that will help make you a better test taker and, hopefully, a better scorer on the AP Computer Science exam. However, there are some things you just have to know. Although you'll have a Quick Reference for the AP Java Classes as part of the exam, review the AP Java library classes beforehand and know what methods are available, what they do, and how to use them. The Quick Reference will help, but it won't substitute for knowing the classes.

Preconditions and Postconditions

Read these carefully when given. They may provide the clue needed to answer the question. For instance, a precondition may state that the array passed to a method is in sorted order.

Parameter Passing

Remember that arguments passed to methods do not keep changes made to them inside the method. For instance, it is impossible to write a method that swaps the value of two integer primitives. Don't confuse this, however, with changing the contents (attributes) of an object that is passed to a method.

Client Program vs. Method

There is likely to be at least one question that defines a class and asks you to choose among different implementations for a method. Pay close attention to whether the method is a "client program" or a method of the class. If it's a client program, the implementation of the method may not access any private data fields or private methods of the class directly. If it's a method of the class, the implementation is free to access both private data fields and private methods.

Boolean Short-Circuiting

Conditionals in if statements and while statements "short-circuit". For example:

```
if ((a ! = 0) && (b / a = = 5))
```

is *not* the same as

```
if ((b / a = = 5) && (a ! = 0))
```

Memorize DeMorgan's Laws

There will be at least one question on the exam where they will be useful.

```
!(p || q) is equivalent to !p && !q
!(p && q) is equivalent to !p || !q
```

Find Data in a Class

Watch out for answer choices that have code segments that attempt to change a data field declared final. This is illegal code.

Mixing double and int in an Expression

In operations that have both an int variable and a double variable, unless explicitly cast otherwise, the int is converted to a double and the result of the operation is a double.

Chapter 2
How to Approach
Free-Response
Questions

FREE-RESPONSE STRATEGIES

Write Java Code, Not Pseudocode

Only Java code is graded; pseudocode is not graded. Don't waste time writing pseudocode if you don't know how to code the solution to a problem. (On the other hand, write pseudocode as a starting point to writing your Java code if it helps you to do so.)

Don't Comment Your Code

Unless you write some code that is extremely tricky (and see below for whether or not you should do that!), there's no need to write comments. It just takes time (that you don't have a lot of) and the comments will be largely ignored by the graders anyway (you won't get points if your comment is correct but your code is wrong). You also run the risk of misleading the grader if your code is correct but your comments are incorrect.

Write Legibly

This seems obvious, but if a grader can't read your code, you won't get any points.

Don't Erase Large Chunks of Code

If you make extensive changes to the code you're writing, it's better to put a big "X" through the bad code rather than erase it. It saves you time and makes it easier for the graders to read.

Don't Write More Than One Solution to a Problem

Graders will grade the first solution they see. If you rewrite a solution, be sure to cross out the old one.

Don't Leave any Problem Blank

You don't get any points if you don't write anything down. Even if you're unsure how to answer a particular problem (or part of a problem), analyze the problem and code the method's "infrastructure." For instance, if the method signature indicates that it creates and returns an ArrayList, writing

```
ArrayList returnedList = new ArrayList ( ) ;
return returnedList;
```

is likely to get you at least partial credit—even if you don't know how to fill the `ArrayList` with the correct objects.

KISS (Keep It Simple, Student)

The problems are designed to make the solutions relatively straightforward. If your solution is getting complicated, there's probably an easier or better way to solve the problem. At the same time, don't try for seemingly elegant but unreadable code. Remember that graders must read hundreds of exams in a week—they may not be able to figure out all of the nuances of your code. KEEP IT SIMPLE!

Write Standard Solutions

Use AP-style variable, class, and method names and follow the indentation style of the AP sample code (even if you don't like their style!). Although graders always try to be fair and accurate, they are human and do make mistakes. The closer your answer adheres to the sample solution given to the graders, the easier it will be for them to grade.

Wherever possible, use clear and intuitive nomenclature. For example, use r and c or row and col for looping through the rows and columns of a two-dimensional array, don't use x and y or a and b or *jack* and *jill*. This ensures that graders can easily follow the flow of your code.

If the Pseudocode for an Algorithm is Given, Use it!

Sometimes you will have to create your own algorithm for a method. Often though, the pseudocode for the algorithm or method is given to you as part of the problem; all you need to do is implement the algorithm. In that case, use the pseudocode that's given to you! Don't make it harder on yourself by trying to re-create the algorithm or implement your own special version. Furthermore, you can often write the code for a method based on given pseudocode even if you don't understand the underlying algorithm.

Answer Part (c) to a Problem Even If You Can't do Parts (a) and (b)

Many parts of free-response problems build on previous parts. For example, the question in part (c) may use the methods you wrote in parts (a) and (b). However, you do not need to have answered parts (a) and (b) correctly in order to get full credit for part (c). In fact, part (c) is sometimes easier than either part (a) or (b). If part (c) states that you should use parts (a) and (b), use them!

Don't Make Easy-to-Avoid Mistakes

Students often lose points on the free-response section because they make common errors. Here are some things you can do to avoid these mistakes.

- Unless the problem *explicitly* asks you to output something (using System.out.print), *never* output anything in a method you write.
- Watch method signatures. Be sure to call methods with the correct name and correct number and type of parameters. If the method is not void, be sure that the method you write returns a value with the correct type as specified in the signature.
- Use the objectName.methodName() syntax when calling methods of a given object; use the ClassName.methodName() syntax when calling static methods such as the random method of the Math class.
- Be sure to declare any variables you use (and give them descriptive names).
- Don't create objects when you don't need to. For instance, if a method you call returns an ArrayList, declare it as

```
ArrayList returnedList;
    returnedList = obj.getList( ) ;
```

not

```
ArrayList returnedList = new ArrayList ( ) ;
    returnedList = obj.getList ( ) ;
```

- Use proper indentation. Even if you use curly braces for all of your conditionals and loops, the indentation will demonstrate your intent should you forget, for example, a closing curly brace.

Design Question

One problem in the free-response section is likely to be a design problem where you will be given a description of a class and asked to write an interface for it. You may also be asked to implement selected methods in your class. Be sure to use appropriate class, method, and private data field names. For example, "method1" is not likely to be a good name for a method that returns the total price of an object; "totalPrice" is a more appropriate name. Be sure to include all methods, private data fields, and *all* of the constructors (including the default constructor) asked for in the problem. If you are asked to implement a method, be sure to use the correct class, method, and private data field names *as you defined them* in the design part.

Arrays and ArrayLists

At least one problem (probably more) on the exam is likely to involve walking through arrays and/or ArrayLists. Know the differences between the two types of structures and how to loop through elements in the array or an ArrayList. Know how to use iterators and how to work with two-dimensional arrays.

GENERAL STRATEGIES

The following strategies apply to both the multiple-choice and free-response sections of the exam.

Pace Yourself and Keep Track of Time

On the multiple-choice section, you should take an average of 2 minutes per problem. This will give you 3 minutes to look over the test at the beginning and 7 minutes for a final check at the end. As a comparison, if you take 3 minutes per problem, you're only going to answer 30 questions; if you take 5 minutes per problem, you're only going to answer 18 questions.

On the free-response section, you should pace yourself at a rate of 20 minutes per complete problem. This will give you roughly 2 minutes per problem to check your answer and a minute at the beginning to look over the problems.

Write in the Test Booklet

Don't try to do the questions in your head. Write things down! Take notes on the question. In addition to making the problem easier to solve, having notes in the test booklet will make it easier to go back and check your work if you have time at the end of the test.

Underline Key Words in Questions

Words like *client program*, *sorted*, *ordered*, *constant*, *positive*, *never*, *always* and *must* all specify conditions to a problem. On both the multiple-choice and free-response sections, underline these key words as you read the question to reinforce their importance to the problem.

Don't Do More Work Than You Need to

You are not graded for your work at all on the multiple-choice section, and you are not given extra credit for clever or well-documented answers on the free-response section. Keep it simple and strive to get the answer right rather than impress the graders.

Look Through the Exam First—Use the Two-Pass System

Keep in mind that all of the multiple-choice questions are worth the same number of points, and each free-response question is worth the same number of points as the other free-response questions. There is no need to do them in order. Instead use a two-pass system.

Go through each section twice. The first time, do all the questions that you can get answers to immediately. That is, the questions with little or no analysis or the questions on computer science topics in which you are well versed.

On the first round, skip the questions in the topics that make you uncomfortable. Also, you might want to skip the ones that look like number crunchers (you might still be expected to crunch a few numbers—even without a calculator). Circle the questions that you skip in your test booklet so you can find them easily during the second pass.

Once you've done all the questions that come easily to you, go back and pick out the tough ones that you have the best shot at.

That's why the two-pass system is so handy. By using it, you make sure that you get to see all the questions that you can get right, instead of running out of time because you got bogged down on questions you couldn't do earlier in the test.

A word of caution though: If you skip a multiple-choice question, be sure that you take extra care in marking your answer sheet. Always be sure that the answer you bubble in on the answer sheet is for the correct question number. In addition, don't forget to circle the skipped question in the multiple-choice booklet so that you remember to come back to it if you have time at the end of the test.

Finally...

Don't panic. If you've prepared, the test is easier than it looks at first glance. Take your time, approach each question calmly and logically, remember the tips in this chapter, and you'll be fine.

Get Ready to Move On...

Now that you have the hints, strategies, and background information locked in, it's time to move on to the serious business at hand...the subject review (Part V). Read over the following chapters, take notes, and compare them to your textbook and class notes as preparation to take Practice Test 2 in the back of the book. Once you've mastered what's in this book and learned from your mistakes on the practice tests, you'll be ready to ace the real AP exam.

REFLECT

Think about what you learned in Part IV, and respond to the following questions:

- How much time will you spend on multiple-choice questions?

- How will you change your approach to multiple-choice questions?

- What is your multiple-choice guessing strategy?

- How much time will you spend on free-response questions?

- How will you change your approach to the free-response questions?

- Will you seek further help, outside of this book (such as a teacher, tutor, or AP Students), on how to approach multiple-choice questions, free-response questions, or a pacing strategy?

Part V
Content Review for the AP Computer Science A Exam

Chapter 3
Basic Techniques

Computer Science ("CS") is a fancy title used for many aspects of computing, usually on the developing end; its areas include computer programming, which is exactly what we will be doing in AP Computer Science A ("APCS"). APCS focuses on the language of Java and its components, and in many cases, you will be the programmer. Although the person using your program ("the user") will typically only see the end result of your program, CS gives you the tools to write statements ("code") that will ideally make the user's experience both functional and enjoyable.

PROGRAMMING STYLE

Computer programming is similar to a foreign language; it has nouns, verbs, and other parts of speech, and it has different forms of style, just like speaking languages. Just as you might use different words and ways of speaking—tone, expressions, etc.—with your family versus your friends, CS has many different languages and, within each language, its own ways of getting the job done. In both the CS world and the APCS world, a particular **programming style** is expected in order to show fluency in the language. A company that might hire you for a CS job will likely expect you to conform to its own unique programming style; similarly, the College Board will expect you to conform to its accepted programming style based on its research of CS styles accepted at universities around the world.

Comments, Identifiers, White Space

Commenting is an extremely vital style technique in the programming world. Comments do not actually cause the program to behave any differently, whether absent or present; however, comments serve many purposes including:

- Allowing the programmer to make "notes" within the program that she or he may want to reference later;
- Allowing the person reading and/or using the program ("the reader" and/or "the user") to understand the code in a less cryptic way, when applicable;
- Revealing to the programmer/reader/user aspects of the program that are required to make the program operate as intended and/or are produced as a result of the program's execution.

There are two types of commenting in Java. **In-line** or **short comments** appear after or near a statement and are preceded by two forward slashes ("//") followed by the comment. **Long comments** that extend beyond a single line of code are surrounded by special characters; they begin with ("/*") and end with ("*/")

For example,

```
//  This is a short comment
/*  This is a
    long comment */
```

Identifiers are names that are given to represent data that is stored in the memory of the computer during the program's execution. Rather than using a nonsensical memory address code to reference data, Java allows the programmer to name an identifier to perform this job. When we name identifiers in Java, there are guidelines that we *must* use and guidelines that the College Board *expects* us to use:

- An identifier may contain any combination of letters, numbers, and underscore ("_"), but *must* begin with a letter and may not contain any other characters, including spaces.
- An identifier *should* be a logical name that corresponds to the data it is associated with; for example, an identifier associated with the side of a triangle would be more useful as *side1* instead of *s*.
- An identifier *should* begin with a lowercase letter and, if it is composed of several words, should denote each subsequent word with a capital letter. If we decided to create an identifier associated with our triangle's number of sides, numberOfSides or numOfSides would conform to this style; NumberOfSides and numofsides would not.

White space is another element of style that does not affect the overall functionality of the program. Rather, it enhances the readability of the program by allowing the programmer to space out the code so as to separate specific statement or tasks from others. Much like a book may leave empty space at the end of a chapter and begin the next chapter on the next page without affecting the overall story, white space has a similar effect.

Compiling & Errors

When the programmer writes Java code, statements are written that are understood within a Java development environment. The computer, however, does not understand this language, much like you would likely not understand a foreign language spoken in its native environment. Therefore, an **interpreter** (sound familiar?) is used within the developer environment, enabling the computer to understand the Java code. A computer only operates using code written in **binary** (zeroes and ones, literally!) and so the interpreter "translates" your Java code into binary. This process is called **compiling**. As a result, in most instances as well as on the AP Exam, modern computer programmers do not need to understand binary code directly.

When an interactive development environment ("IDE") is used to compile your code, the code will be automatically checked for basic programming errors. If an error is found within the code, the compiling is halted and an error message is produced (this feedback is where the "interactive" part comes in); this situation is called a **compile-time error**. Although the error message/code is not always helpful in a direct way, it does allow the programmer to troubleshoot the issue in a more directed way. Unfortunately, since the AP Exam is a pencil-and-paper test, you will have access to neither a computer nor a compiler. Your code must be absent of errors in order to receive full credit for the response (or any credit if it's a multiple choice question).

A **logical error** is more difficult to troubleshoot; rather than a problem with the syntax of the Java code itself, a logical error lies in the desired output/purpose of the program. Similar to ordering dinner and receiving a perfectly prepared dessert instead, you are getting a good result, but it is not appropriate for the desired task.

A **runtime error** is an error that is not caught by the compiler, yet produces an error during the execution of the program. In many ways, this is the worst (and most) embarrassing error for the programmer, because it is not realized until the task is supposedly "done." An analog to this situation is when you are editing your favorite image in a graphics program, and it suddenly crashes. It's frustrating for the user and annoying for the programmer when you leave negative feedback on the company's website!

1. Assuming all other statements in the program are correct, each of the following statements will allow the program to compile EXCEPT

   (A) `// This is a comment`
   (B) `/* This is a comment */`
   (C) `// myName is a good identifier name`
   (D) `// myname is a good identifier name`
   (E) All of the above statements will compile

Here's How to Crack It
Choices (A), (B), and (C) are all valid comments in Java, regardless of their contents and the fact that (B) is not actually any longer than a single line. Choice (D) uses a poor identifier name, not a good one, but neither of these situations will result in a non-compiling program. Therefore, (E) is correct.

OBJECTS & PRIMITIVE DATA

Output (and some input)

In order for your program to "do anything" from the user's perspective (at this level, anyway!) it must produce output to the screen. A program may produce output to many devices, including storage drives and printers, but APCS only requires us to produce output to the screen.

There are two similar statements that we use to produce output to the screen in this course:

```
System.out.print (…);
System.out.println (…);
```

The ellipses in these statements will contain the data and/or identifiers that will be displayed on the screen. We will see the difference between these statements in a minute.

For example, if a triangle has a side length of 2 stored in the memory using the identifier side1 and we wanted to output that information to the screen, we could use one of the following two commands:

```
System.out.print (2);
System.out.print (side1);
```

Since both 2 and side1 represent numerical values, they can be outputted to the screen in this way. If the programmer wanted to display non-numerical data, however, he or she would use a **string literal** (or simply a **string**) to accomplish this task. A string literal is simply one or more characters combined into a single unit. The previous sentence, and this sentence, can be considered as string literals. In a Java program, string literals must be surrounded by double quotes ("") to avoid a compile error. In our triangle example, we can use a string literal to make the output more user-friendly:

```
System.out.println ("The length of side 1 is:");
System.out.print (side1);
// side1 may be simply substituted with 2, in this case
```

Note the usage of the println statement rather than the print statement, which will output the string literal and then put the cursor at the beginning of the next line for further output, rather than displaying the next output on the same line. Note, also, that the statement

```
System.out.print (side1);
```

will display the *value* stored using the `side1` identifier, 2. In contrast, the statement

```
System.out.print ("side1");
```

will literally display

```
side1
```

because the double quotes create a string literal here. The College Board loves to ask multiple choice questions that determine whether you understand these differences.

———————————◯———————————

2. Assuming all other statements in the program are correct, each of the following statements will allow the program to compile EXCEPT

(A) `System.out.print (1);`
(B) `System.out.print ("1");`
(C) `System.out.print (side1);`
(D) `System.out.print ("side1");`
(E) All of the above statements will compile

Here's How to Crack It

Choices (A) and (B) will both display 1, although (A) is numerical and (B) is a string literal. Choice (D) will display the string literal side1. Since there is no indication in the question that side1 has been associated with any data, (C) will generate an error because Java does not know what to display. Therefore, (C) is the answer. Be very careful when choosing "all of the above" or "none of the above" answer choices!

———————————◯———————————

As you might imagine, input is also important in programming. Although you may learn some techniques of getting user input (the Scanner class, for example), the AP Exam will not test any input methods or classes. Instead, the exam will indicate input using code similar to this:

```
String s  = IO.readString();
```

where IO.readString is a method used to read input. You will not be asked to prompt the user for input, unless there is pre-existing code in the task that does it for you. Nice.

Variables & Assignment

Let's put those identifiers to work.

In order to actually "create" an identifier, we need to **assign** a data value to that identifier. This task is done by writing an assignment statement.

The syntax of an assignment statement is:

type identifier = data;

Continuing with our triangle example, if we wanted to actually assign the data value of 2 to a new identifier called side1, we could use this statement:

```
int side1 = 2;
```

This statement tells the compiler that (1) our identifier is called side1, (2) the data assigned to that identifier should be 2, and (3) our data is an integer (more on this in the next section). The equals sign ("=") is called an **assignment operator** and is required by Java. The semicolon, which we also saw in the output statements above, denotes that the statement is finished. Note that an assignment statement does NOT produce any output to the screen.

When data is associated with an identifier, the identifier is called a **variable**. The reason we use this term is because, like in math, the value of the variable can be changed; it can *vary*! Look at the following code:

```
int myFavoriteNumber = 22;
myFavoriteNumber = 78;
System.out.print ("My favorite number is " +
myFavoriteNumber);
```

Can you predict the output? The variable myFavoriteNumber is first assigned the value of 22, but it is then reassigned to the value 78. Therefore, the original value is no longer stored in the computer's memory and the 78 remains. The output would be:

```
My favorite number is 78
```

A few items to note in this example:

- Once a variable is given a type (again, more on this later), its type should not be restated. This fact explains why the second assignment statement is missing int.
- The string literal is outputted as written, but the variable's *value*, not its name, is outputted.

- In order to output a string literal and a numerical value using the same output statement, use the **concatenation operator** between the two items. Although this operator looks like a typical + sign, it does not "add" the values in the traditional sense; instead, it simply outputs the two values next to each other. For example, two plus two equals four in the mathematical sense, but two concatenated with two produces 22.

———————

3. Assuming all other statements in the program are correct, each of the following statements will allow the program to compile EXCEPT

(A) `System.out.print ("Ilove Java");`

(B) `System.out.println ("Ilove" + "Java");`

(C) `System.out.print (1 + "love" + Java");`

(D) `System.out.println (1 + "love" + "Java");`

(E) `System.out.print ("I love"+ " " + "Java");`

Here's How to Crack It

Choices (A) and (B), although their output may not look grammatically correct (they love to do this on the AP Exam—remember, it's not a grammar test!), will compile without error. Choice (D) is fine because the numerical value is concatenated with the string literals, producing a string literal that can be displayed. Choice (E) uses string literal that is simply an empty space, which is valid. Therefore, (C) is the answer because "Java" is missing the left hand quotation mark.

———————

The Four Data Types—int, double, boolean, char

When the programmer wants to assign data to a variable, he or she must first decide what *type* of data will be stored. For the AP Exam, there are four data types that comprise the **primitive data** forms; i.e., the basic types of data. More complex data forms will be discussed later.

integer *(int)* represents an integer number: positive numbers, negative numbers, and zero, with no decimals or fractions. Integers can store non-decimal values from -2,147,483,648 to 2,147,483,647, inclusive. That's a lot of values.

double represents a number that can be positive, negative, or zero, and can be a fraction or decimal… pretty much any number you can think of. It also has a much bigger breadth of upper and lower limits than an integer; it can express numbers with decades of significant digits. If you have to store an integer that is larger than the limits listed above, you must store the data as a double.

On the AP Exam, you do not have to memorize the upper and lower limits of these numerical data types; you do, however, need to know that a double must be declared for a number that is larger than an integer can store.

boolean represents a value that is either true or false. In machine code, true is represented by 1 (or any non-zero value) and false is represented by 0. This data type is excellent for storing or using yes/no data, such as the responses to: Are you hungry? Are you excited about the AP Exam? Is this chapter boring?

character (*char*) represents any single character that can be represented on a computer; this type includes any character you can type on the keyboard, including letters, numbers, spaces, and special characters like slashes, dashes, and the like. Backspace, Enter, and other commands also have char values, although they are not tested on the AP Exam. Char values are stored using a single quotation mark or apostrophe ('). The values of the capital letters A thru Z are 65-90 and lowercase letters are 97–122 (browse to http://unicode-table.com/en for a fancier, more complete listing of these values). Although the AP Exam does not require the memorization of these codes (thankfully), you should know their relative placement in the table. For example, you should know that character "A" comes before (has a lower numerical value) than character "B"; you should also note that every capital letter character comes before the lowercase letters. Therefore, "a" actually comes *after* "Z."

Arithmetic Operations

The most primitive uses for the first computers were to perform complex calculations. They were basically gigantic calculators. As a result, one of the most basic operations we use in Java involves arithmetic.

The symbols +, -, *, and / represent the operations of addition, subtraction, multiplication, and division, respectively. The operator % is also used in Java; called the "modulus" operator, this symbol will produce the numerical remainder of a division. For example, 3%2 would evaluate to 1, since 3 divided by 2 yields 1, with 1 as a remainder. These operations can be performed intuitively on numerical values; they can also be performed on variables that store numerical values.

Speaking of math, back to our triangle example…

Consider the following statement in a program:

```
int side2 = 2, side3 = 3;
```

(Note that you can write multiple assignment statements in a single line, as long as the data types are the same.)

If the programmer wanted to write a statement that found the sum of these data and assigned the result to another variable called sumOfSides, he or she could easily write

```
sumOfSides = 2 + 3;// method 1
```

But this statement is less useful than

```
sumOfSides = side2 + side3;// method 2
```

Since the data is assigned to variables, for which values can vary, method 2 will reflect those changes while method 1 will not.

This same technique can be applied to all of the mathematical operators. Remember that a mixture of mathematical operations follow a specific order of **precedence**. Java will first perform the multiplication and division operations, from left to right, followed by the addition and subtraction operations in the same order. If the programmer wants to change the order of precedence of the operators, he or she can use parentheses.

Consider these lines of code:

```
System.out.print ( 3 - 4/5 ); // statement 3
System.out.print ( 3 -( 4/5 ) ); // statement 4
System.out.print ( ( 3 - 4 )/5 ); // statement 5
```

In statement 3, the division would occur first, followed by the subtraction of three minus the answer.

In statement 4, the same thing would happen, so it is mathematically equivalent to statement 3.

In statement 5, the parentheses override the order of operations, so the subtraction occurs followed by the answer being divided by 5.

Okay, here's where it gets crazy. Can you predict the output of these statements? Believe it or not, the output of statements 3 and 4 is 3; the output of statement 5 is 0. These results demonstrate the fact that data in Java is **strongly typed**.

When you perform a mathematical operation on two integers, Java will return the answer as an integer, as well. Therefore, although 4/5 is actually 0.8, Java will return a value of 0. Likewise, Java will evaluate 5/4 to be 1. The decimal part is cut off (not rounded) so the result will also be an integer. Strange, huh?

As is true with all computer science, there is a workaround for this called casting. Casting is a process through which data is forced to "look like" another type of data to the compiler. Think of someone who is cast in a show to play a part; although the actor has a personal identity, he or she assumes the new identity for the audience. The following modifications to statement 3 demonstrate different ways of casting:

```
System.out.print ( 3 -(double)( 4 )/5 ); // statement 3.1
System.out.print ( 3 - 4/(double)5 ); // statement 3.2
```

These statements will cast 4 and 5, respectively, to be double values of 4.0 and 5.0. As a result, the division will be "upgraded" to a division between double values, not integers, and the desired result will be returned. The following statements, although they will compile without error, will not display the desired result of 2.2.

```
System.out.print ( (double)3 - 4/5 ); // statement 3.3
System.out.print ( 3 - (double)( 4/5 )); // statement 3.4
```

Casting has a higher precedence than arithmetic operators, except parentheses, of course. Therefore, statement 3.3 will first convert 3 to 3.0, but will then perform integer division before completing the subtracting. The result is 3.0. In statement 3.4, the result of dividing the integers is casted to a double; since the integer division evaluate to 0, the cast will simply make the result 0.0, yielding an output of 3.0 once again. Very tricky!

The **increment operator** (++) is used to increase the value of a number by one. For example, if the value of a variable x is 3, then x++ will increment the value of x to 4. This has the exact same effect as writing $x = x + 1$, and is nothing more than convenient shorthand.

Conversely, the **decrement operator** (--) is used to quickly decrease the value of a number by one. For example, if the value of a variable named x is 3, then x-- decreases the value of x to 2. This has the exact same effect as writing $x = x - 1$.

Understanding operator precedence is essential for multiple choice questions on the AP Exam and, perhaps more importantly, for showing off on social media when those "solve this problem" memes pop up and everyone argues over the right answer.

---

4. A math teacher is writing a program that will correctly calculate the area of a circle. Recall that the area of a circle is pi times the radius squared (πr^2). Assuming Math.PI returns an accurate decimal approximation of pi, which of the following statements WILL NOT calculate an accurate area of a circle with radius 22?

(A) `r*r*Math.PI; // r is the int 22`
(B) `r*r*Math.PI; // r is the double 22.0`
(C) `(double)r*r*Math.PI; // r is the int 22`
(D) `(double)(r*r)*Math.PI; // r is the int 22`
(E) All of the above choices will calculate an accurate area.

Here's How to Crack It

Choice (A) will use integer multiplication for r*r but will then convert everything to doubles when it multiplies by Math.PI, a double. Choice (B) is obviously correct. Choices (C) and (D) will cast some of the values to double, but as stated above, this will not impact the result in an undesired way. Therefore, the answer is (E).

Give Me a Break

Humans are pretty smart when it comes to guessing intent For instance, you probably noticed that there's a missing period between this sentence and the one before it. (If not, slow down: AP Computer Science Exam questions require close reading when looking for errors.) Computers, on the other hand, are literal—more annoyingly so, probably, than those teachers who ask if you're physically capable of going to the bathroom when you ask if you can go. To that end, then, it's crucial that you end each complete statement (i.e., sentence) with a semicolon, which is our way of telling the Java compiler that it's reached the end of a step. This doesn't mean that you need to place a semicolon after every line—remember that line breaks exist only to make code more readable to humans—but you must place one after any complete declaration or calculation.

CHAPTER 3 REVIEW DRILL

Answers to the review questions can be found in Chapter 9.

1. Consider the following code segment:

```
Line 1:  int a = 10;
Line 2:  double b = 10.7;
Line 3:  double c = a + b;
Line 4:  int d = a + c;
Line 5:  System.out.println(c + " " + d);
```

   What will be output as a result of executing the code segment?

   (A) 20   20
   (B) 20.0   30
   (C) 20.7   31
   (D) 20.7   30.7
   (E) Nothing will be printed because of a compile-time error.

2. Consider the following code segment:

```
Line 1:  int a = 10;
Line 2:  double b = 10.7;
Line 3:  int d = a + b;
```

   Line 3 will not compile in the code segment above. With which of the following statements could we replace this line so that it compiles?

   I.   int d = (int) a + b;
   II. int d = (int) (a + b);
   III. int d = a + (int) b;

   (A) I
   (B) II
   (C) III
   (D) I and III
   (E) II and III

3. Consider the following code segment.

```
Line 1:  int a = 11;
Line 2:  int b = 4;
Line 3:  double x = 11;
Line 4:  double y = 4;
Line 5:  System.out.print(a / b);
Line 6:  System.out.print(", ");
Line 7:  System.out.print(x / y);
Line 8:  System.out.print(", ");
Line 9:  System.out.print(a / y);
```

What is printed as a result of executing the code segment?

(A) 3, 2.75, 3
(B) 3, 2.75, 2.75
(C) 2, 3, 2
(D) 2, 2.75, 2.75
(E) Nothing will be printed because of a compile-time error.

4. Consider the following code segments:

```
I.   int x = 10;
     int y = 20;
     int z = 0;
     if (x < y && 10 < y / z)
         System.out.println("Homer");
     else
         System.out.println("Bart");
II.  int x = 10;
     int y = 20;
     int z = 0;
     if (x > y && 10 < y / z)
         System.out.println("Homer");
     else
       System.out.println("Bart");
III. int x = 10;
     int y = 20;
     int z = 0;
     if (x < y || 10 < y / z)
         System.out.println("Homer");
     else
         System.out.println("Bart");
```

Which of the code segments above will run without error?

(A) I only
(B) II only
(C) III only
(D) II and III
(E) I, II, and III

KEY TERMS

Computer Science
programming style
commenting
in-line or short comments
long comments
identifiers
white space
interpreter
binary
compiling
compile-time error
logical error
runtime error
string literal (string)
assignment operator
variable
concatenation operator
primitive data
integer
double
Boolean
character
precedence
strongly typed
casting
increment operator (++)
decrement operator (--)

Chapter 4
Flow Control and Constructs

Now that we have some tools to make the computer accomplish a simple task, let's discuss how to make our programs a little more...interesting.

When you wake up in the morning, some tasks occur automatically, while others may depend on a decision. For example, if your alarm clock sounds at 6:00 A.M....wait, what if it doesn't? If it sounds at 6:00 A.M., you proceed with your morning rituals; if it does not sound, you wake up late and have to speed up, or change, your routine. When you sit down to eat your favorite breakfast cereal... none is left! Now what?

Most, if not all, of the actions we perform depend on decisions. These decisions affect whether or not we perform the action, or even how we perform the action. Programs possess this exact ability to make decisions and react accordingly. In this way, the programmer can *control the flow* of the program.

THE IF STATEMENT

If you read the above examples closely, you will literally find the word *if* as a pivotal word in your decision of what action to perform next. The reserved word **if** is a **conditional statement** used in Java when the programmer wants to **control the flow** of the program; i.e., if he or she wants Line 2 to occur ONLY if a condition in Line 1 is true.

The syntax of a simple if statement is:

    if (condition) statement;

Syntax statements in this book will be presented in *pseudocode* in order to illustrate the general form, and then further examples will be given. Pseudocode is not Java code that will compile, but it shows the format of the Java statements that we will write later.

Consider an instance when you are asking a parent whether you can go out to the mall with a friend on Friday night. The (classic) parent response usually looks something like: *If you clean your room, you can go to the mall on Friday.*

In pseudocode, the parent's response could be written as:

    if (you clean your room) go to the mall;

In this example, "you clean your room" is the **condition** of the if statement and "go to the mall" is the *statement*. The condition in an if statement must have a boolean result. Note that if you do clean your room (true), you will go to the mall; however, if you do not clean your room (false), you will not go to the mall. The if statement is written in this way; the programmer is now controlling the flow of the program. Thus "go to the mall" will occur if the condition is true, but will be skipped if the condition is false. Another popular (pseudocode) way to write this statement is:

> if (you clean your room)
>   go to the mall;

This construction simply uses white space to make the code more readable. The AP Exam may present an if statement in either of these formats.

Let's try a code example. Consider the following lines from a Java program:

```
int num1 = 4, num2 = 5;
if (num1 == num2)
    System.out.print ("The numbers are the same.");
```

Since we have an if statement, one of two possibilities could occur, based on whether num1 has the same value of num2...(1) the program would display the string literal "The numbers are the same." if the condition is true, or (2) the program will not display any output if the condition is false.

Note the use, here, of the **boolean operator** ==; do not confuse this boolean operator with the assignment operator =. A boolean operator asks a question, while an assignment operator executes a command. num1 = 4 *assigns* the value of 4 to the variable num1, while num1 == num2 *determines whether* the two values are equal. The assignment statement produces no other result, while the boolean statement returns a truth value based on the comparison.

Wouldn't it be nice if conditions in life depended on just one comparison, as our previous code example did? If we dig a bit deeper into our alarm clock example from before, there are probably a few more decisions that need to be made in order to begin your morning rituals; a few of these decisions might be, "is it a school day?"... "do I feel healthy?"... "is my blanket glued to my mattress, trapping me between them?" Note that each of these questions, regardless of its plausibility, has a true or false (boolean) answer.

If (see how many times we use this word?) the programmer wants to incorporate a more complicated condition into our code, he or she must create a **compound condition**. Compound conditions include at least one boolean operator; each of these and their meaning are as follows:

&&	logical *and*
||	logical *or*
!	logical *not*
==	is equal to
!=	is not equal to

Let's explore how each of these can be incorporated into a program.

Consider a situation in which you need a study break and decide to visit your local bakery for a snack. Your favorite dessert is typically Italian cannoli but you will also accept an apple turnover. But apple turnovers are somewhat dry, so you will only buy one if they are selling coffee that day.

Since this example is relatively complicated, let's break it into chunks.

> When attacking a complicated programming situation, break it into chunks and tackle each part, one by one.

We will use pseudocode for this example.

Let's outline the conditions presented in this example, in order:

- The bakery has cannoli

- The bakery has apple turnovers

- The bakery has coffee

The complication here is that some of these decisions depend on others. For example, if the bakery DOES have cannoli, then it doesn't matter whether it has apple turnovers. Again, step by step...start with condition (1)

```
if (bakery has cannoli) buy dessert;
```

Now, another decision must be made, based on this decision; if the bakery DOES have cannoli, we get our desired dessert. If it does NOT have cannoli, we must try the apple turnover.

```
if (bakery has cannoli)

        buy dessert; // only occurs if bakery has cannoli

else if (bakery has apple turnovers) // only occurs if bakery has no cannoli

        buy dessert; // only occurs if bakery has apple turnovers
```

Note the *else* keyword used here. else is used if the programmer wants a statement to execute if the condition is false. It's not that easy, though...we must consider the coffee. Since you will only buy an apple turnover if there is ALSO coffee for sale, the && operator is appropriate here:

```
1 if (bakery has cannoli)

2       buy dessert; // bakery has cannoli

3 else if (bakery has apple turnovers && bakery has coffee) // no cannoli

4       buy dessert; // bakery has apple turnovers AND coffee
```

This pseudocode seems to work, but we must check for logical errors.

> Remember that logical errors will not be caught by the compiler, and that we cannot test for logical errors on a pencil-and-paper test.

Using the numbered lines of pseudocode, let's trace the possibilities using a *trace table*.

has cannoli: line 1, condition is true -> line 2, buy dessert

no cannoli, no turnovers, no coffee: line 1, false -> line 3, false -> no dessert

no cannoli, yes turnovers, no coffee: line 1, false -> line 3, false -> no dessert

no cannoli, no turnovers, yes coffee: line 1, false -> line 3, false -> no dessert

no cannoli, yes turnovers, yes coffee: line 1, false -> line 3, true -> line 4, buy dessert

Moral of the story: This bakery better get itself together.

There is a lot of Java here! Controlling the flow of a program can be difficult and confusing, which is why it is a popular topic on the AP Exam. But it is also important because most programs, like most things we do in life, rely on conditions and react accordingly.

To make things more complicated (or more life-like…) consider a further idea…. What if we want to execute SEVERAL commands when a condition is true (or false) instead of just one? For example, using the bakery case, let's say that buying cannoli is so exciting that we must devour it right away. In other words, if the conditions are met for the bakery having cannoli, we want to buy it AND it. The pseudocode would look something like:

```
1 if (bakery has cannoli)

2 {
```

3   buy dessert; // bakery has cannoli

4   eat dessert;

5 }

6 else if (bakery has apple turnovers && bakery has coffee) // no cannoli

7   buy dessert; // bakery has apple turnovers AND coffee

The { and } symbols in lines 2 and 5 indicate **blocking**, a technique used in flow control statements that allows the programmer to execute a series of commands (instead of just one) when a given condition is satisfied.

Use blocking to execute more than one statement based on a condition.

---

1. Consider the following code.

```
int x = 0;
if (x == 0)
    System.out.print ("1");
else
    System.out.print ("2");
    System.out.print ("3");
```

Which of the following best describes the result of executing the code segment?

(A) Since the value of x is 0, the first print statement will be performed, producing 1 as the output

(B) Since the value of x is 0, the first print statement will be performed, producing 13 as the output

(C) Since the value of x is 0, the first print statement will be performed, producing 123 as the output

(D) == is not the correct boolean operator, so a syntax error will be produced by the compiler prior to execution

(E) == is not the correct boolean operator, so a logical error will be produced by the compiler prior to execution

Here's How to Crack It

Since x is assigned to 0, the condition of the if statement will be true, performing the first print statement and outputting 1. The else statement will then be skipped, so 2 will not be outputted, eliminating (C). The trick here, however, is that the third print statement is NOT part of the else statement since it is not blocked with {}, even though it is (incorrectly) indented. This will output 3, eliminating (A), (D), and (E). Furthermore, == is a valid boolean operator so (D) and (E) are clearly incorrect (and a compiler will never produce a logical error). The correct answer is (B).

Before we move on, let's scrutinize the boolean operator situation a bit further.

Often, the truth values of a situation are simply abbreviated to a single letter. This action occurs because most real programs involve dozens, or more, of conditions and variables. As a result, it is important (and essential for the AP Exam) to evaluate the **truth value** of a bunch of random boolean variables, completely out of context.

If we look at the bakery example one more time (seriously, just once), the line

    buy dessert;

occurs twice. Good programming style attempts to repeat the same lines of code as little as possible, if ever. Therefore, we can rearrange the boolean operators in the following way, creating the same result:

if (bakery has cannoli OR (bakery has apple turnovers AND bakery has coffee))

    buy dessert;

That is a hefty boolean condition; however, it (1) eliminates the repetition of code and (2) provides a more "elegant" programming solution. "elegant" is a relative term, of course, but the AP Exam often uses this subjective term to write code and to confuse you. Either way, you should be familiar with both ways.

> The AP Exam FRQs do not require you to write code with "elegance" in the FRQs; they will accept any code solution as long as it fulfills the specifications of the question.

To sum up, let's create a truth table of various combinations of boolean conditions, simply called A and B, and the truth possibilities based on those combinations. Since there are two variables, there are four possible combinations of their truth values: they are both true, only one of them is true (both ways), and neither is true. These possibilities are shown in the first two columns below. In subsequent columns, the truth values are shown for the boolean statements shown in the first row.

A	B	A&&B	A||B	!A	!B	!(A&&B)	!A||!B
T	T	T	T	F	F	F	F
T	F	F	T	F	T	T	T
F	T	F	T	T	F	T	T
F	F	F	F	T	T	T	T

An && (and) expression is true if BOTH A and B are true; a || (or) expression is true if EITHER A and B are true, or if they are both true. The ! (not) operator simply reverses the truth value of the variable. Note that the truth values of the last two expressions are identical; these results are an illustration of De Morgan's Law, which is similar to the "distributive property" of boolean expressions. Applying a ! (not) operator to an expression reverses the truth value of each variable and changes an && to an ||, or vice versa. If this law is applied to !(A&&B), the result is !A||!B, as shown in the last column.

> The intricacies of if statements that we just explored will apply to all flow control statements, so understand them here before you move onto the next section.

2. Consider the following code segment.

```
boolean a = true, b = false;
if (<missing code>)
    System.out.print ("Nice job.");
else
    System.out.print ("Nicer job.");
```

Which of the following could be used to replace <missing code> so that the output of this block of code is "Nicer job."?

   I. `a && !b`
  II. `!a || b`
 III. `!a && b`

(A) I only
(B) I and II only
(C) I and III only
(D) II and III only
(E) I, II, and III

Here's How to Crack It

Ahh, the dreaded "roman numeral" problems that the College Board loves to torture us with. If "Nicer job." has to be displayed then the condition must evaluate to *false*. if(b) would work, but that's too easy. The options show relationships between a and b, and boolean "and" is easier to evaluate since it's false whenever *any* variable is false. a&&b would accomplish the job because b is false, and so would !a&&b because b is still false…. This happens to be option III. We can then eliminate (A) and (B), since they do not include III. Option I would be true,

Roman numeral problems are only as annoying as their hardest option; look at the options and do the easiest one first, which is often not I. Then use process of elimination.

because !b is true and therefore a&&!b would be true, but we want false. We can now eliminate answer choices leftover with I, which are (C) and (E). By process of elimination, there is only one choice left, and we didn't even have to evaluate option II. The answer is (D).

–––––––––––––––––○–––––––––––––––––

–––––––––––––––––○–––––––––––––––––

3. Suppose p and q are declared as boolean variable and have been initialized to unknown truth values.

What does the following boolean expression evaluate to?

```
(!p && !q) || !(p || q)
```

(A) The expression always evaluates to true.
(B) The expression always evaluates to false.
(C) The expression evaluates to true whenever p is false.
(D) The expression evaluates to true whenever q is false.
(E) The expression evaluates to false whenever p and q have opposite truth values.

Here's How to Crack It

Using DeMorgan's law, we can see that the truth value of the left expression (!p && !q) will be the same as the truth value of the right expression !(p ||q), so we can test our choices using the easiest side, which is the right side. Through a quick trial-and-error and looking at the answer choices, let p and q be false; the right expression will evaluate to true, making the whole expression true and eliminating (B). Now let both p and q be true; the right expression will evaluate to false, making the whole expression false and eliminating (A), (C), and (D). Similar guess-and-check can be used to finish the job, but you've already eliminated four choices. Through process of elimination, (E) is correct.

–––––––––––––––––○–––––––––––––––––

Trial-and-error and process of elimination are both useful techniques for boolean expression problems.

THE WHILE STATEMENT

When the programmer wants a statement (or multiple statements) to occur repeatedly, he or she has two options: (1) copy and paste the statement as many times as necessary (inefficient and ugly) or (2) write a conditional statement called a **loop** (efficient and "elegant").

> On the AP Exam, you will be expected to know two types of loops: *while* and *for*.

The syntax of a **while loop** is as follows:

      while (condition) statement;

Note its similarity to the if statement. The *while* statement is a loop that does exactly what its name implies: the loop cycles again and again, *while* the condition is true. Consider a paint-soaked paintbrush that you just used to paint your bedroom. Hopefully, you will not store the paintbrush away until it is no longer dirty. A while loop that could represent this situation in pseudocode would look like:

1 while (paintbrush is dirty)

2   do not put away paintbrush;

3 put away paintbrush;

Note that if the condition is true (paintbrush is dirty), line 2 will continue to execute, over and over again, until the condition is false (paintbrush is not dirty). Once the condition is false, line 2 is skipped and line 3 is finally executed.

Unfortunately, this loop is fundamentally flawed. Although its logic SEEMS to be correct, it is not. Within the statement(s) of a loop, the variable(s) in the condition must be modified so that there is a chance that the truth value of the condition to be changed. How will the paintbrush become less dirty--is this a self-cleaning paintbrush? Probably not. Therefore, the paintbrush will actually remain dirty and Java will keep executing line 2, forever. When this happens, the programmer has written an **infinite loop**, which is a logical error and is therefore undesirable. Ever have your computer randomly "freeze" in the middle of your work, leaving it unresponsive and causing you to lose that perfectly sculpted digital picture that you just spent an hour perfecting? That is an infinite loop and it is definitely not desirable.

On the AP Exam, you must trace code in MCQs and detect infinite loops. You must also write code in FRQs that is free of infinite loops.

While loops, like if statements, are therefore dependent on the condition. If the condition is more intricate, as it usually is (Do we put the paintbrush away if it is not dirty but it is wet? Not dirty but it is still not CLEAN?), we can use the techniques outlined in the previous section. Boolean operators are mandatory and compound conditions and/or blocking are appropriate, when necessary. A more realistic pseudocode representation of our paintbrush example could be:

1   while (paintbrush is dirty && paintbrush is wet) // ! means NOT wet

2   {

3   clean paintbrush; // is it COMPLETELY clean?

4   dry paintbrush; // is it COMPLETELY dry?

5   do not put paintbrush away;

6   }

7   put paintbrush away;

In this example, the paintbrush will continue to be cleaned and dried (and not put away) until it either NOT dirty or NOT wet, or both, at which point the condition will be false and the paintbrush will be put away. Remember that an && condition is only true if both conditions are true; therefore, if the paintbrush is not dirty but is still wet (or vice versa), it will be put away. Is this the desired result? Who cares?! Reading code is not about logical understanding of a situation; rather, it is about understanding the code and its result.

It is also worth noting here that an and statement may be **short-circuited**. Since both Boolean statements on either side of the && must be true, a false result from the first statement will automatically render the condition false. As a result, Java will completely skip the second condition, bypassing the rest of the condition.

4. Consider the following code segment.

```
int val1 = 2, val2 = 22, val3 = 78;
while (val2 % val1 == 0 || val2 % 3 == 0)
{
    val3++;
    val2--;
}
```

What will val3 contain after the code segment is executed?

(A) 77
(B) 78
(C) 79
(D) 80
(E) None of the above

Here's How to Crack It

Tracing the loop is the best way to handle this type of problem. Remember that % returns the remainder of the division between the two numbers. In order for the condition to be true, there first must be no remainder when dividing val2 by val1. Since 22/2=11, there is no remainder, and the condition will be true (an "or" statement will be true if its first condition is true) and the loop statements will execute, incrementing val3 to 79 and decrementing val2 to 21. Since there are no visible statements that would decrement val3 below 79, we can eliminate (A) and (B). Execution then returns to the condition; this time, we have 21/2 which does yield a remainder so we check the rest of the division, and 21 % 3 does not yield a remainder so the condition is true overall and the loop statements execute again. We now have val3 = 80 and val2 = 20, eliminating (C). Again we try to evaluate the condition, which will be true since 20/2 has no remainder, increasing val3 to 81 and decreasing val2 to 19. We can now eliminate (D). By process of elimination, (E) is the answer. (In case you are wondering, it will take several more loop iterations before the condition is finally false, but it will get there eventually. Try it for practice!)

When tracing loops, make a table of values for each variable to organize your work.

5. What will be the output when the following code is evaluated?

```
for (int k = 0; k < 3; k++)
{
    for (int j = 1; j < 4; j++)
    {
        System.out.print (j + " ");
    }
}
```

(A) 1 2 3 4
    1 2 3 4
    1 2 3 4

(B) 0 1 2
    0 1 2
    0 1 2
    0 1 2

(C) 1 2 3
    1 2 3
    1 2 3

(D) 1 2 3
    1 2 3
    1 2 3
    1 2 3

(E) 1 2 3 4
    1 2 3 4
    1 2 3 4
    1 2 3 4

Here's How to Crack It

One glance at the condition in the outer for loop reveals that it will iterate a total of 3 times (k=0, 1, and 2). The same will occur for the inner loop (j=1, 2, and 3). Answers that involve loops of 4 can be eliminated, ruling out every choice except (C). The answer is (C).

6. Consider the following code fragments. Assume someNum has been correctly defined and initialized as a positive integer.

```
I.  for (int i = 0; i < someNum; i++)
    {
            i++;
            someNum--;
    }
II. for (int i = 1; i < someNum - 1; i++)
    {
            i++;
            someNum-=1;
    }
III.int i = 0;
    while (i < someNum)
    {
            i++;
            someNum--;
    }
```

All of the following statements are true about these code fragments EXCEPT

(A) The for loops in I and II can be rewritten as while loops with the same results as written above
(B) The value of someNum after execution of I and III is the same
(C) The value of i after execution of II and III is the same
(D) I, II, and III will all have a different number of loop iterations
(E) I, II, and III all produce different results

Here's How to Crack It

For an "except" question, cross out the original sentence and rewrite it without the negative so it's easier to understand. In this case, rewrite the question to say, "Which is false?" Eliminate (A) since virtually every for loop can be rewritten as a while loop, and vice versa. For the remaining choices, let someNum equal a positive nonzero value (not too big)...let's try 5.

I.	i	someNum
	0	5
	1	4
	2	3
	3	
	4	

II.	i	someNum	someNum-1
	1	5	4
	2	4	3
	3		

III.	i	someNum
	0	5
	1	4
	2	3
	3	2

From these trace tables of values, (C), (D), and (E) are all true. Choice (B) is the only false statement, so (B) is the answer.

THE FOR STATEMENT

A *for* statement is another type of loop. **for loops** and while loops are equally effective in controlling the flow of a program when a statement (or set of statements) is to be executed repeatedly. The syntax is quite different, however:

    for (initializer; condition; incrementer) statement;

Since the for loop requires more components, it can potentially avoid an infinite loops situation, although there is no guarantee. Let's try a pseudocode example. Consider a younger brother or sister who is learning to count to 22. He or she will start with 1 and continue counting until he or she reaches 22, and then stop. The counting process repeats until the condition is met. Pseudocode may look like:

for (start with 1; not yet reached 22; go to the next number)

    count the number;

The execution of a for loop is more difficult to understand. Here are the steps:

1. The initializer will occur first, beginning the process
2. The condition will be checked to make sure it is true
3. The statement(s) will execute
4. The incrementer will occur, changing the number
5. See step (1) and keep repeating (1) to (4), until (2) is false
6. Loop ends

A code example of this situation, outputting the current number to the screen, could be:

for (int num = 1; num <= 22; num++)

    System.out.println (num);

This code will produce each counting number and output it to the screen, each on a separate line. Once again, remember that boolean operators are mandatory and compound conditions and/or blocking are appropriate, when necessary.

> for loops and while loops are interchangeable in most cases, although one method may look more elegant than the other

On the AP Exam, MCQs may show you several loop structure in both formats and ask you questions that compare the results, so you should practice working between them. FRQs that ask you to write a loop are equally as correct if you decide to write a for loop or a while loop.

for and while statements are loops; if statements are not

The following two code examples involving loops have identical results:

```
char myInitial = 'X';
while (myInitial <= 'Z')
{
    System.out.print (myInitial);
    myInitial++;
}
System.out.print ("Done");
```

```
for (char myInitial = 'X'; myInitial <= 'Z'; myInitial++)
    System.out.println (myInitial);
System.out.print ("Done");
```

Each set of code is equally as effective and equally as respected in both the programming world and on the AP Exam. But MCQs could use either format, or both, so you should familiarize yourself with both.

> while loops perform the blocked statement(s) once, and then evaluate the condition to determine whether the loop continues; for loops evaluate the condition first and then perform the blocked statement(s) if the condition is initially true

7. Consider the following code segment:

```
for (int i = 1; i < 100; i = i * 2)
{
    if (i / 50 == 0)
        System.out.print (i + " ");
}
```

What is printed as a result of executing the code segment?

(A) 1 2 4 8 16 32 64
(B) 1 2 4 8 16 32
(C) 2 4 8 16 32 64
(D) 2 4 8 16 32
(E) 4 8 16 32 64

Here's How to Crack It

The initial condition for execution to enter the loop is i = 1. Since 1/50 = 0 in integer division, 1 will be displayed, so eliminate (C), (D), and (E). The difference between (A) and (B) is the 64 at the end, so let's skip the output in between and focus on the 64. If i = 64, the if statement will be false, and thus 64 will not be printed. Therefore, the answer is (B).

Hardware and Software

The official AP Computer Science Course Description lists hardware and software topics as one of the requirements of an AP Computer Science course. It is very unlikely that you will see questions about these topics on the exam, but you should at least be familiar with the following:

Processor: Also known as a CPU or Central Processing Unit. This is the brain of the computer, where the processing takes place.

Random Access Memory: Also known as RAM, or simply "memory." This is where programs and the data that they use are kept. RAM is volatile: When a computer is turned off, anything stored in RAM disappears.

Peripherals: Extra devices that you use with a computer, such as a mouse or printer.

Source Code: This is the code that you write, which is readable by humans. In Java, source code files end in .java.

Compiler: A program that reads source code and translates it into a set of low-level instructions that the computer understands. In Java, the compiler translates source code to bytecode—an intermediate level of instructions that can be understood by many different types of computers. A compiler also detects errors in code. For example, if you forget to include a semicolon at the end of a statement, the compiler will give you an error message. Files of compiled code in Java end with a .class extension.

Bytecode: An intermediate step between source code, which is readable by humans, and machine code, which is very low-level code read by the hardware. A Java compiler produces bytecode.

Java Virtual Machine (JVM): A piece of software that reads the bytecode produced by the compiler and runs the program. Different JVMs exist for different types of computer operating systems (such as Windows, Unix, or Macintosh). Each JVM can take the same bytecode and run it on the particular operating system for which the JVM is designed.

Responsible Use of Computer Systems

The College Board also lists "Responsible Use of Computer Systems" as a requirement of an AP Course. This is another topic that you are unlikely to actually see on the exam, however.

In the unlikely event that you do see a question related to this topic, just use common sense. Obviously, computer professionals should respect the privacy of the people who use their software, and they should strive to produce software that is useful and error free. Now that software is in many of the things that we use every day, such as cars, phones, and airplanes, whether or not software is reliable and well designed can quite literally be a matter of life or death.

Synopsis

Here's a quick synopsis of which concepts from this chapter you can expect to find on the exam, and which you won't.

	Concepts Covered on the AP Computer Science Exam	Concepts Not Covered on the AP Computer Science Exam
Primitives	• int • double • boolean	• short • long • byte • char • float
Increment / Decrement Operators	• x++ • x - -	• ++x • - -x
Logical Operators	• = = • != • < • <= • > • >= • && • || • !	• & • | • ^ • << • >> • >>>
Conditional Statements	• if/else • for • while	• do/while • switch • plain and labeled break • continue
Miscellaneous		• ?: (ternary operator) • User input • JavaDoc comments

AP Connect

Head over to your online student tools—what we call AP Connect—to download a printable version of this chart and other important pages from within this book.

CHAPTER 4 REVIEW DRILL

Answers to the review questions can be found in Chapter 9.

1. Consider the following code segment:

```
for (int i = 200; i > 0; i /= 3)
{
    if (i % 2 == 0)
        System.out.print(i + "   ");
}
```

What is output as a result of executing the code segment?

(A) 200 66 22 7 2
(B) 66 22 7 2
(C) 200 66 22 2
(D) 200 66 22
(E) 7

2. Consider the following statement:

```
int i = x % 50;
```

If *x* is a positive integer, which of the following could NOT be the value of i after the statement above executes?

(A) 0
(B) 10
(C) 25
(D) 40
(E) 50

3. Consider the following output:

```
0   1
0   2   4
0   3   6   9
0   4   8   12   16
```

Which of the following code segments will produce this output?

(A)
```
for (int x = 1; x < 5; x++)
{
  for (int z = 0; z <= x; z++)
  {
      System.out.print(x * z + "  ");
  }
  System.out.println(" ");
}
```

(B)
```
for (int x = 1; x <= 5; x++)
{
  for (int z = 0; z < x; z++)
  {
      System.out.print(x * z + "  ");
  }
  System.out.println(" ");
}
```

(C)
```
for (int x = 1; x < 5; x++)
{
  for (int z = 0; z <= 4; z++)
  {
      System.out.print(x * z + "  ");
  }
  System.out.println(" ");
}
```

(D)
```
for (int x = 1; x < 5; x++)
{
  for (int z = 0; z <= 4; z += 2)
  {
      System.out.print(x * z + "  ");
  }
  System.out.println(" ");
}
```

(E)
```
for (int x = 1; x <= 5; x++
{
  for (int z = 0; z <= x; z++)
  {
      System.out.print(x * z + "  ");
  }
  System.out.println(" ");
}
```

4. The speed limit of a stretch of highway is 55 miles per hour (mph). The highway patrol issues speeding tickets to anyone caught going faster than 55 miles per hour. The fine for speeding is based on the following scale:

Speed	Fine
greater than 55 mph but less than 65 mph	$100
greater than or equal to 65 mph but less than 75 mph	$150
greater than or equal to 75 mph	$300

If the value of the int variable speed is the speed of a driver who was pulled over for going faster than 55 mph, which of the following code segments will assign the correct value to the int variable fine?

```
I.      if (speed >= 75)
            fine = 300;
        if (speed >= 65 && speed < 75)
            fine = 150;
        if (speed > 55 && speed < 65)
            fine = 100;
II.     if (speed >= 75)
            fine = 300;
        if (65 <= speed < 75)
            fine = 150;
        if (55 < speed < 65)
            fine = 100;
III..   if (speed >= 75)
            fine = 300;
        if (speed >= 65)
            fine = 150;
        if (speed > 55)
            fine = 100;
```

(A) I only
(B) II only
(C) III only
(D) I and II
(E) I and III

5. Consider the following code segment:

```
int x = 10;
int y = 3;
boolean b = true;
for (int i = 0, i < 15; i += 5)
{
    x = x + y;
    b = (x % y = = 2);
    if (!b)
    {
        y++;
        i += 5;
    }
}
```

What is the value of x after the code segment executes?

(A) 10
(B) 15
(C) 17
(D) 22
(E) 25

6. In the following statement, a and b are boolean variables:

```
boolean c = (a && b) || !(a | | b);
```

Under what conditions will the value of c be true?

(A) Only when the value of a is different than the value of b.
(B) Only when the value of a is the same as the value of b.
(C) Only when a and b are both true.
(D) Only when a and b are both false.
(E) The value of c will be true for all values of a and b.

7. Consider the following code segment:

```
while ((x > y) || y >= z)
{
    System.out.print("*");
}
```

In the code segment above, x, y, and z are the variables of type int. Which of the following must be true after the code segment has executed?

(A) x > y || y >= z
(B) x <= y || y > z
(C) x > y && y >= z
(D) x < y && y <= z
(E) x <= y && y < z

8. Consider the following code segment:

```
int a = 0;
for (int i = 0; i < 10; i ++)
{
    for (int k = 0; k <= 5; k++)
    {
        for (int z = 1; z <= 16; z = z * 2)
        {
            a++;
        }
    }
}
```

What is the value of a after the code segment executes?

(A) 31
(B) 180
(C) 200
(D) 300
(E) 400

9. Consider the following code segment:

```
int x = 10;
int y = x / 3;
int z = x % 2;
x++;
System.out.println(x)
```

What is printed as a result of executing the code segment above?

(A) 2
(B) 4
(C) 10
(D) 11
(E) 15

10. Consider the following code segment:

```
int a = 10;
double b = 3.7;
int c = 4;
int x = (int) (a + b);
double y = (double) a / c;
double z = (double) (a / c);
double w = x + y + z;
System.out.println(w);
```

What is printed as a result of evaluating the code above?

(A) 10
(B) 15
(C) 15.5
(D) 17
(E) 17.5

11. Consider the following code segment:

```
int i = 1;
int k = 1;
while (i < 5)
{
    k *= i;
    k++;
}
System.out.print(k);
```

What is printed as a result of executing the code above?

(A) 6
(B) 10
(C) 24
(D) 120
(E) Nothing is printed.

KEY TERMS

if
conditional statement
flow control
condition
boolean operator ==
&& - logical and
|| - logical or
! - logical not
== - is equal to
!= - is not equal to
truth value
loop
while loop
infinite loop
short-circuited
for loops
processor
Random Access Memory
peripherals
source code
compiler
bytecode
Java Virtual Machine (JVM)

Chapter 5
Classes

When a group of statements, including control structures, are assembled into a single unit, the unit is called a **class**. Similar to a word processing document or a picture file stored on your computer, a class is stored on your computer in a file. Unlike a word processing document, however, a class must follow specific rules in order to conform to Java and, as a result, to be understood by the compiler. Remember that your brilliantly constructed program is useless unless the compiler can successfully translate it into machine code.

DESIGN & STRUCTURE

The structure of a class, at this level anyway, is straightforward. Take all of the statements you've written before this chapter, put curly brackets around them, kind of like a huge block, name it, and save it. The naming conventions for a class are similar to those of a variable, except that they should begin with a capital letter. The name of the class should reference the purpose or function of the class. For example, a class that calculates a GPA might be called GPA or GradePointAvg. The way we declare a class in Java is using the header:

```
public class GradePointAvg
{
    // statements not shown
}
```

Note that the statements in the class reside at least one tab stop across the page. If the programmer would like to use more white space within the structures of the class, they will be tabbed further into the page:

```
public class GradePointAvg
{
    // other code and variable declarations not shown

    while (/* condition not shown */)
    {
        // looped statements not shown
    }
}
```

Typically, variable declarations are placed into the code first, right after the class header, as a sort of "setup" for the rest of the class. Of course, this is not a rule, but it is a good guideline in order to keep your code readable.

On the AP Exam, your code must be readable (not just legible), quickly and easily.

This class would be saved to the computer as GradePointAvg.java; the .java extension helps the compiler to recognize the file as containing Java code. If the code compiles (there are no syntax errors), the compiler will create another file in the same folder called GradePointAvg.class; this file is unreadable to the programmer because it is encoded in machine language. The computer, however, uses this file to execute the program. The .java file is called the **source code** of the program, since defines the program's actions and funtions.

Remember that classes are executed top-down; i.e., line 1 followed by line 2, etc. If the programmer wants to alter top-down execution, he or she must use a flow control structure, as we studied before.

———————————○———————————

1. Which of the following class declarations would NOT cause a compile-time error? Assume the rest of the code compiles as intended.

    (A) `public class Calculus`
    (B) `public class apCalculus`
    (C) `public class APCalculus`
    (D) `public class 4APCalculus`
    (E) `public class APCalculus extends Math`

Here's How to Crack It

Choice (A) and (C) follow the format as discussed above. The naming conventions of a class name are that we *should* begin with a capital letter; however, this is not required by the compiler, so (B) does not cause an error. Be careful when the College Board uses programming techniques in the answer choices that you may not know; in this case, the *extends* keyword comes in a later section of this book, so you may choose it here if you have never seen it. However, it is used properly, so (e) does not cause an error, but you would not be able to use POE if you didn't know this. The real problem with (D) is that it begins with a numerical character, which is not allowed in a class name. The answer is (D).

———————————○———————————

POE is a great tool, but it isn't always enough on an AP Exam. Know your stuff!

METHODS

Picture a Java class as a closet, with essentially limitless possibilities. If you were to declare a single shelf to hold, say, board game boxes…that would be a great way to organize your collection of games, toys, and other sophisticated possessions.

A class is organized in this way using **methods**.

> A method is a group of code that performs a specific task.

Although a class can simply contain a list of commands, any program that accomplishes a task could easily balloon to 100 lines of code, or more. Instead of writing a class that contains a giant list of disorganized code, writing separate methods for each small task (within the overarching task) is an excellent way to make your code more readable. In addition, method-based classes enable easier flow control.

To understand this concept, let's break down a bright, sunny Saturday in the middle of the summer (don't worry—you will make it). Perhaps some of the activities you would do might include, getting out of bed (obviously), eating breakfast, taking a shower, getting ready for the beach, driving to the beach, enjoying the beach, and eating lunch. Each of these activities has its own specific components; that is, part of eating breakfast includes drinking orange juice and taking a daily vitamin supplement. The pseudocode of a program that simulates these Saturday's activities might look like:

```
public class Saturday1
{
    hear alarm;
    turn off alarm;
    get out of bed;
    make breakfast;
    eat breakfast; ...
```

You get the idea…. A long list of commands that occur top-down. Now, consider each of these general activities as a separate grouping of smaller activities, called a method. Each small activity will be defined later, but your Saturday class would look much cleaner:

```
public class Saturday2
{
    wake up method; // includes alarm
    eat breakfast method; // includes preparation, OJ,
                          // vitamin, etc.
    take a shower method; // includes preparing for the
                          // shower, etc.
    beach method; // includes prep for the beach, driving
                  // to the beach, etc.
    eat lunch method;
}
```

The result is a cleaner, more structured class that is easier to read. A class that is created to control a larger program, such as Saturday2, is called a **driver class** because it *drives* the program through its general structure which will, in turn, execute the smaller commands. Note also that if, for some reason, the programmer wanted the simulation to take a shower before eating breakfast, the two lines would be switched in Saturday2 and the job is done. Performing the same change in Saturday1 would involve switching multiple lines of code. Even more poignant would be a simulation that repeats method calls, such as one that represents your extra hungry older brother, who eats breakfast twice. The driver would simply call the breakfast method twice (or use a loop to call it more than twice) and the job is completed.

An **object class** is a different kind of class which houses the "guts" of the methods that the driver class calls. As you understand this setup, you will see that your driver classes begin to shorten, while your object classes expand. For example, the driver of a car truly performs a relatively small set of actions in order to drive the car: start the engine, buckle the seatbelt, check the mirrors, accelerate, brake. The driver does not actually understand (nor does he need to) exactly how these operations work, he just does them. How does the accelerator pedal ACTUALLY make the car move more quickly? Doesn't matter. The "driver" just operates the pedal and the rest happens under the hood. The object class is the "under the hood" class. It defines all of the aspects of an object; more specifically, it defines what the object *has* and what the object *does*.

> For the AP Exam, you must be able to write, troubleshoot, and understand object AND driver classes, as well as understand how they interact. These skills are HUGE in the FRQs!

Back to the breakfast example…

Pseudocode for the object class might look something like this:

```
public class Saturday3
{
    wake up (...)
    {
        hear alarm
        turn off alarm
        get out of bed
    }


    breakfast (...)
    {
        make breakfast;
        eat breakfast;
    }
    ...
```

Since our object class could be used for any day of the week, not just Saturday, *BeachDay* might be a more appropriate name for this class. The driver class from before, which executes a series of actions for this particular day, might be called *Saturday*.

———————————○———————————

2. Which of the following statements would best describe an efficient design to represent a pair of sunglasses?
    (A) A Sunglass driver class with methods that unfold, clean, and wear the objects in the class.
    (B) A Sunglass object class with methods that unfold, clean, and wear the objects in the class.
    (C) A PairOfSunglasses driver class with methods that unfold, clean, and wear the objects in the class.
    (D) A PairOfSunglasses object class with methods that unfold, clean, and wear the objects in the class.
    (E) A UseSunglasses driver class with statement that unfold, clean, and wear the sunglasses; no object class is needed for this task.

Here's How to Crack It

Design questions must account for efficiency and "beauty", since the former isn't formally tested on the FRQs and the latter is not tested in the FRQs. Since a pair of Sunglasses is best represented as an object—is has attributes and can do tasks—(E) is not appropriate. A sunglass object does not properly represent this object; does a Sunglass class represent a single lens of the glasses? A piece of glass that blocks the sun? Both? This is too ambiguous and therefore eliminates (A) and (B). Since a PairOfSunglasses object would be defined in an object class, (C) is not appropriate. The answer is (D).

———————————○———————————

One more item that needs to be mentioned...do you see how each method in the object class has a "title," or **header**? Driver classes must, for our purposes in this course, have a method header called **main**. Therefore, every driver class will contain the method header for main, as shown below.

This is a Java book, right? So let's look at some Java. These two classes, one driver and one object, are designed to simulate a phone downloading and opening a new app.

```
1 public class UsePhoneApp
2 {
3   public static void main (String[] args) // just do
it, we'll explain later
4   {
5       Phone myPhone = new Phone ();
6       myPhone.downloadApp();
7       myPhone.openApp();
8       myPhone.closeApp();
9   }
10}
```

```
1 public class Phone
2 {
3   private boolean hasApp;
4   public Phone ()
5   {
6       hasApp = false;
7   }
8   public void downloadApp()
9   {
10      hasApp = true;
11  }
12
13  public void closeApp() // closes the app
14  {
15      if (hasApp)
16          System.out.println ("App is closed.");
17  }
18
19  public void openApp() // opens the app
20  {
21      if (hasApp)
22          System.out.println ("App is running...");
23  }
24 }
```

OUTPUT:

```
App is running...
App is closed.
```

There are many components in this program; first, note that we now have two classes that make up a single program. In isolation, neither of these classes would produce a useful result. The driver class would not compile because the compiler does not understand the methods if they are not present (compiler: what does openApp mean?); the object class would compile but would not actually perform any actions without the driver (compiler: when do I openApp, and on which phone?).

Line 5 in the driver coordinates with lines 4–7 in the object class. Lines 4–7 in the object class comprise a special kind of method called a **constructor**. An object must be constructed before it can perform any actions, just as a car must be built before it can be driven. Line 5 in the driver calls this constructor method, which "builds" the Phone object; this command must occur before the non-constructor methods are called, otherwise the compiler will return an error. Imagine someone pressing an imaginary accelerator pedal and trying to drive somewhere, without a car. Interesting, but not possible.

Line 3 of the object class defines whether the Phone has an app (true) or does not (false). This is the sole attribute of a Phone object in our program; more complex programs may have dozens or even hundreds of attributes (a phone, in reality, has many more attributes, such as a screen, volume buttons, etc.). The programmer should write these attributes, called **instance data** or **data fields**, directly after the class header. Following the data fields is the constructor, as we stated before, and then a series of methods that control what the Phone *can do*.

> An object class defines what an object HAS and DOES.

A method has several components. The method header is built in a very specific way; its syntax is as follows:

```
visibility returnType methodName (param1, param2, …)
```

The visibility of a method can be public or private, depending on the situation (more on this later). The **return type** identifies what type of data, if any, will be returned from the method after its commands are executed. The name of a method, similar to the name of a variable, should be an intuitive name that summarizes the function of the method; it should conform to the same specifications as a variable name (begin with a lowercase letter, etc.). The **parameters**, which are optional, are the data that the method needs in order to perform its job.

In our previous example, the method header for closeApp was

```
public void closeApp()
```

This is functional, but it is also relatively simple for the example. Its visibility is public, its return type is void (there is no information returned), and it does not have parameters. A more realistic method to close an app on a phone might require information regarding when it should be closed, and might return data whether or not it was closed successfully. Thus, the revised method header might look like:

```
public boolean closeApp (int minutes)
```

Note that the single parameter, minutes, is defined with its type. Since minutes will be a temporary variable that exists only during the execution of this method, it must be defined as new, right in the header. A method can have any number of parameters, depending on the programmer's design decisions for the program.

A method must begin with a header, containing a visibility modifier (private or public), a return type or void if no information will be returned, and a method name. Parameter(s) are optional, depending on the method's requirements to perform its task.

The ultimate purpose of a method is to perform some sort of task with respect to the object. Note that openApp() and closeApp() simply access the data field hasApp and react accordingly; i.e., the message is only displayed if the value hasApp is true. downloadApp() is more profound, in a way; rather than simply accessing data, it actually changes the value of a data field—in this case, updates hasApp to true once the "app" is "downloaded". As a result, it is common in Java to label methods like openApp() and closeApp() as **accessor methods** and to label methods like downloadApp() as **mutator methods**.

We have mentioned a car in several examples in this chapter, but it's a great way to understand these concepts. When you want to start a car, you have to go through a series of steps. Since all of those steps perform, ultimately, a single action—the car starting—a method would be a great way to keep the "car starting" commands in a single, convenient unit. As a programmer, you would have to decide what data the method would need in order to work (parameter(s)) and what data, if any, the method would return. Does the car need a key to start? A password code? Does the brake pedal have to be depressed? This information would all be accepted through parameters. Should the method return whether the car has started? How long it took to start? A code that represents whether it needs an oil change? These are all examples of possible return data.

In some cases, there may be a situation in which the car can be started multiple ways; i.e., the owner has a push-button starter and a remote starter. The designer could write two startCar methods (or three, or four…), each one performing the same task but requiring different information (parameters) to do the task. This process is called **overloading** and can be accomplished by writing two or more methods with identical names but different types and/or numbers of parameters.

A method may accept any number of parameters, but may only return one data value or object.

As a final example for this section, consider a programmer who is trying to write an object class that represents a book (like this book, only arbitrarily more interesting). Some of the data the programmer may consider are:

- What does a book *have*? A cover, pages, words, …

- What does can a book *do*? It can be read, be skimmed, be put away, …

From this information, the programmer can begin to write the object class. He or she must first determine which item(s) on his or her list are relevant to the situation, so as to keep the object class as efficient as possible. For example, if the programmer is designing a book to be used as a paperweight, it is probably not important to discuss how many words are in the book, so that data field would not be incorporated into the program. Likewise, if the programmer is not a student studying a ridiculous amount of books in a short amount of time (sound familiar?) then it may not be relevant to have a method that skims the book, rather than reading it closely. The class will then be built based on these decisions.

As you can see, the **planning** of the program is equally as important, if not more important, than the actual writing of the program. In some classes, your teacher may remind you to "write an outline" or "write a first draft" before you compose the final product, and you might skip that step and go right to end unit, and still be successful. For programming at any profound level, which is required in this course to some extent, planning is essential in order for your program to work well and in order to increase your efficiency. Remember, the AP Exam is strictly timed.

> The AP Exam tests the planning of a class by presenting a LENGTHY description of the requirements, along with other interacting classes in the project.

RELATIONSHIPS

Now that we have written a driver class and an object class (or several, depending on the program), we must get these classes to interact correctly in order to create a functioning program. We have the driver, we have the car, now we need to put the driver into the car so he or she can eagerly drive to his or her APCS Exam on exam day.

The driver and object classes must reside in the same folder on the computer. If you are using an interactive development environment (as opposed to command line programming), you often have to create a "Project" or some similar structure in the software that will hold all of the program's files in one place. Remember that the driver depends on the object class in order to compile, and the object class depends on the driver to make it actually do anything.

Consider a program that will take "flower" objects and "plant" them into a garden. The flower objects might be outlined in an object class called…Flower. The driver class would perform the planting, so we can call it MakeGarden.

Suppose the Flower constructor method has the following header:

```
public Flower (int xPosition, int yPosition)
```

where xPosition and yPosition are horizontal and vertical coordinates in the garden, respectively, where the flower object will be planted. Our driver would have to first "create" the flowers, and then plant them accordingly.

> In order to create an object, we must instantiate the object using its corresponding class.

Each time we instantiate a flower object, we must assign it an *object reference variable*; like the fancy name implies, this is just a variable name. Some lines in a driver class might look like:

```
Flower f1 = new Flower (2, 1);
Flower f2 = new Flower (2, 2);
Flower f3 = new Flower (2, 3);
```

These lines will instantiate three different flower objects, each containing its own instance data. f1, f2, and f3 are used to distinguish between the objects. We can then use these objects to perform methods. Consider a plant method in the Flower class; this method would "plant" the flower and might have the following header:

```
public void plant ()
```

In the driver, we must invoke this method through the objects. Let's say we only want to plant f1 and f3, but not f2. We would add the following lines to the driver:

```
f1.plant();
f3.plant();
```

Now let's say the plant method, instead, returns whether or not the plant was successfully planted. This altered plant method might have the header:

```
public boolean plant ()
```

Now we can use the returned data to output an appropriate message in the driver:

```
if (f1.plant())

  System.out.print ("Planted successfully.");

else

  System.out.print ("There was a problem.");
```

Because we are invoking f1.plant, f1 should be planted as requested. Since the plant method returns a boolean value, we can place f1.plant in the context of an if statement (it produces a truth value so it is considered a condition) and now it also functions as part of a control structure. Awesome!

Let's add to our garden situation. As you know, other items can appear in a garden, besides flowers. Plants, bushes, and weeds can appear in gardens. Each of these items would probably have its own object class, since their instance data and methods would be different from those of a flower. For example, a flower has flower pedals, while a plant does not; a weed grows on its own without water, while flowers and plants do not. Regardless, separate object classes can be created for each of these object types, and the driver can hold them all together, as long as they are all stored in the same folder on the computer.

Assuming each of these object classes have been created and each corresponding object class has a plant method as outlined above, the new driver might include these lines:

```
Flower f1 = new Flower();
Flower f2 = new Flower();
Plant p1 = new Plant();
Plant p2 = new Plant();
Weed w1 = new Weed();
if (f1.plant())
System.out.println ("Planted successfully");
if (f2.plant())
System.out.println ("Planted successfully");
if (p1.plant())
System.out.println ("Planted successfully");
if (w1.plant())
System.out.println ("You have a weed.");
```

Note that this driver does not instantiate any Bush objects, and does not attempt to plant the p2 object. Note also that we cannot see the entire driver class! The programmer has the task of deciding which objects to instantiate of which type, when and if to use them, and how to use them appropriately, based on their class specifications. Still think you can go directly to the final draft?

Let's add another layer. Programmers often recognize that an object is actually composed of many smaller, or more basic, objects. If you think about a flower, it actually has several parts, each of which *has* data and *does* particular actions. As a result, we could write an object class for, say, the stalk and the root system. The Stalk class and the RootSystem class, then, would reside as attributes of each flower. Their classes, again, must be placed in the same folder as the rest of the program's classes. The programmer can the set up the Flower class as follows:

```
public class Flower
{
    // other data not shown
    private Stalk st;
    private RootSystem rootSys;

    public Flower ()
    {
        st = new Stalk();
        rootSys = new RootSystem();
        // other commands not shown
    }

    // other methods not shown
}
```

This means that every Flower object *has* a stalk and a root system. The Flower class, then, is called an *aggregate class* because it is made up of, among other data, instances of other classes. This setup is more realistic; think of any object in your room, and you can probably see pretty quickly that it is made of smaller objects, each with its own data and methods. A laptop computer has keys, ports, and a screen, which can all be considered as objects because they *have* stuff and *do* stuff. A dresser has drawers, but we can go even deeper…a drawer has walls and a floor and can be opened or closed…the floor of a drawer has a shape and is made of a certain material and can be broken if the drawer is overstuffed…you get the idea. Luckily, as the programmer, we get to decide the detail of the object classes, and the answer typically lies in the desired function of the program, as we stated before. Do you REALLY need to know what material the floor of the drawer is made of? Most people do not, although a furniture retailer might. Again, it all depends on the application.

The FRQs on the AP Exam will present some sort of context and will often tell you exactly what class(es) and/or method(s) to write, so they don't get a wild variety of solutions from testtakers around the world.

Otherwise, they could literally be forced to read thousands of completely different approaches to a given task. This fact is not good for our creativity, but it's great for scoring a 5; save your creative juices for those extra college classes you can take when you AP out of CS!

Use following class Chair and incomplete class SitOnChair to answer Questions 3 and 4.

```
public class Chair
{
    private int numberOfLegs = 4;
    private boolean padded;

    public Chair (boolean soft)
    {
        if (soft) padded = true;
        else padded = false;
    }
}

public class SitOnChair
{
    public static void main (String[] args)
    {
        <program statements>
    }
}
```

3. SitOnChair is supposed to allow the user to "sit" on a Chair if the chair is padded. Which of the following code segments could be used to replace <program statements> so that SitOnChair will work as intended?

I.   Chair c = new Chair(true);
      c.sit();
II.   Chair c = new Chair (true);
III. Chair chair = new Chair (true);
      if (c.padded) System.out.print ("You are sitting.");

(A) I only
(B) II only
(C) III only
(D) I, II, and III
(E) None

Here's How to Crack It

Since (A), (B), and (C) allow the selection of only one option, we must test check all of them. We've got this! Remember that an object must (1) be instantiated in the executing class and (2) only be associated with methods that are defined in its class. Option I instantiates a Chair correctly, but then attempts to invoke a sit() method, which is not defined in Chair (or anywhere); eliminate (A) and (D). Option II correctly instantiates a Chair but does not attempt to "sit"; eliminate (B). Option III is incorrect because it also attempts to access padded, which is private data in Chair and therefore not accessible directly; eliminate (C). Since no option is valid, (E) is the answer.

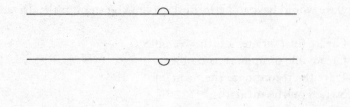

4. Which of the following modifications, if any, would help to make the Chair class MOST useful to the driver class, based on the task attempted in Question 1?

   (A) Adding an accessor method that returns the value of numberOfLegs.
   (B) Adding an accessor method that returns the value of padded.
   (C) Adding a mutator method that changes the value of numberOfLegs.
   (D) Adding a mutator method that changes the value of padded.
   (E) Adding an accessor method that returns the values of both numberOfLegs and padded.

Here's How to Crack It

The situation presented in Question 3 requires the information regarding whether the chair is padded. numberOfLegs is irrelevant here, regardless of your personal bias; eliminate (A), (C), and (E). Since the padded attribute of the chair does not have to be changed, eliminate (D). The answer is (B).

Do not get "emotional" about a situation presented; follow the specifications carefully and don't imply the programmer's intentions.

REFERENCES

All of this data that is passed from driver classes to object classes and vice versa, creates a complicated operation that's occurring behind the scenes. Consider this example: The programmer decides that he or she wants to write a class that represents a vinyl record player (for music), or "turntable." The driver class will then operate the turntable, turning it on and off, controlling it, and putting on/taking off the desired record. For this program, we will have three classes: Turntable and Record, which represent each of these objects, and PlayRecord will be the driver that relates them.

In theory, we would have to perform the following steps in the driver:

- Create (instantiate) a turntable object
- Create one or more record objects
- Place the record onto the turntable
- Switch on the turntable

Some code from these classes might look like:

```
public class Record
{
    // data not shown

    public Record ()
    // constructor code and other methods not shown
}
public class Turntable
{
    private Record r;
    // other data not shown

    public Turntable (Record r1)
    {
        r = r1;
        // other statements not shown
    }

    // other methods not shown
}
public class PlayRecord
{
    public static void main (String[] args)
    {
        Record rec = new Record();
        Turntable tt = new Turntable(rec);
        // other statements not shown
    }
}
```

In this example, note that Turntable is an aggregate class since part of its instance data involves another object. More importantly for this section, note the instantiation of the Record object in the driver, the "passing" of that object to the Turntable class, and the assignment r=r1. When an object is passed to another class and, as a result, received through a parameter, a *reference* is created to the object. Think of it this way: If you just picked up your favorite Taylor Swift record (you know you love her) and wanted to play it, you wouldn't need two copies of the album. In the same way, we don't have to create a copy of the Record object, we just need to create another reference to it in order for it to be used in the Turntable class. This is the only way the Turntable class can use this record, since it was instantiated in the driver. The record can then be used in context (in this case, assigned to the data field r) and then the reference will disappear once the constructor is over. Since the reference is not an actual copy of the object, its life is not affected.

Another way to think of references is to think of a superhero with his or her secret identity. Superman used to pose as Clark Kent in order to mask his superpowers and all of those realistic things that happen in those movies. Although Clark Kent was another name for the person, he was still actually Superman. They were the same guy with the same superpowers, the same attributes, and the same ability to perform cool superhero actions. Therefore, "Clark Kent" was simply a reference created to *refer* to the same guy.

It is extremely important to know that primitive data is not copied by reference, it is copied by value itself.

> When received as a parameter, primitive data is actually copied, while object data will simply receive a new reference to the object itself. Primitives are copied by value; objects are copied by reference.

Here's the really confusing part or maybe, not really. If a copy of a primitive data value is made, then the two copies (the original and the new one) exist exclusively. Therefore, if I change the value of one copy, the other is not affected. On the other hand, if a new reference to an object is made, then a modification of the object through the reference will be reflected by all references. Again, the superhero example: if Superman dyed his hair blonde because it was all the rage, then both Clark Kent and Superman will have blonde hair. They are two names that reference the same guy, so any changes will be reflected in all the references. If we suddenly decided that Superman/Clark Kent should be called "Blue Guy" instead of either of these two names, we are *still* referring to the same guy, he now has three *aliases* instead of two.

Use the following incomplete class declarations to answer Questions 5 and 6.

```
public class Number
{
    private int value;

    public Number (int someNum)
    {
        if (someNum >= 0)
            value = someNum;
    }

    public int changeVal (int newVal)
    {
        /* missing code */
    }

    public int getValue()
    {
        return value;
    }
}

public class NumChanger
{
    public static void main (String[] main)
    {
        Number n1 = new Number (5);
        Number n2 = new Number (5);
        int sum1 = n1.getValue() + n2.getValue();
        int oldn1Val = n1.changeValue (10);
        n2 = n1;
        int sum2 = n1.getValue() + n2.getValue();
        System.out.print (sum1 + " " + sum2);
    }
}
```

5. The changeVal method in Number should reassign value to be the value taken as the parameter and return the original value. Which of the following code segments should be used to replace /* missing code */ so that changeVal will work as intended?

(A) `value = newVal;`
    `return value;`
(B) `value = newVal;`
    `return 5;`
(C) `int oldVal = value`
    `value = newVal;`
(D) `int oldVal = value;`
    `value = newVal;`
    `return value;`
(E) `int oldVal = value;`
    `value = newVal;`
    `return oldVal;`

Here's How to Crack It

To accomplish the task, two events must occur: value must be reset to the parameter value and the old value must be returned. Choice (C) does not attempt to return any value, so it cannot be correct. The remaining answer choices attempt to accomplish the both events; however, if value is reset and its new value is returned, the second event is done incorrectly. The original value must be stored, so eliminate (A) and (B) as a result. Choice (D) stores the old value but returns the new value, since it has been reassigned to newVal, so it is not correct. Since (E) stores the old value, reassigns value, and returns the old value, (E) is the answer.

————————⚬————————

————————⚬————————

6. What will be printed as a result of executing the program? Assume changeVal in the Number class works as intended.

(A) 5 5
(B) 5 10
(C) 10 5
(D) 10 10
(E) None of these

Here's How to Crack It

The College Board LOVES to write MCQs with confusing object references like this. Remember that setting an object "equal" to another object merely means that the two identifiers reference the same object (like Superman and Clark Kent). sum1 will be assigned to the sum of the values of n1 and n2, which is 10, so the first number printed will be 10. Eliminate (A) and (B) a a result. oldn1Val is irrelevant here but n1.changeValue(10) makes n1 have a value of 10. n2 = n1 will now have variable n2 reference the same object as n1, which has a value of 10 from the previous statement. Therefore, n1.getValue and n2.getValue will both return 10, so sum2 will be 10+10=20. As a result, the second number printed will be 20 and (C) and (D) can be eliminated. The answer is (E).

————————⚬————————

STATIC MODIFIER

The *static* keyword can appear in two contexts at this level. A *static variable* is an attribute that shared among all instances of a class. When the valuable of this variable is changed, the alteration is reflected by all of the objects instantiated through that class. A classic example of a static variable is the high score list on a video game. Consider video game MKA, the latest in a series of popular games on portable devices. After you fire up the MKA app, you start a new game and play until you lose…then, since you are addicted to the game, you start over. If each game of MKA you play is considered an object of the same class, a static variable might be the high score. Every time you start (or instantiate) a new game, the high score remains the same from when it was initially set. Once the a new high score is set, every new game will reflect the new high score, rendering the old high score non-existent (or 2nd best, etc.).

In an object class, a static variable is declared with the rest of the instance data at the top of the class, preceded by the keyword static. Static variables are often used for identification numbers or for counters. Consider this short program:

```
public class Box
{
    private static int boxNumber = 0;
    // other data fields not shown

    public Box ()
    {
        boxNumber++;
        // other statements not shown
    }
}
public class BoxCreator
{
    public static void main (String[] args)
    {
        Box box1 = new Box();
        Box box2 = new Box();
    }
}
```

As each box object is instantiated in BoxCreator, the static variable in the Box class will be updated. That way, the next time a box is created, it is literally given a new box number. As a result, no box will be assigned the same number. Contrast this setup with a non-static declaration of boxNumber; every time a box is instantiated, its boxNumber would start as 0 and then be incremented, making every box have the same boxNumber value of 1.

In order to show this structure is actually working, let's create an *accessor method* to let the driver "see," or access, the value of boxNumber. This method is necessary for this result since boxNumber has been declared private. A non-constructor method that is designed to access and/or modify a static variable is a *static method* and must be declared as such. To add this functionality and test it, here are our new object and driver classes:

```
public class Box
{
    private static int boxNumber = 0;
    // other data fields not shown

    public Box ()
    {
        boxNumber++;
        // other statements not shown
    }

    static public int getBoxNum ()
    {
        return boxNumber;
    }
}
public class BoxCreator
{
    public static void main (String[] args)
    {
        Box box1 = new Box();
        Box box2 = new Box();
        System.out.print (Box.getBoxNum() + " boxes cre-
        ated so far.");
    }
}
```

Notice the method call from the driver does not use an object reference variable; rather, the class is used directly. Since static variables are shared among all instances, the programmer needs to access static methods (and therefore, static variables) through the class itself.

---

7. A class called ComputerMouse has a static variable connector and a static method getConnector. Which of the following statements is true based on this information?

   (A) In order to invoke getConnector, a new ComputerMouse object does not need to be instantiated; getConnector must be called directly through the object class.

   (B) In order to invoke getConnector, a new ComputerMouse object must be instantiated and then getConnector must be called through that object.

   (C) Since connector is declared static, getConnector is shared among all objects in the program.

   (D) Since connector is declared static, ComputerMouse objects cannot be mutated during execution.

   (E) Since connector is declared static, all of the methods in ComputerMouse must also be declared static.

Here's How to Crack It

The AP Exam tests rote knowledge as well as reasoning; this question can only be answered correctly if you know how static works. A static method must be called directly through the class, so (A) looks good so far, but eliminate (B). Choice (C) is incorrect because getConnector will be shared among all ComputerMouse objects, not all objects in general. Choice (D) is nonsensical since static is not related to mutations. Choice (E) would be correct if it said "all of the methods in ComputerMouse that access or mutate connector." The answer is (A).

Do not be afraid of choices (A) or (E).

INTERFACES

Just in case you are not convinced that a powerful, efficient program requires proper planning before the code is written, let's complicate things further. An *interface* is sometimes defined as a blueprint for a class. This definition is somewhat misleading; let's call it a template that must be followed.

Let's say, for example, that you have a low-paying job at the local bookstore. As an employee, you must *have* and *be able to do* specific items; in fact, every employee at your level has this same list of requirements. Here is a short list of what some of those requirements might be:

- Must *have* a name tag
- Must *have* an employee ID number
- Must *be able to* put books on a shelf
- Must *be able to* speak to a customer respectfully

The first two items would serve as private instance data, while the last two would translate into methods. An *interface* class could be used to plan the construction of an Employee class, but it's more powerful than just a planning tool. If the interface is required to be used, then the Employee class MUST contain the required elements of the interface, or it will not compile. Here is some code:

```
public interface Employable
{
    abstract static int employeeID;
    abstract public boolean putBooksOnShelf();
    abstract public void speakToCustomer();
}
```

```
public class Employee implements Employable
{
    String nameTag;
    static int employeeID = 0; // required by interface
    // other data fields not shown

    public Employee (String empName)
    {
        nameTag = empName;
        employeeID++;
        // other constructor statements not shown
    }
    public boolean putBooksOnShelf ()
    { /*statements not shown */ }
    public void speakToCustomer ()
    { /* statements not shown /* }
    // other methods not shown
}
```

Note that (1) the driver *implements* the Employable interface. If this line were not included (the header was simply public class Employee) then the interface would not have to be followed, but this setup does not enforce the rules of employment. Note (2) that all three components of the interface are *overridden*, meaning they are explicitly defined with statements, and they have the EXACT same method headers (without *abstract*). Finally, note (3) that the object class that implements an interface may (and often, does) include extra data fields and/or methods, besides the items required from the interface. Finally, finally, note (4) that data variables enforced in the interface must be declared as static; since the object CLASS is implementing the interface, each object of the class will share the enforced data field, which renders it static, by definition.

---

8. A restaurant is attempting to digitize some of its inventory, including food items and non-food items. Which of the following is the best idea for designing a program that accomplishes this task?

(A) Create a driver class that accomplishes the tasks top-down.

(B) Create an object class for each of the edible and non-edible items.

(C) Create an object class for each of the edible and non-edible items, along with a driver class that instantiates one of each object.

(D) Create an object class for each of the edible and non-edible items, along with an interface that provides a "blueprint" for edible items.

(E) Create an object class for each of the edible and non-edible items, along with an interface that provides a "blueprint" for edible items and an interface for non-edible items.

Here's How to Crack It

Design questions can be difficult because you have no code to rely on. Remember that an interface provides "quality control"—the programmer must conform to certain standards when accomplishing his or her task. Choice (A) is clearly incorrect, since few projects are accomplished this way in any context except very basic Java. Simply creating a class for each item does not demonstrate control, so (B) and (C) are incorrect; furthermore, arbitrarily instantiating one of each object is senseless. Choice (D) only provides a blueprint for edible items, which is not sufficient here. Choice (E) is the answer.

THROWING EXCEPTIONS

Your own programs can be written to easily throw exceptions for dealing with any number of error conditions that might occur. For example, if you want to indicate that a method should not be called at the current time, you might instantiate an IllegalStateException and then throw it using the throw keyword. Recall that instantiation is merely the process of creating an object based on a given class. In the following example, lines 4 and 5 instantiate an "ise" object based on the IllegalStateException class. Note that the exception is explicitly instantiated on line 5 and explicitly thrown on line 8.

```
Line 1: public void throwIllegalStateException( )
Line 2: {
Line 3:    //create an object of type
Line 4:    //IllegalStateException
Line 5:    IllegalStateException ise =
Line 6:    new IllegalStateException ("not right now");
Line 7:    //now throw the IllegalStateException
Line 8:    throw ise;
Line 9: }
```

If you wanted to indicate that your method did not have access to a requested element, you might instantiate a NoSuchElementException and then throw it using the throw keyword. Note that the exception is explicitly instantiated on lines 7 and 8 and explicitly thrown on line 10.

```
Line 1: public void throwNoSuchElementException( )
Line 2: {
Line 3:    //create the error message
Line 4:    String msg = "That element doesn't exist";
Line 5:    //create an object of type
Line 6:    //NoSuchElementException
Line 7  java.util.NoSuchElementException nse =
Line 8:    new java.util.NoSuchElementException(msg);
Line 9  //now throw the NoSuchElementException
Line 10:   throw nse;
Line 11: }
```

Finally, note that you do not need to explicitly create an exception object to throw an exception. A call to the throwIllegalStateException() method illustrated above could more concisely be replaced by one line of code.

```
throw(new IllegalStateException("not right now"));
```

CHAPTER 5 REVIEW DRILL

Answers to the review questions can be found in Chapter 9.

1. A development team is building an online bookstore that customers can use to order books. Information about inventory and customer orders is kept in a database. Code must be developed that will store and retrieve data from the database. The development team decides to put the database code in separate classes from the rest of the program. Which of the following would be an advantage of this plan?

    I.   The database access code could be reused in other applications that also need to access the database.
    II.   The database access code can be tested independently. It will be possible to test the database access code before the interface is developed.
    III. A team of programmers can be assigned to work just on the code that is used to access the database. The programmers can work independently from other programmers, such as those who develop the user interface.

    (A) I only
    (B) II only
    (C) III only
    (D) I and II only
    (E) I, II, and III

2. In Java, data fields and methods can be designated public or private. Which of the following best characterizes the designation that should be used?

    (A) Data fields and methods should always be public. This makes it easier for client programs to access data fields and use the methods of the class.
    (B) Data fields should be either public or private, depending on whether or not it is beneficial for client programs to access them directly. All methods should be public. A private method is useless because a client program can't access it.
    (C) Keep all methods and data fields private. This enforces encapsulation.
    (D) Data fields should always be private so that clients can't directly access them. Methods can be either public or private.
    (E) All data fields should be public so client programs can access them, and all methods should be private.

3. Which of the following are signs of a well-designed program?

    I.   Clients know how data is stored in the class.
    II.   Classes and methods can be tested independently.
    III. The implementation of a method can be changed without changing the programs that use the method.

    (A) I only
    (B) II only
    (C) II and III
    (D) I and II
    (E) I, II, and III

4. Consider the following classes:

```java
public class Sample
{
    public void writeMe (Object obj)
    {
        System.out.println("object");
    }
    public void writeMe (String s)
    {
        System.out.println("string");
    }
}
```

What will be the result of executing the following?

```java
Sample s = new Sample ( );
String tmp = new String("hi");
s.writeMe(tmp);
```

(A) Compile-time error
(B) "hi"
(C) "object"
(D) "string"
(E) Run-time error

5. Consider the following class:

```java
public class Sample
{
    public void writeMe (Object obj)
    {
        System.out.println("object");
    }
    public void writeMe (String s)
    {
        System.out.println("string");
    }
}
```

What will be the result of executing the following?

```java
Sample s = new Sample( );
Object tmp = new Object( );
s.writeMe(tmp);
```

(A) Compile-time error
(B) "string"
(C) "object"
(D) "hi"
(E) Run-time error

6. Consider the following class:

```
public class Sample
{
    public void writeMe (Object obj)
    {
        System.out.println("object");
    }
    public void writeMe (String s)
    {
        System.out.println("string");
    }
}
```

What will be the result of executing the following?

```
Sample s = new Sample( );
Object tmp = new String("hi");
s.writeMe(tmp);
```

(A) Compile-time error
(B) "hi"
(C) "object"
(D) "string"
(E) Run-time error

7. Consider the following class:

```
public class Sample
{
    public void writeMe (Object obj)
    {
        System.out.println("object");
    }
    public void writeMe (String s)
    {
        System.out.println("string");
    }
}
```

What will be the result of executing the following?

```
Sample s = new Sample( );
String tmp = new Object( );
s.writeMe(tmp);
```

(A) Compile-time error
(B) "hi"
(C) "object"
(D) "string"
(E) Run-time error

8. Consider the following class:

```
public class Sample
{
    int val = 0;
}
```

Is val an attribute or a method?

(A) Neither: a compile-time error occurs when we try to execute this code.
(B) val is an attribute.
(C) val is a method.
(D) val is both an attribute and a method.
(E) Neither, val is a primitive.

9. Consider the following class:

```
public class Sample
{
    public String writeMe(String s)
    {
        System.out.println("object");
    }
    public void writeMe(String s)
    {
        System.out.println("string");
    }
}
```

What will be the result of executing the following?

```
Sample s = new Sample( );
Object tmp = new Object( )
s.writeMe(tmp);
```

(A) Compile-time error
(B) "hi"
(C) "object"
(D) "string"
(E) Run-time error

KEY TERMS
class
source code
methods
driver class
object class
header
main
constructor
instance data
data fields
return type
parameters
accessor methods
mutator methods
overloading
planning

Chapter 6
Arrays

Now that we understand how to store data and manipulate it, the next step is to understand how to organize it. Imagine creating a program that keeps track of hundreds of entries per day, such as a factory that produces bottles of aspirin. Using the skills we have learned thus far, you would have to write a class representing an aspirin bottle, instantiate each individual bottle separately, and use an object reference variable for each. Imagine invoking a method on every one of those objects? You're looking at some serious lines of code…not to mention, some serious *repetition* of code, which is bad style. Let's discuss an **array** structure, the fundamental object that organizes data in an intuitive way.

PRIMITIVES & OBJECTS

In order to instantiate an array, you must first decide what type of data will be contained in the array. Suppose you are creating a program that will keep track of your test grades in your APCS class. Since grades are usually represented by an integer number, you will create an array of integers. The syntax for instantiating an array of integers is:

```
int <identifier> [] = new int [<array size>];
```

This format is used if you do not yet know the values that will be stored in the array. Alternatively, if you already know the data values, you can instantiate the array using an **initializer list**:

```
int <identifier> [] = {<data1>, <data2>, …, <data n>};
```

Notice the square brackets—these are standard characters in Java that signify that an array is present. The braces (curly brackets) indicate an initializer list. In the beginning of the semester, you do not yet know your grades. In order to create an array called testGrades that will eventually store your first 5 test grades, you could write a statement like this:

```
int testGrades[] = new int[5];
```

This array object will store your test grades and keep them organized using **index numbers**. Just like your tests might be organized as Chapter 1 Test, Chapter 2 Test, etc., your data will be accessed through particular index numbers in the array. The tricky part is that array indexes start with the number 0 instead of 1. Therefore, if your Chapter 1 Test is the first test score in the array, it will be stored at index 0. Think of it as, the first test you have in APCS reviews a previous course, so it's Chapter 0 instead of Chapter 1. If you did not instantiate the array using an initializer list, then you will assign data values, using the index number; you will do the same process to access the data, regardless of how you created the array. For example, if you scored a 95 on the first test, you could write the line:

```
testGrades[0] = 95;
```

Let's say that, after looking over your test, you realize that your teacher made a grading error and you actually scored a 98. You can either increment the data value or reassign it:

```
testGrades[0] += 3;
```

or

```
testGrades[0] = 98;
```

You can also perform any integer operation, including displaying the value to the user, with that same format.

Let's step it up a notch. Suppose, after all 5 tests are complete, your teacher feels that the scores are too high and decides to deflate the grades. (You didn't think this book would only discuss *nice* teachers, did you?) The programmer can use a simple loop in order to **span** the array and change every value accordingly, rather than writing 5 separate lines. Since an array's length is well-defined, a for loop is usually appropriate for arrays. Provided that the array is **full**, meaning all 5 values are assigned, the following loop with span the array and subtract 2 points from every grade:

```
for (int index = 0; index < 5; index++)
    testGrades[index] -= 2;
```

Note the values of index will be 0, 1, 2, 3, and 4, even though it stores 5 elements. Since the index numbers start at 0, you must stop spanning the array before index 5, or your will receive an **ArrayIndexOutOfBoundsException** and the program execution will be interrupted, which is never desirable.

Much better than writing multiple lines, right? Whether you use an array or not, the loop systematically changes every value. We are just scratching the surface of the usefulness of arrays, and we have already improved our coding efficiency.

The AP Exam will require you to read, interpret, and write arrays; FRQs are loaded with arrays and will specifically state that an array must be created.

The programmer needs to ensure that every element of the array contains a value, or undesired results may occur. In an array of primitives, the value of an unassigned element will default to 0. Consider the following code segment that will calculate the average of your 5 test grades:

```
int total = 0, len = testGrades.length;
double average;
for (int index = 0; index < len; index++)
    total += testGrades[index];
average = (double)total / len;
```

If all 5 of your test grades are stored in the array, this code segment will calculate the average. If you did not input one of your scores, however, it will remain stored as 0 and incorrectly drag down your average, which is (definitely) an undesired result. Even worse, your teacher's grade deflation will make that grade negative!

1. Consider the following code segment:

```
final int[] a1 = {1, 2};
int[] b1 = {3, 4};
a1 = b1;
System.out.print(a1[1]);
```

What is printed as a result of executing the code segment?

(A) 2
(B) 3
(C) 4
(D) Nothing is printed due to a compile-time error
(E) Nothing is printed due to a run-time error

Here's How to Crack It

This is an easy one if you know your compiler. Since a1 is declared final, its reference cannot be changed. In the third line, the programmer attempts to change a1 to reference the second array, which is not allowed. The answer is (D).

2. Consider the following incomplete method:

```
public static int Mod3(int[] a)
{
    int count = 0;
    for (int i = 0; i < a.length; i++)
    {
        // code not shown
    }
    return count;
}
```

Method Mod3 is intended to return the number of integers in the array numbers that are evenly divisible by 3. Which of the following code segments could be used to replace // code not shown so that Mod3 will work as intended?

I. ```
    if (i % 3) == 0)
    {
      count++;
    }
    ```
II. ```
    if (a[i] % 3 == 0)
    {
      count++;
    }
    ```
III.```
    while (a[i] % 3 == 0)
    {
      count++;
    }
    ```

(A) I only
(B) II only
(C) III only
(D) I and II
(E) II and III

## Here's How to Crack It

I is checking whether i—the counter—is divisible by 3, rather than the element in the array itself, so I is incorrect, eliminating (A) and (D). The process needs to be looped in order to span the entire array, but the hidden code is already in a loop, so III is incorrect, eliminating (C) and (E). By process of elimination, (B) is the answer.
    ```

Since objects are typically used to represent real-world phenomena, arrays are also commonly used to organize and manipulate objects. Suppose you have an object class that represents a pair of sneakers. The following code segment would instantiate an array that would store 5 of these objects:

```
PairOfSneakers collection[] = new PairOfSneakers[5];
```

Since each element is an object, however, the default value for each object is **null**. Since null is not a valid object, operations performed on null will result in a **NullPointerException**, another error that will halt the execution of the program. Without getting into the specifics of the PairOfSneakers class, a statement that could assign an instantiated pair of sneakers called jordans is:

```
collection[0] = jordans;
```

Now suppose PairOfSneakers has a tie() method that will tie the laces of the corresponding pair of sneakers; i.e., jordans.tie() will tie that pair. At this point, index 0 references the jordans object—remember objects are referenced, not copied—but indexes 1-4 are null. As a result, the following statement will cause a NullPointerException:

```
for (int i = 0; i < collection.length; i++)
    collection[i].tie();
```

When using a loop to span an array of objects, be sure the array is full to avoid undesired results.

Use the following method to answer Questions 3 and 4.

```
public int[] someMethod (int[] array, int value)
{
    for (int i = 1, i < array.length-1; i++)
        array[i-1] += value;
    return array;
}
```

3. Which of the following statements is true about the method someMethod?

    (A) The method will not return any value.
    (B) The method will not return the correct value.
    (C) The method will not cause any runtime errors.
    (D) The method will not increment the first element of the array by value.
    (E) The method will not increment the last element of the array by value.

Here's How to Crack It

The return value must be an array of integers, so eliminate (A) and (B) because array[i] is an integer. This fact will prevent the method (and thus, the program) from compiling, so (C) in incorrect because runtime will not occur. The remaining answer choices prove that this question is messing around with the spanning of the array (and with your brain). The loop purposely offsets the way it (supposedly) spans the array because...well, you don't expect a straightforward MCQ on this exam, do you? Index 0 is incremented because the method increments element i-1, and I is initialized with a value of 1. By the same reasoning, index 4 is not addressed because the last value of i will be less than array.length-1. The answer is (E).

4. Which of the following modifications will make the method compile, based on the information given?

(A) Change int[] array in the method header parameter to int[] numbers.
(B) Change array.length-1 to array.length in the loop statement.
(C) Change array[i-1] = 0; to array[i] = 0;
(D) Change the return statement to return array;
(E) None of these choices will make the method compile.

Here's How to Crack It

The problem with this method is the discrepancy between the return type (int[]) and the type of value that the method attempts to return (int); (D) addresses this issue. Choice (A) will have no effect on the outcome of the method because array is simply the name of the variable that references the array. Choices (B) and (C), although valid, will not correct the return type issue. Choice (C) will cause a problem. Choice (E) is incorrect, again, because the return type issue is keeping the method from compiling. The answer is (D).

One last item before we start manipulating the data contained in the array.... The constant value returned by arrayName.length is very useful when spanning the area and/or attempting to identify the size of the array. This constant is always available for the programmer's use.

SEARCHES

Once data is stored in an array, a common task is to methodically search the array for given data. Consider a line of parked cars in the "Curbside To Go" section of your local chain restaurant. When the server is bringing the food to a particular car, he or she must use a given attribute—say, a license plate number—to find the correct car. Once the correct car is found, he or she can deliver the food and then go back inside for the next order, beginning the process all over again…and again…and again. Poor kid.

This same technique is used for searching an array. In APCS, we have two methods of searching arrays, the **linear search** and the **binary search**. Since each of these search methods using a distinct formula to search through the arrays, they are commonly referred to as **search algorithms**.

The chain restaurant example given above is an example of a linear search. All of the cars are "lined up" and the server begins with the first car, checking its license plate number against the one he or she is looking for. If it's correct, he or she delivers the food and returns. If not, he or she moves on to the next car and repeats the process; this all ends when either (1) the correct car is found or (2) the correct car is not in the line at all. This linear process works just fine, although it can be very tedious. The server would have to do much more work if the desired car was at the end of the line, as opposed to the beginning. Remember, we are programming a computer: the server cannot simply "look" at all of the plates at once, like we would in real life. The computer does not know how to "look," unless we know how to write the program that enables it!

A code segment that performs a linear search for a number target in array of integers nums might look like:

```
for (int i = 0; i < nums.length; i++)
    if (nums[i] == target)
        System.out.print ("Found at " + i);
```

This segment will correctly traverse the array, searching for target, starting with index 0 and continuing to index length-1, as desired. Remember that nums.length is the size of the array and therefore nums[length] would be out of bounds. When target is found, the print statement displays its index number. This process will continue until the end of the array is reached. Note that, if target is never found, there will be no output.

When writing search algorithms and other structures that span entire arrays, programmers often implement the **for-each loop**, which is designed specifically for spanning entire arrays. The for-each loop will automatically search through the ENTIRE array, so it should not be used if there are empty elements. Assuming nums from the previous example is full, the same code segment can be written as a for-each loop structure like this:

```
for (int i: nums)
    if (nums[i] == target)
        System.out.print ("Found at " + i);
```

Each time the loop iterates, i will be assigned the value of the next element in the array. This structure automatically ensures that i does not go out of bounds. Nice! Just remember that a for-each loop is only appropriate for full arrays.

A binary search is much more efficient; think of it as a "divide-and-conquer" mechanism. Instead of our restaurant server starting with the beginning of the line of cars, he or she will start with the middle car. Depending on whether the license plate is "greater" than that car's or less, he or she will move in the appropriate direction. (It is the programmer's decision to decide what "greater" or "lesser" means with respect to license plates.)

There is a huge obstacle with binary searches, however, or at least, for us with our current level of Java knowledge. Suppose the top 21 students in the senior class are lined up in a row. You are looking for a top 21 student named Kathy, who you have never met, but you are not sure where she is in the line. If the students are not lined up in a particular order, a linear search is your only option, and you might need all 21 tries to get to her if she is the last person. If they were sorted in alphabetical order by first name, though, you could divide and conquer. Go to the middle person and find out his or her name…if her name is Sara, you would move toward the front of the line and ignore the back. You then perform the same process, asking the name of the person halfway between the front of the line and Sara, and then ignore the appropriate side. Within a few tries, you will have Kathy.

Here is a code example of how a binary search might look for array nums when searching for target, assuming nums is sorted:

```
int front = 0, back = nums.length-1, middle = 0;
for (int i = front; i <= back; i++)
{
    middle = (front + back)/2;
    if (nums[middle] < target)
        front = middle + 1;
    else if (nums[middle] > target)
        back = middle - 1;
}
if (nums[middle] == target)
    System.out.print ("Found target at element " + middle);
else
    System.out.print ("Target not found.");
```

On the AP Exam, you will not be required to WRITE a search algorithm; however, you will be required to RECOGNIZE a search algorithm and trace it, which can be done the easy way if you understand the algorithm, or the hard way by actually tracing the code, step by step. Try to identify the key characteristics of each search; for example, the "sum divided by 2" line is a good indicator of a binary search. The for-each loop will span the entire array, which may indicate a linear search.

5. Which of the following statements is true, regarding search algorithms?

   (A) Searching for a Twix in a row of unsorted candy is most efficient using a linear search

   (B) Searching for a Twix in a row of unsorted candy is most efficient using a binary search

   (C) Searching for a Twix in a row of sorted candy is most efficient using a linear search

   (D) Searching for a Twix in a row of sorted candy is most efficient using a binary search

   (E) None of these

Here's How to Crack It

Searching is usually more efficient using a binary search, provided the array is sorted. However, a binary search will require more than one comparison if the target is not in the middle, whereas a linear search will only need one comparison if the target is first in line. Therefore, each of the four situations presented in (A) through (D) could be the most efficient, depending on the position of the Twix. The answer is (E).

6. Assuming target is in array a, which of the following methods will correctly return the index of target in sorted array a?

I.
```
public int findTarget (int[] a, int target)
{
for (int x = 0; x < a.length; x++)
  if (a[x] == target)
      return x;
}
```

II.
```
public int findTarget (int[] a, int target)
{
  for (int x: a)
  if (a[x] == target)
     return x;
  else return -1;
}
```

III.
```
public int findTarget (int[] a, int target)
{
  int f = 0, h = a.length, g = 0;
for (int i = 0; i < h; i++)
{
      g = (f + h)/2;
      if (a[g] < target)
            f = g + 1;
      else if (a[g] > target)
            h = g - 1;
}
if (a[g] == target)
      return g;
else
      return -1;
}
```

(A) I only
(B) II only
(C) I and II only
(D) II and III only
(E) I, II, and III

Here's How to Crack It

Notice that options I and II look like linear searches, while III looks like a binary search. Option I will not compile because a non-void method must return data. An if statement without an else implies data may not be returned—even though the assumption states that will not occur—so the compiler will stop here. Eliminate (A), (C), and (E). Looking at (B) and (D), they both include option II so it must be correct; skip to option III. Note that the variables are a bit confusing—but front/middle/back correspond to f/g/h, so they are in alphabetical order. Option III is a nice binary search and it avoids the return problem in option I by returning -1 if target is not found, a common practice when writing search algorithms. Therefore, options II and III are correct and (D) is the answer.

SORTS

Probably the most useful algorithms you will learn in this course are **sorting algorithms**—but they are also probably the most annoying to understand. If you've been keeping up, then you have a good start.

As the name implies, sort algorithms will take data in an array and rearrange it into a particular order. We already know that this technique is useful if we want to search for data using the binary search algorithm. But imagine this automated process in real life: a process that automatically sorts the cups in your cabinet in height order, a process that automatically takes your homework assignments and arranges them in time order, and a process that sorts your to-do list in priority order. Needless to say: sorting algorithms are extremely powerful.

The **selection sort** is the first sort algorithm we will discuss, and one of the three sorting algorithms you need to know for the AP Exam. I like to call this sort a search-and-swap, and remember that the selection sort searches and swaps. Similar to a linear search, the sort will first span the array for the lowest value. Once it finds the lowest value, it will swap its position in the array with the data at index 0. Now the first element is sorted. The process then repeats for index 1. The rest of the array will be searched for the lowest value and swapped with the data at index 1. Note that if the lowest value is already in position, it will stay there.

Consider the array below. We would like to sort this array from least to greatest.

| 8 | 6 | 10 | 2 | 4 |

Our strategy will be to first find the smallest element in the array, and put it in the first position. We will then find the smallest of the remaining elements and put that in the second position. We will continue to do this until the array is ordered.

We can start by looking at every element in the array (starting with the first element) and find the smallest element. It's easy for a person to quickly glance through the array and see which element is smallest, but the sorting algorithm that we will implement can only compare two elements at once. So here's how we can find the smallest element: Take the number in the first cell in the array and assign it to a variable called smallestSoFar. We'll also assign the position of that value to a variable called position. In this case, smallestSoFar will equal 8 and position will be 0. Note that even though we are assigning 8 to smallestSoFar, the first cell of the array will contains 8; we didn't actually remove it.

Next we'll walk through the array and compare the next value to smallestSoFar. The next value is 6, which is less than 8, so smallestSoFar becomes 6 and position becomes 1.

```
smallestSoFar = 6;
position = 1;
```

| 8 | 6 | 10 | 2 | 4 |

Now let's look at the next value in the array. 10 is larger than 6, so smallestSoFar remains 6.

```
smallestSoFar = 6;
position = 1;
```

| 8 | 6 | 10 | 2 | 4 |

The next value in the array is 2. Two is smaller than 6.

```
smallestSoFar = 2;
position = 3;
```

| 8 | 6 | 10 | 2 | 4 |

And finally we look at the last element, 4. Because 4 is greater than 2, and we are at the end of the array, we know that 2 is the smallest element.

```
smallestSoFar = 2;
position = 3;
```

| 8 | 6 | 10 | 2 | 4 |

Now we know that 2 is the smallest element in the array. Because we want to order the array from least to greatest, we need to put 2 in the first cell in the array. We don't simply want to overwrite the 8 that is in the first cell, though. What we'll do is swap the 2 with the 8 to get

| **2** | 6 | 10 | **8** | 4 |

We now have the smallest element in place. Next we'll need to find the second smallest element in the array. We can do this using the same approach we employed to find the smallest element. Because we know that 2 is the smallest element, we only have to look at the elements in positions 1 to 4 for the second smallest element.

Start by assigning 6 to smallestSoFar and 1 to position and then compare 6 to 10. Six is the smaller. Next, compare 6 to 8; 6 is still the smaller. Finally, compare 6 with 4. Four is smaller and because we have no more elements in the array, 4 must be the second smallest element in the array.

Swap 4 with the second element in the array to get

2	4	10	8	6

Make another pass through the array to find the third smallest element, and swap it into the third cell. The third smallest element is 6.

2	4	6	8	10

Finally, we look at the last two elements. Eight is smaller than 10, so we don't need to do anything. Our array is now sorted from least to greatest.

Implementation of Selection Sort

Here is how a selection sort can be implemented in Java. The following implementation will sort the elements from least to greatest and will begin by sorting the smallest elements first.

```
//precondition: numbers is an array of ints
//postcondition: numbers is sorted in ascending order
Line 1:  public static void selectionSort1(int[] numbers)
Line 2:  {
Line 3:    for (int i = 0; i < numbers.length - 1; i++)
Line 4:    {
Line 5:      int position = i;
Line 6:      for (int k = i + 1; k < numbers.length; k++)
Line 7:      {
Line 8:        if (numbers[k] < numbers[position])
Line 9:        {
Line 10:           position = k;
Line 11:        }
Line 12:      }
Line 13:      int temp = numbers[i];
Line 14:      numbers[i] = numbers[position];
Line 15:      numbers[position] = temp;
Line 16:    }
Line 17:  }
```

How could this be useful? Consider a case in which you have an unsorted array of 1,000 Student objects, and each Student object has a method that returns a grade-point average for that Student. What if you would like to find the five students with highest grade-point average? In this case, it would be a waste of time to sort the entire array. Instead, we can just run through five cycles of the second implementation of the selection sort shown above, and the top five students will be sorted.

The **insertion sort** is a little less intuitive. Rather than traversing the entire array, it compares the first two elements and depending on the comparison, inserts the second value "in front" of the first value into index 0, moving the first value to index 1. The first two elements are now sorted. Then the third element is checked, and the inserting continues. Note that here, also, an already-sorted element will remain in its position.

Below is an array with 9 elements. This array is sorted from least to greatest except for the last element.

2	3	5	8	11	14	17	22	15

We would like to move 15 so that the entire array is in order. First, we'll temporarily assign 15 to a variable. This will give us room to shift the other elements to the right if needed.

```
temp = 15
```

2	3	5	8	11	14	17	22	

We then compare 15 to the first element to its left: 22. Because 22 is larger than 15, we shift 22 to the right.

temp = 15

2	3	5	8	11	14	17	->	22

We then compare 15 to the next element: 17. Because 17 is larger, we shift that to the right also.

temp = 15

2	3	5	8	11	14	->	17	22

Next we compare 15 to 14. Because 15 is larger, we don't want to shift 14 to the right. Instead, we insert 15 into the empty cell in the array. Now the array is correctly sorted.

Insert 15

2	3	5	8	11	14	15	17	22

Now we'll look at how we can use the idea illustrated above to sort an entire array. This example will start at the beginning of the sorting process.

Here is the array that we are going to sort.

8	6	7	10

First, we'll look at just the first two elements of the array and make sure that they are sorted relative to each other.

8	6	7	10

To do this, we'll pull 6 (the number that is farthest to the right in our subarray) out of the array and temporarily assign it to a variable. We'll then compare 6 to 8. Because 8 is larger, shift 8 to the right and then put 6 in the cell where 8 was.

temp = 6

8 ->		7	10

Here's what the array looks like.

6	8	7	10

Now we need to put 7 in the proper place relative to 6 and 8. We start by assigning 7 temporarily to a variable.

temp = 7

6	8		10

We then compare 7 to the first number to its left: 8. Because 7 is less than 8, we shift 8 one place to the right.

temp = 7

6	->	8	10

Next, we'll compare 7 to the next number in the array: 6. Because 6 is less than 7, we don't want to shift 6 to the right. Instead, we will put 7 in the second cell. Our array now looks like the following:

6	7	8	10

Now we need to put 10 in its place relative to the first 3 elements in the array.

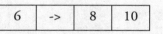

6	7	8	10

temp = 10

6	7	8	

First we compare 10 to 8; because 8 is smaller than 10, we don't need to shift 8 to the right. In fact, we can put 100 right back into the cell from which it came.

6	7	8	10

Iterative Implementation of Insertion Sort

Here is how an insertion sort can be implemented in Java.

```
//precondition: x is an array of integers; x.length >= 0
//postcondition: x is sorted from least to greatest.
Line 1:    public static void insertionSort(int[] x)
Line 2:    {
Line 3:        for (int i = 1; i < x.length; i++)
Line 4:        {
Line 5:            int temp = x[i];
Line 6:            int j = i - 1;
Line 7:            while (j >= 0 && x[j] > temp)
Line 8:            {
Line 9:                x[j + 1] = x[j];
Line 10:               j--;
Line 11:           }
Line 12:           x[j + 1] = temp;
Line 13:       }
Line 14:   }
```

Note that like the selection sort, the insertion sort contains nested loops. In this case, we have a while loop nested within a for loop.

The for loop, beginning on line 3, proceeds from index 1 to the end of the array. The while loop goes through the array from i to 0 and shifts elements that are larger than temp to the right on line 9. On line 12, we put the value in temp into its proper place in the array.

2-D ARRAYS

Two-dimensional, or 2-D, arrays are structures that have entered, exited, and re-entered the required topics for the AP Exam. They are quite powerful and, at the same time, not too difficult to understand once you have mastered 1-D array structures, which we studied in previous sections.

A great example of a 2-D array is a stand-up soda machine, like you see in the mall or in front of the supermarket. You know the type, the one in which you drop money and hope desperately that the soda actually drops out.

Think of the soda machine as a set of **rows** across the machine, each having a different type of soda (i.e., first row has cola, second has orange, etc.). Each of those rows can be considered as an array. Now consider the vertical **columns** down the machine; each column will have one of each type of soda, since it travels down the rows (i.e., first item is cola, second item is orange, etc.). *That* vertical column can also be considered in array. The result is an "array of arrays," which Java quantifies as a 2-D array, with index numbers assigned independently to each row and column location.

In the soda machine example, the very first cola in the upper left location of the 2-D "array" would be located at index 0 of the first horizontal array, as well as index 0 of the first vertical array. The code to access this element (soda) in a 2-D array (soda machine) already instantiated as sodaMachine would be sodaMachine[0][0], with the first 0 being the row and the second 0 being the column. The second cola would be located at [0, 1] and the first orange would be located at [1, 0], and so on. For an *m* by *n* 2-D array, with *m* being the number of rows and *n* being the number of columns, the last element in the lower right corner would be located at [*m*-1, *n*-1]. But you didn't forget that index numbers begin at 0 and end at (array.length-1), did you?

The methods and constants available for use with array structures are available for 2-D array structures as well, because a 2-D array is an array—just a fancy one. it's a little tricky, however; in order to, say, return the number of cola slots across the soda machine, you would use sodaMachine.length, as expected. In order to access the number of slots down the left side of the machine, however, you would use sodaMachine[0].length, meaning you want the length of the first column of the 2-D array.

---

7. Consider the following code segment:

```
int[][] sum = new int [4][4];
for (int i = 0; i < num.length; i++)
{
    for (int k = 0; k < num[0].length; k++
    {
        num[i][k] = i * k;
    }
}
```

What are the contents of num after the code segment has executed?

(A) 0 0 0 0
     0 1 2 3
     0 2 4 6
     0 3 6 9

(B) 0 1 2 3
     1 2 3 4
     2 3 4 5
     3 4 5 6

(C) 0 3 6 9
     0 2 4 6
     0 1 2 3
     0 0 0 0

(D) 1 1 1 1
     2 2 2 2
     3 3 3 3
     4 4 4 4

(E) 0 0 0 0
     1 2 3 4
     2 4 6 8
     3 6 9 12

Here's How To Crack It

2-D array questions are always intimidating. The first iteration of the outer loop will occur with i = 0. Looking at the inner loop, the k values will range from 0 to 3 before it terminates. Since i = 0 and each iteration of the inner loop will multiply i times k, the first row of the array will be all zeroes. Eliminate (B), (C), and (D). Wow! Once that finishes, the outer loop will have its second iteration with i = 1. The inner loop will then start over with k = 0, and i times k will equal zero, as a result. The first number in the second row, then, will be 0. Eliminate (E) because its first number in the second row is 1, and the answer is (A).

Remember that an array, regardless of its dimensions, can store any one type of data, but not multiple types. Also remember that, as is true for most computer programming language rules, there is always a workaround! More on this later.

LISTS & ARRAYLISTS

There are two big limitations of the powerful array structure in Java: an array has a fixed length and it can only store one type of data. If you wanted to represent, say, a friend's collection of action figures, an array would require all of the action figures to be the same type. Generally speaking, they must *all* be flying superheroes, or they must *all* have protective body armor, etc.

Likewise, a collection of action figures represented as an array could only store a fixed number of action figures, no more and no less. If there are extra, unused slots, they stay there, which could be problematic if you have an array of helmeted heroes and you try to remove the helmet from every element in every index of the array. Once you reach the first empty spot, there is no hero and therefore no helmet, so the directions do not make sense; in Java, the compiler will return a *NullPointerException* for this situation.

There are advantages and disadvantages to every structure that we study in Java.

A *List* object—more specifically for our purposes, an ArrayList—addresses both of these issues. An *ArrayList* object is **dynamically sized**, expanding and compressing as elements are added and removed. An ArrayList can also store multiple types of data, without limit.

Let's use an example to understand the advantages and disadvantages of arrays versus ArrayLists. Consider your lunch bag that you bring to school. If you wanted to represent your lunch bag using an array or ArrayList structure, which would be more accurate?

Naturally, the answer to this question depends on (1) the details of the objects in the bag—in this case, the types of lunch items—and (2) the programmer's choice of which is more appropriate. If your lunch contains a sandwich object, a fruit object, and a drink object, the ArrayList structure might be a better choice. Furthermore, as the components of the lunch are removed, the lunch bag theoretically shrinks (or can shrink). An ArrayList seems appropriate.

Let's consider the same lunch example, but this time, suppose the items are stored in a plastic container with compartments. Regardless of whether you have not yet eaten your lunch or you are done with your lunch, or anytime in between, the number and setup of the compartments does not change. We will discuss a workaround for "tricking" the array to think the lunch objects are all the same type. These facts and abilities render an array structure more appropriate, versus an ArrayList.

To further demonstrate the usefulness of an ArrayList structure, it is also possible to create a **typed** ArrayList which only allows objects of the same type to be stored in the list. This structure combines useful aspects of both arrays and ArrayLists.

In order to instantiate an ArrayList called lunchBag that will store our various componenets of our lunch, we use the following line of code:

```
ArrayList lunchBag = new ArrayList();
```

Note that, unlike the syntax we use for instantiating an array, neither the type of object nor the length of the list are defined initially.

In order to access data from within the list, particular methods must be invoked; unlike array structures in Java, there is not a convenient bracket notation available with lists. To return the second object, an Apple object, in the ArrayList and store it using the variable food, the line of code would be:

```
Apple red = lunchBag.get (1);
```

There are several other useful methods available in the List class, and they are all mentioned in the AP Exam Quick Reference, although their functionality is (obviously) not given. These methods include add, set, remove, and size.

> Bracket notation can only be used with array objects; lists must use the appropriate methods.

If the programmer decides it is more appropriate to keep the dynamic sizing ability of the ArrayList while fixing the type of data it can hold (just like an array) it would be instantiated as follows:

```
ArrayList<Apple> lunchBag = new ArrayList<Apple>();
```

8. Consider the following code segment:

```
ArrayList list = new ArrayList;
for (int i = 1; i <= 8; i++)
{
    list.add (new Integer(i));
}
for (int j = 1; j < list.size(); j++)
{
    list.set (j / 2, list.get(j));
}
System.out.println (list);
```

What is printed as a result of executing the code segment?

(A) [2, 4, 6, 8, 5, 6, 7, 8]
(B) [1, 2, 3, 4, 5, 6, 7, 8]
(C) [1, 2, 3, 4]
(D) [1, 2, 3, 4, 1, 2, 3, 4]
(E) [2, 2, 4, 4, 6, 6, 8, 8]

Here's How to Crack It

This is an annoying problem, particularly in the second loop. A quick glance at the first loop reveals that list will be filled with eight elements, 1 through 8; eliminate (C). The second loop will traverse list again, changing some values. The first iteration of this loop will go to index 1 / 2, which is 0, and set it to element 1 of list, which is 2. Eliminate (B) and (D). Now, if you trace this loop through for j = 2, list will read [2, 2,...] and (E) looks tempting. However, looping through again reveals that we are reassigning the second element of list again, so it will read [2, 4,...]. The answer is (A).

Arrays	ArrayList
After an array is created, it cannot be resized.	ArrayLists will automatically resize as new elements are added.
No import statement is needed to use an array, unless the array holds elements that require an import statement.	You must import java.util.ArrayList, or use the full package name whenever you use an ArrayList.
Elements are accessed using index notation (e.g., myArray[2]).	Elements are accessed using methods of the ArrayList class (e.g., myList.get(2), myList.add("George")).
Arrays can be constructed to hold either primitives or object references.	ArrayList instances can hold only object references, not primitives. The Integer and Double wrapper classes must be used to store integer and double primitives in an ArrayList.
Each array can be declared for only one type of element. For example, if an array is declared to hold Strings, you cannot store an Integer in it.	An ArrayList can hold a heterogeneous collection of objects. For example, the following is perfectly legal (though not recommended): `ArrayList list = new ArrayList( );` `list.add(new String("A String"));` `list.add(new Integer(4));`

CHAPTER 6 REVIEW DRILL

Answers to review questions can be found in Chapter 9.

1. Consider the following code segment:

```
String[] s = new String[2];
String[] t = {"Michael", "Megan", "Chelsea"};
s = t;
System.out.print(s.length);
```

What is printed as a result of executing the code segment?

(A) 1

(B) 2

(C) 3

(D) Nothing will be printed due to a compile-time error.

(E) Nothing will be printed due to a run-time error.

2. Consider the following code segment:

```
final int[] a1 = {1, 2};
int[] b1 = {3, 4};
a1 = b1;
System.out.print(a1[1]);
```

What is printed as a result of executing the code segment?

(A) 2

(B) 3

(C) 4

(D) Nothing will be printed due to a compile-time error.

(E) Nothing will be printed due to a run-time error.

3. Consider the following code segment:

```
final int[] myArray = {1, 2};
myArray[1] = 3;
System.out.print(myArray[1]);
```

What is printed as a result of executing the code segment?

(A) 1

(B) 2

(C) 3

(D) Nothing will be printed due to a run-time error.

(E) Nothing will be printed due to a compile-time error.

4. Consider the following incomplete method:

```
public static int Mod3(int [] numbers)
{
    int count = 0;
    for (int i = 0; i < a.length; i++)
    {
        // code not shown
    }
    return count;
}
```

Method Mod3 is intended to return the number of integers in the array numbers that are evenly divisible by 3. Which of the following code segments could be used to replace // code not shown so that Mod3 will work as intended?

I.
```
if (i % 3 = = 0)
{
     count++;
}
```

II.
```
if (a[i] % 3 = = 0)
{
     count++;
}
```

III.
```
while (a[i] % 3 = = 0)
{
     count++;
}
```

(A) I only
(B) II only
(C) III only
(D) I and II
(E) II and III

5. Consider the following code segment:

```
ArrayList list = new ArrayList( );
list.add("A");
list.add("B");
list.add(0, "C");
list.add("D");
list.set(2, "E");
list.remove(1);
System.out.println(list);
```

What is printed as a result of executing the code segment?

(A) [A, B, C, D, E]
(B) [A, B, D, E]
(C) [C, E, D]
(D) [A, D, E]
(E) [A, C, D, E]

6. Consider the following data fields and method:

```
private ArrayList letters;
// precondition: letters.size( ) > 0
// letters contains String objects
public void letterRemover( )
{
    int i = 0;
    while (i < letters.size( ))
    {
        if (letters.get(i).equals("A"))
            letters.remove(i);
        i++;
    }
}
```

Assume that ArrayList letters originally contains the following String values:

```
[A, B, A, A, C, D, B]
```

What will letters contain as a result of executing letterRemover( )?

(A) [A, B, A, A, C, D, B]
(B) [B, C, D, B]
(C) [B, A, C, D, B]
(D) [A, B, A, C, D, B]
(E) [A, A, B, C, D, B, D]

7. Consider the following method:

```
private ArrayList myList;
// precondition: myList.size( ) > 0
// myListcontains String objects
public void myMethod( )
{
    for (int i = 0; i < myList.size( ) - 1; i++)
    {
        myList.remove(i);
        System.out.print(myList.get(i) + " ");
    }
}
```

Assume that myList originally contains the following String values:

```
[A, B, C, D, E]
```

What will be printed when the method above executes?

(A) A B C D E
(B) A C E
(C) B D E
(D) B D
(E) Nothing will be printed due to an IndexOutOfBoundsException.

8. Consider the following code segment:

```
int[] [] numbers = new int [4] [4];
initializeIt(numbers);
int total = 0;
for (int z = 0; z < numbers.length; z++)
{
    total += numbers[z] [numbers [0].length - 1 - z];
}
```

The call to initializeIt( ) on the second line initializes the array numbers so that it looks like the following:

```
1 2 5 3
7 9 4 0
3 3 2 5
4 5 8 1
```

What will be the value of total after the code has executed?

(A) 11
(B) 12
(C) 13
(D) 14
(E) 15

9. Consider the following code segment:

```
int[] [] numbers = new int [3] [6];
initializeIt(numbers);
int total = 0;
for (int j = 0; j < numbers.length; j++)
{
    for (int k = 0; k < numbers[0].length; k += 2)
    {
        total+= numbers[j] [k];
    }
}
```

The call to initializeIt( ) on the second line initializes the array numbers so that it looks like the following:

```
2 4 6 3 2 1
5 6 7 4 2 9
4 0 5 6 4 2
```

What will be the value of total after the code has executed?

(A) 18
(B) 35
(C) 37
(D) 72
(E) 101

10. Consider the following code segment:

```
ArrayList list = new ArrayList( );
for (int i = 1; i <= 8; i++)
{
    list.add(new Integer(i));
}
for (int j = 1; j < list.size( ); j++)
{
    list.set(j / 2, list.get(j));
}
System.out.println(list);
```

What is printed as a result of executing the code segment?

(A) [2, 4, 6, 8, 5, 6, 7, 8]
(B) [1, 2, 3, 4, 5, 6, 7, 8]
(C) [1, 2, 3, 4]
(D) [1, 2, 3, 4, 1, 2, 3, 4]
(E) [2, 2, 4, 4, 6, 6, 8, 8]

11. Consider the following code segment:

```
int[] [] num = new int[4] [4];
for (int i = 0; i < num.length; i++)
{
    for (int k = 0; k < num[0].length; k++)
    {
        num[i] [k] = i * k;
    }
}
```

What are the contents of num after the code segment has executed?

(A) 0 0 0 0
     0 1 2 3
     0 2 4 6
     0 3 6 9
(B) 0 1 2 3
     1 2 3 4
     2 3 4 5
     3 4 5 6
(C) 0 3 6 9
     0 2 4 6
     0 1 2 3
     0 0 0 0
(D) 1 1 1 1
     2 2 2 2
     3 3 3 3
     4 4 4 4
(E) 0 0 0 0
     1 2 3 4
     2 4 6 8
     3 6 9 12

KEY TERMS

array
initializer list
index numbers
span
full
arrayindexoutofboundsexception
null
NullPointerException
linear search
binary search
search algorithms
for-each loop
sorting algorithms
selection sort
insertion sort
rows
columns
list object
ArrayList object
dynamically sized
typed ArrayList

Chapter 7
Inheritance

Inheritance is the quintessential way—and the only way, for our purposes—to create direct relationships between classes. An **inheritance hierarchy** is designed in order to quantify this relationship, much like a family tree, and it defines the "parent" class and all of its "child" classes. A carefully designed hierarchy implemented as an inheritance relationship between classes is arguably the most powerful programming technique that you will learn in this course.

HIERARCHIES & DESIGN

The designing of the hierachy is critical in implementing inheritance. As the programmer, there are limitless ways design an interface, so the important of the planning process cannot be understated.

The first decision for the programmer/designer—yes, there are programmers who focus solely on *design*—is to define the parent class of the situation. Typically the parent class (**superclass**) is the most general form of the objects that will be instantiated in the overall program. Every other class in the program will lie lower in the hierarchy (**subclasses** of the superclass), but their objects will be more specific versions of the overall parent. This setup creates an *is-a* relationship between the parent and the child classes.

Let's use potato chips as our example for this discussion (everyone loves food, right? If you don't, you should have realized that you won't like this book by now). If we are designing a hierarchy of classes to properly represent potato chips, there are a ridiculous amount of possibilities—would the parent class be PotatoChip? Potato? Snack? SaltySnack? JunkFood? So we have to make a decision, based on the situation that we are given; if the programmer receives no context whatsoever, the design is very difficult and will produce unpredictable—yet all viable—results.

In this case, let's use Snack as the superclass. A Snack object is very general; there may be many subclasses in our situation. Let's define two subclasses for Snack, one for our purposes and an extra for practice: PotatoChip and Cookie. Since a potato chip (and a cookie) is a snack, the setup makes intuitive sense. Note how we define the relationship from the bottom (lowest subclasses) of the hierarchy to the top (highest superclass). Let us then define another, lower set of classes that will be subclasses of PotatoChip: BBQChip and OnionChip. A visual representation of a hierarchy makes the design much easier to understand:

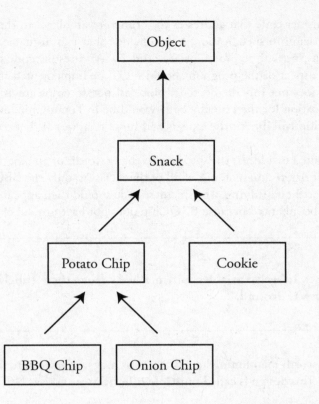

As you can see, there are several is-a relationships here. A BBQChip is-a Potato-Chip, which is-a Snack. A BBQChip also is-a Snack, by inheritance. All of these relationships as designed in the hierarchy should make intuitive sense and/or conform to the given specifications.

> On the AP Exam, at least one FRQ and at least several MCQs typically focus on the design and/or implementation of inheritance relationships. Detailed specifications will be given in order to suppress the variety of exam responses to score.

Let's discuss the benefits of the setup we have created. When the programmer is ready to implement code, he or she should decide which variables and methods should be implemented, as well as their location within the hierarchy. This task is more formidable than it might seem; very general variables and methods should be closer to the top of the hierarchy, while more specifics should reside in lower subclasses. For example, virtually every snack food has some kind of flavor. Therefore, code to address the flavor of the snack food should be implemented in Snack, and it will be subsequently inherited by all of the subclasses…. Since a Snack object has a flavor, and a PotatoChip object is-a Snack, a PotatoChip object will also have a flavor. What about an OnionChip object? It also will have a flavor, as described above.

Now consider code that addresses the crunch of an object in the hierarchy. Without any detail in specification, let's conclude that it is arguable whether a cookie is crunchy, but all potato chips are crunchy. As a result, code that addresses the crunchy aspect of the program should NOT be implemented in Snack, that way Cookie does not inherit the code. Since all potato chips are crunchy, the appropriate location for the crunchy code would be in PotatoChip, and BBQChip and OnionChip will inherit the aspects and functionalities of that code.

If we wanted to address the spiciness (is that a word?) of an object in our hierarchy, we might determine that, out of all of these classes, only the BBQChip has a spice factor worth quantifying. The spiciness code should then appear in BBQChip and will not be inherited because BBQChip does not have any subclasses.

> **Classes inherit variables and methods from their subclasses, not the other way around.**

It is also worth mentioning here that a class may not have more than one direct superclass. This design is called **multiple inheritance** and it is NOT allowed in Java.

---

1. Consider the following two classes:

```
public class A
{
    public int method1 (int x)
    {
        return 2;
    }
}
public class B extends A
{ /* code not shown */ }
```

Which of the following could be the signature of a method in class B that correctly overloads method1 in class A?

(A) `public int method1 (String x)`
(B) `public int method1 (int y)`
(C) `private int method1 (int x)`
(D) `public int method2 (String x)`
(E) `public int method2 (int y)`

Here's How to Crack It

Overloading a method means to create a new method with the same name, visibility, and return type, regardless of whether the method lies in the parent class or the child class. The parameter must be different, however, or the new method overrides the original method. Choice (B) will override method1, (C) and (E) will create all new methods that are independent of method1, and (C) does not have the same visibility as method1. The answer is (A).

―――――――――○―――――――――

Now, suppose there is functionality in a superclass that is inherited, but should be changed based on the level of inheritance. For example, all snacks can be eaten so the programer appropriately implements an eat() method in Snack. As a result, all subclasses will inherit this method and its functionality. But what if, say, an OnionChip must be eaten differently than the other snacks? Perhaps after a few chips, the "eater" would have to wipe his or her hands before he or she keeps eating. The desired eat() method—possessing the identical name, parameters, and return type—would be implemented in OnionChip and all objects of that class (and only that class, in this example) would use this new eat() method. The superclass's eat method has been **overrided** by this new version. The workaround for this situation would be to use the **super** keyword: super.super.eat()

Another level of overriding involves method **abstraction**. Suppose that the programmer wants to force all subclasses to have the eat() method, but he or she decides that an eat() method's code in Snack is inappropriate; for example, all Snack objects can be eaten but the WAY they are eaten depends so much on the type of snack that superclass code for the method seems inappropriate. You would not eat a chip same way you would eat a cookie? Go with it. The eat() method can be declared abstract; in this design, the Snack class has now mandated every subclass to either (1) override the abstract method with code or (2) declare the method abstract once again, forcing its subclasses to override the abstract method.

2. Consider the following two classes:

```
public class Parent
{
    public void writeMe (String s)
    {
        System.out.println ("Object");
    }
}
public class Child extends Parent
{
    public void writeMe (String s)
    {
        System.out.println ("Object");
    }
}
```

Which of the following best describes the writeMe method of the Child class?

(A) an inherited method
(B) an overridden method
(C) an overloaded method
(D) an interface method
(E) an abstract method

Here's How to Crack It

Since the writeMe method in Child has the same name, return type, and parameter types, it is overriding writeMe in Parent. The answer is (B).

POLYMORPHISM

Polymorphism is a technique that, in a way, breaks all of the rules we think would happen in inheritance—and yet, it conforms to them at the same time.

Using our Snack example from above, including the overridden method in OnionChip, suppose several objects from various levels in the hierarchy reside in an untyped ArrayList. The programmer would like to, using a simple loop, simulate the user "eating" the chips in the list, regardless of their type. The loop will iterate through the list and automatically invoke the appropriate eat() method, including the overriden method for OnionChip objects, as desired. This is an example of polymorphism.

The word polymorphism, which means "many forms," can also apply to programs in a more profound manner. This process directly or indirectly involves virtually every technique we have learned in this book.

Suppose an interface called Eatable is implemented by all of the classes in the Snack hierarchy. Every class has either overrriden the abstract methods from the interface, as normally required, or passed on the abstraction to a subclass.

Have you ever seen those snack bags that have multiple forms of snacks (for example, potato chips AND pretzels AND nacho chips...) in them? This example is similar; if you instantiated the "bag" as either a typed ArrayList or an array, you could fill the structure with instances of all of these classes by declaring the type as Eatable. Once the eat() method is invoked on all of the components of the list structure using a loop, each object will automatically invoke its corresponding eat method! Pretty awesome.

Use the information below to answer Questions 3 and 4.

———————————————○———————————————

Consider the following declaration for a class that will be used to represent a rectangle:

```
public class Rectangle
{
    private double width;
    private double height;
    public Rectangle ()
    {
        width = 0;

        height = 0;
    }
    public Rectangle (double w, double h)
    {
        width = w;
        height = h;
    }

    // postcondition: returns the height
    public double getHeight ()
    {
        return height;
    }

    // postcondition: returns the width
    public double getWidth ()
    {
        return width;
    }
}
```

The following incomplete class declaration is intended to extend the above class so the rectangles can be filled with a color when displayed:

```
public class FilledRectangle extends Rectangle
{
    private String color;
    // constructors go here

    public String getColor ()
    {
        return color;
    }
}
```

Consider the following proposed constructors for this class:

```
I.    public FilledRectangle ()
      {
          color = "red";
      }


II.   public filledRectangle (double w, double h, String c)
      {
          super (w, h);
          color = c;
      }


III.  public FilledRectangle (double w, double h, String c)
      {
          width = w;
          height = h;
          color = c;
      }
```

3. Which of these constructors would be legal for the FilledRectangle class?

   (A) I only
   (B) II only
   (C) III only
   (D) I and II
   (E) I and III

Here's How to Crack It

This is an interesting one. II follows all of the rules nicely, invoking the super constructor and initializing the data field in its class, so II is good; eliminate (A), (C), and (E). Note that we do not have to check III now. For I, remember that the superclass's default constructor will be invoked automatically if it is not called. Therefore, I is fine. The answer is (D).

4. Based on the class declarations for Rectangle and FilledRectangle given above, which of the following code segments would be legal in a client class? Assume that the constructor that takes no arguments has been implemented for FilledRectangle.

```
I.   FilledRectangle r1 = new Rectangle ();
     double height = r1.getHeight();
II.  Rectangle r2 = new FilledRectangle ();
     double height = r2.getHeight();
III. Rectangle r3 = new FilledRectangle()
     r3.getColor();
```

Which of the code segments above are legal?

(A) None
(B) II only
(C) III only
(D) I and II
(E) II and III

Here's How to Crack It

Since II appears in the most answer choices, let's check that option first. A FilledRectangle may be declared as a Rectangle because it is a subclass of Rectangle, and a FilledRectangle inherits getHeight from Rectangle as well, so II is legal; eliminate (A) and (C). A Rectangle cannot be declared as a FilledRectangle for the same reason, so I is illegal and (D) can be eliminated. As for III, a Rectangle object can only invoke methods from Rectangle (regardless of r3's identity as a FilledRectangle) so the second line is illegal. The answer is (B).

CHAPTER 7 REVIEW DRILL

Answers to the review questions can be found in Chapter 9.

1. Consider the following two classes:

```java
public class Parent
{
    public void writeMe(String s)
    {
        System.out.println("object");
    }
}

public class Child extends Parent
{
    public void writeMe(String s)
    {
        System.out.println("object");
    }
}
```

Which of the following best describes the writeMe method of the Child class?

(A) An inherited method
(B) An overridden method
(C) An overloaded method
(D) An interface method
(E) An abstract method

2. How many classes can a given class extend?

(A) None
(B) 1
(C) 2
(D) As many as it needs to

3. How many interfaces can a given class implement?

(A) None
(B) 1
(C) 2
(D) As many as it needs to

4. How many other interfaces can a given interface extend?

(A) None
(B) 1
(C) 2
(D) As many as it needs to

5. How many classes can a given interface implement?

(A) None
(B) 1
(C) 2
(D) As many as it needs to

6. Consider the following class:

```
public class Sample
{
    int var = 0;

    public static void writeMe(String string)
    {
        System.out.println("string");
    }
}
```

What is the result of executing the following?

```
Sample.writeMe("hello");
```

(A) This is not a legal call because there is no instance variable.
(B) "hello"
(C) "null"
(D) "string"
(E) Run-time error

7. Consider the following class:

```
public class Sample
{
    int static final var = 0;
}
```

What is the result of executing the following?

```
System.out.println(Sample.var);
```

(A) This is not a legal call because there is no instance variable.
(B) −1
(C) 0
(D) The value is unknowable.
(E) This is not a legal call because var is final.

For questions 8–9, consider the following class:

```
public class Sample
{
    String name;

    public Sample (String in)
    {
        name = in;
    }

    public void writeMe(String s)
    {
        String val = null;

        if (val.equals(s))
        {
            System.out.println("me");
        }
        else
        {
            System.out.println("you");
        }
    }
}
```

8. What will be the result of executing the following?

```
Sample s = new Sample( );
String tmp = new String("hi");
s.writeMe(tmp);
```

   (A) Compile-time error
   (B) Run-time error
   (C) "hi"
   (D) "string"
   (E) "Sample"

9. What will be the result of executing the following?

```
Sample s = new Sample("sample");
String tmp = new String("hi");
s.writeMe(tmp);
```

   (A) "hi"
   (B) Run-time error
   (C) "me"
   (D) "sample"
   (E) "you"

10. An apartment rental company has asked you to write a program to store information about the apartments that it has available for rent. For each apartment, they want to keep track of the following information: number of rooms, whether or not the apartment has a dishwasher, and whether or not pets are allowed. Which of the following is the best design?

(A) Use four unrelated classes: Apartment, Rooms, Dishwasher, and Pets.

(B) Use one class, Apartment which has three subclasses: Room, Dishwasher, and Pet.

(C) Use one class, Apartment, which has three data fields: int rooms, boolean hasDishwasher, boolean allowsPets.

(D) Use three classes Pets, Rooms, and Dishwasher, each with a subclass Apartment.

(E) Use four classes: Apartment, Pets, Dishwasher, and Rooms. The class Apartment contains instances of the other classes as attributes.

11. Consider the following class declaration:

```
public interface Inter
{
    int inter1( );
}
```

Which of the following classes will compile without error?

```
I.   public class A implements Inter
     {
         private int inter1( )
         {
             return 7;
         }
     }
II.  public abstract class B implements Inter
     {
     }
III. public class C implements Inter
     {
         public double inter1 ( )
         {
             return 7;
         }
     }
```

(A) None of the above

(B) I only

(C) II only

(D) III only

(E) I and III

12. Consider the following class declarations:

```
public class Vehicle
{
    private int maxPassengers;
    public Vehicle( )
    {
        maxPassengers = 1;
    }
    public Vehicle(int x)
    {
        maxPassengers = x;
    }
    public int maxPassengers( )
    {
        return maxPassengers;
    }
}
public class Motorcycle extends Vehicle
{
    public Motorcycle( )
    {
        super(2);
    }
}
```

Which of the following code segments will NOT cause a compilation error?

(A) `Motorcycle m1 = new Motorcycle (3);`
(B) `Vehicle v1 = new Motorcycle (4);`
(C) `Motorcycle m2 = new Vehicle ( );`
(D) `Vehicle v2 = new Motorcycle ( );`
(E) `Vehicle v3 = new Vehicle ( );`
     `int max = v3.maxPassengers;`

KEY TERMS
inheritance
inheritance hierarchy
superclass
subclass
multiple inheritance
overrided
super keyword
abstraction
polymorphism

Chapter 8
Advanced Control Structures

RECURSION

The final flow control structure that appears on the AP Exam is called **recursion**. It is not represented in the FRQs and appears at least once in the MCQs, but typically just a few times. This structure has a result similar to a loop, but approaches the task in a different manner.

Remember those little wind-up toys you played with when you were little? You know, the plastic teeth or bunny (or whatever) with the little white knob on the side? You would wind the knob over and over, and when you let go, the little teeth would walk across the table. The more you wound the knob, the longer the teeth would walk. Since the winding is the same action repeated, it can be considered a loop. The UNWINDING action, however, differentiates this situation from a while or for loop. When an unwinding or "winding down" occurs as a result of a "winding up," recursion is lurking in the shadows.

The distinguishing characteristic of a recursive method is a call to the very method itself; this statement is called a **recursive call**. In order to prevent an infinite loop, the recursive method includes a **base case**, which signals execution to stop recursing and return to each prior recursive call, finishing the job for each. Let's use an easy example to illustrate this somewhat confusing topic, and then we'll spice up the example a bit afterwards.

Suppose you have a giant bag of small, multi-colored, candy-coated chocolates. As a programmer, you naturally do not want to eat these candies in a haphazard manner; instead, you want to use some sort of algorithm. (I mean, don't we all do this normally?) You decide that you will eat random candies, one at a time, until you reach your favorite color; when your favorite color is reached, you will systematically eat the same colors you ate previously, in backwards order.

For example, if you eat red -> blue -> orange -> blue -> green, and green is your base case, you will then eat blue ->orange -> blue -> red and the recursion is complete. Pretty tough to remember, right? Well, a recursive method renders this task a cinch. In pseudocode:

```
eatCandy (color of current candy)
{
    if (current candy color is green)
        done eating;
    else
        eat more candy;
}
```

Although there is no for or while loop in the code, the recursive call to the method will exhibit a looping quality; unlike our previous loops, however, there is a forward/backward progression, as described above.

Let's add to this task: I want to tell the user that I'm done eating once I finish. Would adding the following line after the if-else statement accomplish this task?:

display I'm done;

The way recursion works, the task will be accomplished, although perhaps not according to plan. When the base case is reached, execution of the current method is completed, and then the process continues all the way back to the initial recursive call. Since the "I'm done" message is displayed after, and regardless of, the if/else, it will be displayed each time a recursive iteration completes. The result is the displaying of "I'm done" once for every candy that I ate. Ten candies, ten "I'm done" outputs. It works, but probably not as planned.

---

1. Consider the following method:

```
// precondition: x >= 0
public int mystery (int x)
{
    if (x == 0)
    {
        return 0;
    }
    else
    {
        return ((x % 10) + mystery (x / 10));
    }
}
```

Which of the following is returned as a result of the call mystery(3543)?

(A) 10
(B) 15
(C) 22
(D) 180
(E) Nothing is returned due to infinite recursion

Here's How to Crack It

We hate these questions! But here we go, anyway. Eliminate (E) right away because there is a base case. Go through the recursion a few times and you will see that 3543 quickly loses digits because the method returns the sum of the units digit and the other digits. The units digit will be less than 10 and the recursion will occur 4 times, chopping off a digit each time and adding it to the overall sum. Therefore, the result will be 3 + 5 + 4 + 3 = 15. The answer is (B).

RECURSIVELY TRAVERSING ARRAYS

Although it is more common to use a for loop to step through an array, it is also possible to use a recursion. For example, say you have a lineup of football players, each of whom has a numbered helmet. You want to step through the lineup, and find the position of the person who has "9" written on his helmet:

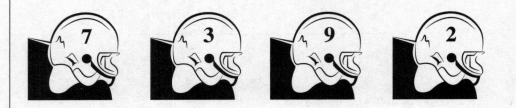

A recursive solution for this problem is very easy to implement. You need to look through an array of int values and find the position of a specific value, if it's there.

First, we'll need describe the problem in recursive terms.

- If we've looked through every item, then return −1.
- If the current item in the array is a match, return its position.
- Or else, restart the process with the next item in the array.

```
public int findPosition
    (int nums[], int key, int currentIndex)
{
    //if we've already looked through
    //the entire array
    if (nums.length <= currentIndex)
        return -1;
    //if the next item in the array is match,
    //then return it
    if (nums[currentIndex] == key)
        return currentIndex;
    //else, step past the current item in the array,
    //and repeat the search on the next item
    return findPosition(nums, key, currentIndex + 1);
}
```

This example is slightly more subtle than the others because we're carrying information from one recursive call to the next. Specifically, we're using the currentIndex field to pass state information from one recursive call to another. Thus, the first recursive call starts looking at position 0, the next one at position 1, and so on.

Let's go back to our football-player example. You want to step through a lineup of football players and return the position of the player who has the helmet with "9" written on it. Your code would be of the form

```
int [] players = //represents the football players
int pos = findPosition(players, 9, 0);
```

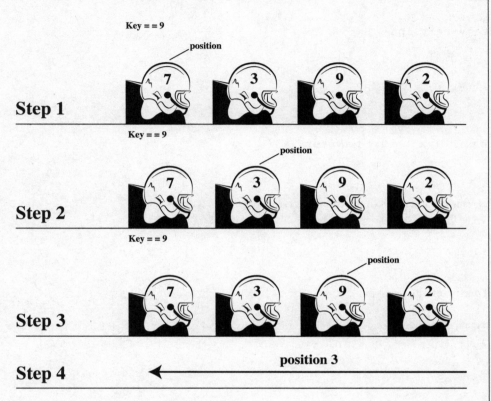

Study Break
Congratulations! You just tackled all of your AP Computer Science A content review! Take a study break and go for a walk or crank up some music or eat your favorite snack.

CHAPTER 8 REVIEW DRILL

Answers to the review questions can be found in Chapter 9.

1. Consider the following method:

```
// precondition: x >= 0
   public int mystery(int x)
   {
      if (x = = 0)
      {
          return 0;
      }
      else
          {
          return ((x % 10) + mystery(x / 10));
          }
   }
```

Which of the following is returned as a result of the call mystery(3543)?

(A) 10
(B) 15
(C) 22
(D) 180
(E) Nothing is returned due to infinite recursion.

2. Consider the following recursive method:

```
public int mystery(int x)
{
    if (x == 1)
        return 2;
    else
        return 2 * mystery(x - 1);
}
```

What value is returned as a result of the call mystery(6)?

(A) 2
(B) 12
(C) 32
(D) 64
(E) 128

3. Consider the following recursive method:

```java
public static int mystery(int x)
{
    if (x == 0)
    {
        return 0;
    }
    else
    {
        return (x + mystery(x / 2) + mystery(x / 4));
    }
}
```

What value is returned as a result of a call to mystery(10)?

(A) 10
(B) 12
(C) 20
(D) 22
(E) 35

4. Consider the following nonrecursive method:

```
//precondition: x >= 0
public static int mystery(int x)
{
    int sum = 0;
    while(x >= 0)
    {
        sum += x;
        x- -;
    }
    return sum;
}
```

Which of the following recursive methods are equivalent to the method above?

I.
```
public static int mystery2(int x)
    {
            if (x == 0)
            {
                return 0;
            }
            return (x + mystery2 (x - 1));
    }
```

II.
```
public static int mystery3 (int x)
    {
            if (x == 0)
                    return 0;
            else
                    return mystery3(x - 1);
    }
```

III.
```
public static int mystery4 (int x)
    {
            if (x == 1)
            {
                    return 1:
            }
            return (x + mystery 4(x - 1));
    }
```

(A) I only
(B) II only
(C) III only
(D) I and II
(E) II and III

5. Consider the following method:

```java
public int mystery(int x, int y)
{
    if (x >= 100 || y <= 0)
    {
        return 1;
    }
    else
    {
        return mystery(x + 10, y - 3);
    }
}
```

What value is returned by the call mystery (30, 18)?

(A) 0

(B) 1

(C) 6

(D) 7

(E) Nothing will be returned due to infinite recursion.

6. Consider the following incomplete method:

```java
public int mystery(int x)
{
    if (x <= 1)
    {
        return 1;
    }
    else
    {
        return (<missing code>);
    }
}
```

Which of the following could be used to replace <missing code> so that the value of mystery(10) is 32?

(A) `mystery(x - 1) + mystery(x - 2)`

(B) `2 * mystery(x - 2)`

(C) `2 * mystery(x - 1)`

(D) `4 * mystery(x - 4)`

(E) `4 + mystery(x - 1)`

KEY TERMS

recursion
recursive call
base case

Chapter 9
Chapter Review
Drill Answers and
Explanations

CHAPTER 3

1. **E** Let's start by examining line 3 in the code segment above: double c = a + b. a is an integer variable and b is a double variable. When a double variable is added to an integer variable, the integer is automatically cast to a double before the addition takes place. Therefore, a + b will be 20.7; this value will be assigned to c.

   Now look at line 4: int d = a + c. Because c is a double, a will once again be cast to a double and a + c will be 30.7. This value, which is double, is then assigned to an integer variable. Because there is a loss of precision when a double value is assigned to an integer variable, the compiler will alert us.

2. **E** The key to this question is remembering that the cast operator (int) has precedence over the addition operator. Let's first take a look at expression I. In that case, a will first be cast to an int (which has no effect because it is already an int) and then it will be added to b, which is still a double: The result of the addition will be a double, so we haven't fixed the problem. You can therefore eliminate (A) and (D).

   In Expression II, a + b is enclosed in parenthesis, so the addition will take place first. The result of adding a and b results in a double (20.7). This double is then cast to an int (20) and assigned to d. This is a legal assignment, so keep answers (B) and (E) and eliminate (C).

   Now, let's look at III. Here the double b (10.7) is first cast to an int (10). This int is added to a, which is also an int. When two ints are added, the result is also an int, so this expression is also valid.

3. **D** In line 5 of the code segment, we divide a by b. Because both of the operands are integers, the result will be truncated to an int. 11 divided by 4 is 2.75, which is then truncated to 2. We now know that the first number printed will be 2 (assuming we don't run into a compilation error later in the code), so we can get rid of (A) and (B).

   In line 7, we once again divide 11 by 4. This time, however, the variables that hold these values are doubles. Therefore the result of dividing 11 by 4 will also be a double: 2.75. We can get rid of (C).

   In line 9, we yet again divide 11 by 4. The variable that holds 11 is an integer, while the variable that holds 4 is a double. With arithmetic operators, if one of the operands is a double and the other an integer, the integer is automatically cast to a double and the result of the operation is a double. Therefore, we get 2.75 again.

4. **D** This question tests your understanding of short-circuit evaluation. In each code segment, pay attention to the conditional in the if statement.

   In the first code segment, the conditional statement is x < y && 10 < y/z. First x < y is evaluated.

Because x is 10 and y is 20, x < y evaluates to true. We then need to check 10 < y / z. Because we divide by zero here, a run-time exception occurs. You can eliminate answers (A) and (E).

Now let's look at the second code segment. The conditional statement is x > y && 10 < y / z. Once again, we first evaluate the operand to the left of the && operator. Because x is no greater than y, x > y evaluates to false. There's no need to evaluate the right-hand operand. With the && operator, if the left operand is false, the whole condition is false. Because the right-hand operand is not evaluated, y is never divided by z and a run-time exception does not occur. This means (B) and (D) are still possible.

In the third code segment, the conditional statement is x < y || 10 < y /z. The left-hand side, x < y evaluates to true. Notice that this time we have the or operator (||) in the middle of the conditional. With an or statement, if the left-hand side is true, the condition is true regardless of the value of the right side. Because the left side is true, there is no need to evaluate the right-hand side, and the division by 0 error never occurs.

CHAPTER 4

1. **C** This question is very similar to the previous one. This time, though, i starts at 200 and is divided by 3 after each pass through the for loop. Note that i /= 3 is equivalent to i = i / 3, and integer division truncates the results. As we iterate through the loop, the values of i will be: 200, 66, 22, 7, 2.

    In the body of the loop, i is printed if i % 2 equals 0. i % 2 gives the remainder when i is divided by 2; i will give a remainder of 0 when divided by 2 whenever i is even. Therefore, 200, 66, 22, and 2 will be printed; 7 will not be printed.

2. **E** In this question, we are trying to find the answer choice that doesn't work. If the answer to this question is not obvious to you, the best approach is to try each answer choice and see if it could be the a value of i. If it can, then get rid of it.

    Let's start with (A). Could i be equal to 0? Because x % 50 gives the remainder when x is divided by 50, for i to equal 0, x would have to be evenly divisible by 50. There are plenty of integers that would work for x (50, 100, 150…). In fact, any multiple of 50 would work.

    How about (B)? Is there a positive integer we can pick for x that leaves a remainder of 10 when divided by 50? Well, because 50 is evenly divisible by 50, 50 + 10, or 60, would leave a remainder of 10 when divided by 50. Other numbers that would work include 110 and 160. In fact, if you add 10 to any positive multiple of 50, you will get a number that leaves a remainder of 10 when divided by 50.

    Following the same logic, we find numbers that leave a remainder of 25 and 40 when divided by 50. For example, 75 and 90 would work. Therefore, we can get rid of (C) and (D).

The only choice left is (E). So why is it that we can't get a remainder of 50 if we divide a positive integer by 50? Consider what happens if we divide 98 by 50. We get a remainder of 48. What if we divide 99 by 50? Now the remainder is 49. It seems if we increase 99 to 100, our remainder will increase to 50! But wait—100 divided by 50 actually leaves a remainder of 0.

The upshot of this example is that the value returned by the modulus operator will always be less than the operand to the right of the modulus operator.

3.   **A**   This question tests your ability to reason through a nested loop. The first thing you should note is that the output is triangular. The first row has two elements, the second has three elements, and so on. Generally, the output of a nested loop will be triangular if the conditional statement of the inner loop is dependent upon the value of the outer loop. If the two loops are independent, the output is usually rectangular.

Let's trace through each answer choice and see which one will give us the first row: 0 1.

The first time we go through the inner loop in (A), x will be 1, because z starts at 0 and the loop continues while z is less than or equal to 1, the inner loop will print out 0 1. So let's keep this choice. For (B), the condition of the inner loop is that z is strictly less than x, so this will only print out 0. We can get rid of (B). Choice (C) will print out 0 1 2 3 4, so we can get rid of that too. Choice (D) will print 0 2 4 for the first line. Get rid of it. Choice (E) prints 0 1 for the first line, so we will keep it for now.

We are now down to (A) and (E). Rather than tracing through each segment in its entirety, let's see what the differences are between each segment.

The only difference is the outer for loop. In (A) it is

for (int x = 1; x < 5; x++)

And in (E) it is

for (int x = 1; x <= 5; x++) (note the extra equal sign)

In (E), because the body of the outer loop is evaluated 5 times, it will print out 5 rows of numbers. Because the answer we are looking for only prints out 4 rows, the correct answer must be (A).

4.   **A**   Segment 1 works correctly, so we can get rid of our second and third possible answers.

Segment 2 is incorrect, because the conditional 65 <= speed < 75 is illegal. A variable can't be compared to two numbers at once. This code will therefore cause a compile-time error. We can get rid of (D).

Segment 3 will compile and run, but it contains a logical error. Assume, for example, that a driver's speed is 85 mph. The driver should receive a fine of $300. If we trace through the code in segment

3, we see that the value of the variable fine is, in fact, set to $300 in the body of the first if loop because the driver's speed is greater than or equal to 75. The problem is that the condition in the second if loop is also true: The driver's speed is greater than 65. The body of the second loop is executed and the fine is set to $150. Finally, the condition in the third loop is also true, so the fine is then set to $100. Because Segment 3 is incorrect, we can get rid of our final possible answer. Note that segment 3 would have been correct if we had put "else" in front of the second and third loops.

5. **C** This questions tests your ability to trace through a convoluted piece of code. A few things to note:

The body of the if loop is executed only if b is false.

The variable i is incremented by 5, not by 1, in the for loop.

The variable i is also incremented by 5 in the body of the if loop. This is something you would do normally do in your own code, but it is something you may see on the exam. Don't assume the variable in the conditional of the for loop is only modified in the for loop.

6. **B** Keep in mind that && returns true if both operands are true, || returns true if one or more of its operands are true, and ! reverses a boolean value.

The best way to crack questions involving Booleans is often to just assign true or false to the variables and evaluate the expression.

We can break (a && b) || !(a || b) into two pieces: (a && b) and !(a || b). The variable c will be assigned true if either of these pieces are true. (a && b) is true when both a and b are true. Therefore we can get rid of (A) and (D).

Let's see what happens if both a and b are false. Clearly (a && b) evaluates to false in this case, but what about !(a || b)? (a || b) is false if both a and b are false, but the ! operator inverts the value to true. So because !(a || b) is true, (a && b) || !(a || b) evaluates to true. Therefore c will be assigned true when both a and b are false. We can therefore get rid of (C).

We are left with answer choices (B) and (E). Let's see what happens when a is false and b is true. (a && b) evaluates to false. (a || b) is true, so !(a || b) is false. Therefore, (a && b) || !(a || b) is false and we can get rid of (E).

7. **E** The code will finish executing when the conditional in the while loop is false. In other words, when !(x > y || y >= z) is true. So we need to figure out which of the answer choices is equivalent to !(X > y || y >= z).

Here's how to solve it step by step:

Recall that !(a || b) is equivalent to !a && !b. So !(x > y || y >= z) becomes !(x > y) && !(y >= z)

!(x > y) is equivalent to x <= y, so we now have x <= y && !(y >= z)

!(y >= z) is equivalent to y < z, so we have x <= y && y < z.

8. **D** Each time the incremental statement (a++) is evaluated, the value of a is increased by one. So to answer this question, we need to figure out how many times a is incremented.

The outer loop will be evaluated 10 times. The inner loop will be evaluated 6 times for each time that the outer loop is evaluated. The code in the body of the second loop will therefore execute 6 * 10 or 60 times. Note that the condition k <= 5 evaluates to true when k equals 5. In the third loop, the value of z starts at 1 and is doubled after each pass through the loop. So the body of the inner-most loop will execute when I equals 1, 2, 4, 8, and 16—or 5 times for each time the middle loop executes. Because 60 * 5 is 300, a will be incremented 300 times.

9. **D** The trick to this question is that arithmetic operators don't modify their operands. So if x is 10 when we divide x by 3, the result is 3 but x remains the same. Likewise, taking the modulus of a number does not change the number itself. On the other hand, the post-increment operator (++) does change the value of the number it operates on, so x++ will increase the value of x by 1.

10. **E** On the fourth line, a + b will be 13.7, but this result is cast to an int, so x will be 13. On the next line, a is first cast to a double and then divided by c. Because a is a double, c is automatically promoted to a double and the result of dividing the two is also a double. Therefore, y is 2.5.

On the next line, the parentheses cause the division to take place before the cast. Because a and c are ints, the result of dividing the two is truncated to an int, 2 in this case. The fact that we then cast the result to a double does not bring back the truncated decimal. Then z is equal to 2, so w = 13 + 2.5 + 2.

11. **E** Before the while loop is entered, i is equal to 1. The while loop will continue to execute as long as i is less than 5. Because the value of i is never changed in the code, i will always be less than 1 and an infinite loop will occur.

CHAPTER 5

1. **E** Because the database code can, in fact, be developed separately, tested separately, and possibly reused, all of the answers are correct. With questions like these, the easiest approach is to consider each candidate statement suspect, and look for ways in which they could be incorrect. If you find an incorrect one, cross it off, and cross any other answer that might "and" with that answer, because a combination of a true statement and a false statement is a false statement. Alternatively, when a candidate answer is true, put a star next to it. When you're done reading the questions, the one with the most stars wins.

In the above, because all three answers are true statements, we can cross of (A), (B), and (C), because they each say that only one statement is correct. Similarly, we can cross of (D), because it dismisses the third statement.

2. **D**   While the Java language makes it possible to make data fields public, one of the golden rules on the AP Computer Science Exam is that data fields should always be designed private. Note that constants that are declared as static and final can be public, however static constants apply to the class as a whole (because of the keyword static) and thus, aren't data fields.

Because data fields must be private, we can get rid of any answer choice that states it can be public. So we can get rid of (A), (B), and (E).

Now let's look at (C). What would happen if all methods in a class were private? Instances of the class would be useless, because clients couldn't ask the class to do anything for them. Classes need public methods to be useful.

What about (D)? The first part is good, because data fields should be private. What about the second sentence? We just saw above that methods can be public. They can also be private. A private method is used internally by a class to help out a public method, but is not directly accessible by client programs.

3. **C**   We know that statement I is incorrect, because it violates encapsulation. Thus, any answer that includes statement I can be dismissed out of hand. Thus, we dismiss (A), (D), and (E). The implementation of a method can be changed without changing its client programs, so III is correct. We can therefore eliminate (B), which dismisses III. Thus, the answer must be (C).

4. **D**   Both writeMe methods completely ignore the input that's passed into them, so there's no opportunity for "hi" to be printed. So (B) cannot be the answer. The code is syntactically correct, so (A) cannot be the answer. Along the same lines, we're not doing anything that requires casting, or dealing with null, or dividing by a number that could potentially be 0, so (E) is not the answer. That leaves (C) and (D). Because we're creating a String object and passing to a method that takes a String as a parameter the existence of the writeMe(Object obj) method is inconsequential. Thus, the only valid answer is (D).

5. **C**   Both writeMe methods completely ignore the input that's passed into them, so there's no opportunity for "hi" to be printed. So (D) cannot be the answer. The code is syntactically correct, so (A) cannot be the answer. Along the same lines, we're not doing anything that requires casting, or dealing with null, or dividing by a number that could potentially be 0, so (E) is not the answer. That leaves (B) and (C). Because we're creating an Object and passing to a method that takes an Object as a parameter, the existence of the writeMe(String s) method is inconsequential. Thus, the only valid answer is (C).

6. **C**   Both writeMe methods completely ignore the input that's passed into them, so there's no opportunity for "hi" to be printed. So (B) cannot be the answer. We can use an Object reference to refer to a String instance, because a String IS-A Object. Thus, the code is not syntactically incorrect, so (A) is not the answer. That leaves (C), (D), and (E). Because we're not doing any sort of casting, (E) is also an unlikely candidate. That leaves (C) and (D). Now the question becomes, when making overloaded calls, does Java pay attention to the type of the reference (which in this case is Object)

or the type of the variable (which in this case is String)? It turns out that Java always pays attention to the type of the object, so (C) is correct.

7. **A** tmp is an Object, not a String, thus the code snipped "String tmp = new Object" is illegal. This code will generate a compile-time error.

8. **B** This class is not declaring any methods at all, so (C) cannot possibly be correct. The code does not have any syntactical errors, so (A) cannot be correct. Choice (D) is nonsense, because nothing can be both an attribute and a method, and (E), while true, is irrelevant. Being a primitive does not imply that val cannot be an attribute, so the "neither" part of the question is a red herring.

9. **A** Both writeMe methods have the same name and same parameter list, but they return different types. This is illegal. Thus, (A) is the right answer.

CHAPTER 6

1. **C** On line 1, an array of String is created and assigned to reference s. Note that the array to which s refers can only hold two Strings. This does not prevent us, however, from pointing s to another array that is not of length 2. This is exactly what happens on line 3; s is reassigned to the same array that t references. This array has a length of 3.

    Here is what this looks like:

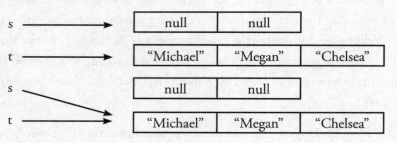

2. **D** In the code segment, the variable a1 is declared as final. This means that once we assign an array to it, a1 must always point to that array. A compile-time error will occur when we try to assign the array referenced by b1 to a1.

3. **C** In the code segment, an array containing two integers is constructed and assigned to a variable named myArray. Because this reference is final, it cannot be assigned to another array. This does not prevent us, however, from changing the contents of the array that the variable myArray points to, as we do in the second line. The key here is that even though we change the contents of the array, it is still the same array.

4. **B**   In the for loop in the method Mod3, the variable I keeps track of the position of the array that we are inspecting for each iteration of the loop. A[i], on the other hand, is the value that is located at position I in the array. Segment I will check to see if the position I is divisible by 3, that is not what we are looking for, so (A) and (D) are incorrect. Segment II will check if the number that is stored in the array at position I is divisible by 3, which is what we are looking for. Segment III will go into an infinite loop the first time it encounters an element in the array that is divisible by 3, so (C) and (E) can be eliminated. Only Segment II will get the program to work as intended.

5. **C**   Let's walk through this step by step. Remember that the add() method that takes just one argument adds the argument to the end of the list. The following two lines of code add "A" and "B" to the ArrayList one after another:

```
list.add("A")
```

```
list.add("B")
```

After the code above executes, the list looks like

```
[A, B]
```

The next statement, list.add(0, "C"), adds "C" to the beginning of the list. Now the list looks like

```
[C, A, B]
```

After list.add("D") executes, the list looks like

```
[C, A, B, D]
```

The set() method replaces the value at the position indicated by the first argument. After list.set(2, "E") executes, the list looks like

```
[C, A, E, D]
```

After list.remove(1) executes, the list looks like

```
[C, E, D]
```

The correct answer is therefore (C).

6. **C**   The key to this question is that as elements are removed from an ArrayList, the elements to the right of the removed element are shifted to the left and their indices are reduced by 1.

On the first pass through the while loop, i will be 0. Because the String in position 0 of letters equals "A", it will be removed and letters will look like

```
[B, A, A, C, D, B]
```

The next time through the while loop, i will be 1. The letter in position 1 is equal to "A", so it is removed. Now letters look like

```
[B, A, C, D, B]
```

On the next pass through the ArrayList, i is 2. The letter in position 2 is a C, so it is not removed. The while loop will continue to iterate through the ArrayList, but because none of the Strings in indices higher than 2 are equal to A, nothing else will be removed.

The correct answer is therefore (C).

7. **D** The first time through for loop, the letter in position 0 is removed and myList looks like

```
[B, C, D, E]
```

The letter that is in position 0, which is now B, is printed.

The next time through the for loop, i is 1, so C, the letter in position 1 is removed. Now myList looks like

```
[B, D, E]
```

The letter that is in position 1, which is now D, is printed.

At this point, i is incremented to 2. The size of myList is also 2, so i is no longer less than myList.size(). The for loop does not execute again.

The correct answer is therefore (D).

8. **D** The variable numbers.length is the number of rows in the two-dimensional array numbers. The variable numbers[0].length is the number of columns. Both the number of rows and the number of columns are 4.

On the first pass through the for loop, z is 0, and numbers[0].length − 1 − z is 3. So the value of numbers[0][3] is added to the total. So, numbers[0][3] is 3.

On the next pass, z is 1, numbers[0].length − 1 − z is 2, so the value of numbers[1][2] (which is 4) is added to the total.

On the next pass, we add the value at numbers[2][1], which is 3, and on the final pass we add the value at numbers[4][0], which is 4.

As you can see, the for loop simply finds the sum of one of the diagonals of the array.

9. **C** Note that k is incremented by 2 in the inner for loop. The code segment will find the sum of all the integers in columns with an even index.

```
numbers[0][0] + numbers[0][2] + numbers[0][4] +

numbers[1][0] + numbers[1][2] + numbers[1][4] +

numbers[2][0] + numbers[2][2] + numbers [2][4]
```

10. **A** The first for loop initializes the ArrayList list so that it looks like

```
[1, 2, 3, 4, 5, 6, 7, 8]
```

Now let's take a look at the second for loop. Note that the highest value that j will reach is 7, one less than the size of the list. In the body of the for loop, the index of the position that we are setting is j divided by 2; the index can therefore never be greater than 3, In other words, we won't be modifying any values other than those in the first 4 positions of the ArrayList. Knowing this, we can eliminate (D) and (E).

On the first pass through the loop, j is 1 and we call list.set(1 / 2, list.get(1)). Because the result of integer division is truncated, this call is equivalent to list.set(0, list,get(1)), so the value of the element at position 0 is the same as that of position 1 and the ArrayList is

```
[2, 2, 3, 4, 5, 6, 7, 8]
```

On the next pass through the for loop, I is 2 and we call list.set(1, list.get(2)). The ArrayList looks like this:

```
[2, 3, 4, 5, 6, 7, 8]
```

On the next pass we call, list.get(1, list.get(3)). The ArrayList now looks like this:

```
[2, 4, 3, 4, 5, 6, 7, 8]
```

If we continue to iterate through the second for loop, the ArrayList will end up looking like this:

```
[2, 4, 6, 8, 5, 6, 7, 8]
```

11. **A** For each cell in the two-dimensional array, the code sets the value to the product of the indices for that cell. For example, num[2][3] is set to 2 * 3 or 6.

CHAPTER 7

1. **B** In this question, the Child class extends the Parent class. In both classes, the writeMe method has the same signature. Therefore, the writeMe method of the Child class overrides the writeMe method of the Parent class. Choice (A) is incorrect because an inherited method is one that would not be implemented in the Child class. Choice (C) is incorrect because an overloaded method is one in which the method name is the same but the signatures are different. Choices (D) and (E) are incorrect because the Child class is neither an interface nor an abstract class. Choice (B) is the correct answer.

2. **B** A class can, at most, directly extend one other class.

3. **D** A class can implement as many interfaces as it needs to.

4. **D** A given interface can extend as many other interfaces as it needs to.

5. **A** This is a trick question. An interface can never implement a class.

6. **D** Choice (A) is not relevant, because writeMe is a static method, and thus doesn't need an instance variable. The only print statement in the code explicitly writes out the hard-coded string "hellostring", so (B) can't possibly be correct. And because we are not casting, dealing with elements that could be null, or dividing anything, (E) is very unlikely. Choice (C) is a possibility, but we're not using a null, nor are we doing anything that could result in a null value. Thus, the answer must be (D).

7. **C** Choice (A) is not relevant, because writeMe is a static method, and thus doesn't need an instance variable. The variable var is never initialized to −1, so (B) can't possibly be correct. Choice (D) can't be correct because Java doesn't allow values to be unknowable. They are always equal to their initialization value, or 0, if left uninitialized. And (E) is partially true, but irrelevant. Variables that are final can be displayed, but not changed. Thus, the answer must be (C).

8. **A** Because we've provided our own constructor for the Sample class we must therefore provide all constructors that our code might use. This code will not compile, because we are attempting to create a Sample object by using the default constructor when we write Sample s = new Sample();.

9. **B** This is a trick question. The only messages that are ever written are the hard-coded strings "me" and "you" so neither (A) nor (D) can be the answer. That leaves (B), (C), and (E). If we trace through the logic of the code into the writeMe method, we can see that "hi" is not equal to null, so (B) and (E) are left. Now comes the tricky part. The variable "var" is initialized to null, yet the code attempts to call methods on it. This will cause a runtime exception to be thrown because you cannot call methods on a null object. Therefore, (B) is the correct answer.

10. **C** This is a good question on which to use Process of Elimination. Don't try to find the best design right away. Instead, first get rid of the answer choices that you know are flawed.

The use of the word unrelated is a tip-off that (A) is incorrect. In general, classes and data fields in a program will be related to each other, otherwise there would really be no point in writing the program in the first place.

Now let's look at (B). Whenever you are trying to decide if one class is a subclass of the other, ask yourself if an instance of the proposed subclass IS-A instance of the proposed super class. For example, in this case you could ask if a Pet IS-A Apartment. Obviously not, so get rid of (B).

Choice (C) looks good. Using primitive data fields allows us to store information about the Apartment within an instance of the class. Let's check the rest of the answer choices though.

Like (B), (D) refers to subclasses. The difference this time is that Apartment is a subclass of the other classes. There are two problems here. First of all, the IS-A relationship doesn't hold. It would be incorrect to say that an Apartment IS-A Pet, Room, or Dishwasher. Here's the other problem: If Apartment is a subclass of all three of the other classes, then that means that Apartment has three immediate super classes; in other words, Apartment extends three of the classes. However, in Java, a class can only extend one other class.

Finally, (E) uses a HAS-A relationship (this is also called composition). This design is similar to that of (C), except we are using objects instead of primitives, as we did in (C). In this case, using objects will be overkill. For example, the specification from the rental company only states that they want to know if the apartment has a dishwasher. A Boolean can be used to store this information, so there's really no point in building a Dishwasher class. On the other hand, if the rental company had specified that they needed to store a lot of information about the type of dishwasher in each apartment, such as its color, manufacturer, and year of installation, then a Dishwasher class would be appropriate.

The correct answer, therefore, is (C).

11. **C** When a class implements an interface, the implemented methods in the class must be declared as public. Because the inter1() method is private in class A, the class won't compile.

Class B declares that it implements Inter, yet it doesn't' have an inter1() method. This won't cause a problem because B is declared abstract. What this means though is that any nonabstract class that extends B will need to implement inter1().

Class C has an inter1() method, but the return type is double, no tint as defined in the Inter interface. Because of this difference, the class will not compile.

12. **D** Choice (A) is incorrect because the Motorcycle class does not define a constructor that takes one argument. Note that unlike other methods, constructors are not inherited, so even though Motorcycle extends Vehicle, and Vehicle defines a constructor that takes on argument, Motorcycles will not inherit this constructor.

Choice (B) is incorrect for the same reason that (A) is incorrect. Even though our reference type is Vehicle, we are still constructing a Motorcycle, and the Motorcycle class does not define a constructor that takes one argument.

In (C), we are creating a Vehicle and assigning it to a reference of type Motorcycle. This is incorrect because a Vehicle is not necessarily a Motorcycle. The reference type of a variable must be the same class or a super class of the object that we are trying to assign to it. It cannot be a subclass.

Choice (D) is correct. Because the Motorcycle class extends the Vehicle class, a Motorcycle IS-A Vehicle and we can assign a Motorcycle instance to a Vehicle reference.

The first line in (E) is correct, however in the second line we are trying to access a private date member. To fix this, we would need to call the public method maxPassengers() instead. This would look like the following:

```
int max = v3.maxPassengers();
```

Always bear in mind that all data members on the exam will be private; only methods are public. Therefore, when you use dot notation on an instance of a class, the part that follows the dot should end in parenthesis. The only exception to this that you will see on the test is the length attribute of an array.

CHAPTER 8

1. **B** In the method above, the base case occurs when x is equal to 0. Because the value that is initially passed to the method is 3543, the base case does not yet apply. Let's see what happens on the line return ((x % 10) + mystery(x / 10)).

Make sure that you understand what (x % 10) and (x / 10) do. If x is a base 10 integer, x % 10 will return the units digit. For example, 348 % 10 returns 8. I*f x is an int variable, then x / 10 will remove the units digit. For example, 348 / 10 returns 34.

The expression within the return statement has two parts (x % 10) and mystery(x / 10).

Let's take a look at (x % 10). This returns the remainder when x is divided by 10. In our case, x is 3543, so 3543 % 10 is 3.

Now what about (x / 10)? 3543 / 10 is 354; integer division truncates the result.

So we now have

```
mystery(3543) - 3 + mystery(354).
```

Following the same logic as above, mystery(354) will be (354 % 10) + mystery(354 / 10) or mystery(354) = 4 + mystery(35).

So what is mystery(35)?

```
mystery(35) = (35 % 10) + mystery(35 / 10)
```

Or simplified

```
mystery(35) = 5 + mystery(3);
```

And mystery(3)?

```
mystery(3) = (3 % 10) + mystery(3 / 10)
```

Or simplified

```
mystery(3) = 3 + mystery(0);
```

But mystery(0) equals 0 (this is the base case), so

```
mystery(3) = 3 + 0 = 3
```

```
mystery(35) = 5 + 3 = 8
```

```
mystery(354) = 4 + 8 = 12
```

```
mystery(3543) = 3 + 12 = 15.
```

2. **D**

```
mystery(6) = 2 * mystery(5)

    mystery(5) = 2 * mystery(4)

        mystery(4) = 2 * mystery(3)

            mystery(3) = 2 * mystery(2)

                mystery(2) = 2 * mystery(1)

                    mystery(1) = 2;
```

So mystery(6) = 2 * 2 * 2 * 2 * 2 * 2 = 64.

3. **D** On the first pass through the method we get

```
10 + mystery(10 / 2) + mystery(10 / 4)
```

Which can be simplified to

```
10 + mystery(5) + mystery(2)
```

So now we need to figure out what mystery(5) and mystery(2) are and add the results to 10.

First we'll solve mystery(5)

```
mystery(5) = 5 + mystery(5 / 2) + mystery(5 / 4) = 5 + mystery(2) + mystery (1)
```

```
mystery(2) = 2 + mystery(2 / 2) + mystery(2 / 4) = 2 + mystery(1) + mystery(0)
```

```
mystery(1) = 1 + mystery(1 / 2) + mystery(1 / 4) = 1 + mystery(0) + mystery(0)
```

Note that mystery(0) is our base case and returns 0. Working our way back up the recursive calls, we find that mystery(1) = 1, mystery(2) = 3, and mystery(5) = 9. Note that in solving mystery(5) we ended up needing to solve mystery(2).

So in our original equation: 10 + mystery(5) + mystery(2), we can replace mystery(5) with 9 and mystery(2) with 3 to get: 10 + 9 + 3, which equals 22.

4. **A** For any value non-negative number n that is passed as an argument to the non-recursive method mystery(), the method will return the 0 + 1 + 2 + 3 + ... + n. For example, a call to mystery(5) will return 15(1 + 2 + 3 + 4 + 5). Note that the border case for mystery() occurs when 0 is passed to the method. In this case, the method returns 0.

Method I (method mystery2()) is equivalent to mystery().

Method II (mystery3()) is not equivalent. Notice that mystery2() does not modify what is returned by the recursive call, whereas mystery2() adds x to the results of each recursive call. The method mystery2() will return 0 regardless of the value that is passed to the method.

Method III (mystery4()) is equivalent to mystery() except when x equals 0. If 0 is passed to the method, the loop will infinitely recurse. Because mystery4() doesn't handle the border case correctly, so III is incorrect.

Only Method I is equivalent to the mystery() method, so (A) is correct.

5. **B** We originally pass 30 and 18 to the method as x and y respectively. Each time the method is recursively called, 10 is added to x and 3 is subtracted from y, therefore x will eventually become larger than 100 and y will become smaller than 0, so we know that the condition of the base case will eventually be met and infinite recursion won't occur.

Note that the base case returns 1. What about the non-base case? The method return mystery(x + 10, y – 3) simply returns whatever was returned by the call to mystery(); it doesn't modify it in any way. Because there's no modification of the return value, 1 is the only thing that is ever returned, no matter how many recursive calls occur.

6. **B** The best way to solve this problem is to trace through each answer choice. But don't necessarily start with (A). Start with the answer choice that you think you can solve most quickly. In this case, (A) will probably take longer to check because it has two recursive calls. Instead, let's start with (D). Why (D)? Because each recursive call reduces the integer that we pass as an argument by 4, there won't be as many recursive calls as there will be with the other choices.

With (D), the first time through the method, we have mystery(10 = 4 * mystery(6). We find that mystery(6) = 4 * mystery(2) and mystery(2) = 4 * mystery(-2). Finally, mystery(-2) equals 1 (the base case). Working our way back up the call stack, we get mystery(2) = 4, mystery(6) = 16 and mystery(10) = 64. So (D) is incorrect.

The choice with the next fewest recursive calls is (B). For this choice, mystery(10) = 2 * mystery(8); mystery(8) = 2 * mystery(6); mystery(6) = 2 * mystery(4); mystery(4) = 2 * mystery(2); mystery(2) = 2 * mystery(0); and mystery(0) = 1. Therefore, mystery(2) = 2; mystery(4) = 4; mystery(6) = 8; mystery(8) = 16; and mystery(10) = 32.

Chapter 10
Required Lab Time
and Suggested Labs

Beginning with the 2015 exam administration, a 20-hour lab requirement replaced a "case study"-type project that was required for previous exams. The lab requirement can be fulfilled with the College Board-provided labs and/or with work using virtually any developing environment, provided that the required topics for lab experience are practiced.

The three College Board-provided labs (Magpie, Picture, and Elevens) can be found by navigating to **https://apstudent.collegeboard.org/apcourse/ap-computer-science-a/course-details/lab-requirements**. *Magpie* discusses Chatbots, which are programs that are supposed to "chat" with the user via a series of programmed responses. *Picture* focuses on manipulation of graphic images, similar to a very rudimentary photo editor. *Elevens* uses a card game simulation and its associated functions to punctuate many topics from the course (who *doesn't* like a video game?).

Although the College Board recommends these labs, you do not have to KNOW them; however, the topics within are always covered, just not in the context of a lab. For example, a question about the String class in previous years, just felt like a random question about the String class. Since 2015, a String question may still seem random, but it may resemble a method seen in one of these labs. The task presented in one of the FRQs on the 2015 exam was structured *very* similarly to one of the labs, so students who were comfortable with the labs had a distinct advantage, even though it wasn't deemed as such, officially. So you do not need to know the labs explicitly, but you should look through the code anyway and, if you don't have a better "lab" option, complete them. The student guides were written for self-study anyway! If your teacher didn't cover them, check them out regardless.

The list below indicates each of the three College Board-provided labs and the topics they address, which you should practice in this context, or in any other, using a compiler. The chapter in this book that addresses the topic is in parenthesis.

- **Magpie Lab**
  - if statements (Ch. 4)
  - String methods (Ch. 5)
  - while loops (Ch. 4)
- **Picture Lab**
  - for loops (Ch. 4)
  - arrays (Ch. 6)
- **Elevens Lab**
  - Objects and classes (Ch. 5)
  - int and String (Ch. 3)
  - Arrays (Ch. 6)
  - Lists and ArrayLists (Ch. 6)
  - Conditionals and loops (Ch. 4)
  - Math.random (Ch. 5)
  - Classes (Ch. 5)
  - Inheritance and abstract classes (Ch. 7)

Part VI
Practice Test 2

Chapter 11
Practice Test 2

AP® Computer Science A Exam

SECTION I: Multiple-Choice Questions

DO NOT OPEN THIS BOOKLET UNTIL YOU ARE TOLD TO DO SO.

At a Glance

Total Time
1 hour 30 minutes
Number of Questions
40
Percent of Total Score
50%
Writing Instrument
Pencil required

Instructions

Section I of this examination contains 40 multiple-choice questions. Fill in only the ovals for numbers 1 through 40 on your answer sheet.

Indicate all of your answers to the multiple-choice questions on the answer sheet. No credit will be given for anything written in this exam booklet, but you may use the booklet for notes or scratch work. After you have decided which of the suggested answers is best, completely fill in the corresponding oval on the answer sheet. Give only one answer to each question. If you change an answer, be sure that the previous mark is erased completely. Here is a sample question and answer.

Sample Question   Sample Answer

Chicago is a
(A) state
(B) city
(C) country
(D) continent
(E) county

Use your time effectively, working as quickly as you can without losing accuracy. Do not spend too much time on any one question. Go on to other questions and come back to the ones you have not answered if you have time. It is not expected that everyone will know the answers to all the multiple-choice questions.

About Guessing

Many candidates wonder whether or not to guess the answers to questions about which they are not certain. Multiple-choice scores are based on the number of questions answered correctly. Points are not deducted for incorrect answers, and no points are awarded for unanswered questions. Because points are not deducted for incorrect answers, you are encouraged to answer all multiple-choice questions. On any questions you do not know the answer to, you should eliminate as many choices as you can, and then select the best answer among the remaining choices.

GO ON TO THE NEXT PAGE.

Quick Reference

class java.lang.Object
- boolean equals(Object other)
- String toString()

class java.lang.Integer
- Integer(int value)
- int intValue()
- Integer.MIN_VALUE   // minimum value represented by an int or Integer
- Integer.MAX_VALUE   // maximum value represented by an int or Integer

class java.lang.Double
- Double(double value)
- double doubleValue()

class java.lang.String
- int length()
- String substring(int from, int to)   // returns the substring beginning at from
       // and ending at to-1
- String substring(int from)   // returns substring(from, length())
- int indexOf(String str)   // returns the index of the first occurrence of str;
       // returns -1 if not found
- int compareTo(String other)   // returns a value < 0 if this is less than other
       // returns a value = 0 if this is equal to other
       // returns a value > 0 if this is greater than other

class java.lang.Math
- static int abs(int x)
- static double abs(double x)
- static double pow(double base, double exponent)
- static double sqrt(double x)
- static double random()   // returns a double in the range [0.0, 1.0)

interface java.util.List<E>
- int size()
- boolean add(E obj)   // appends obj to end of list; returns true
- void add(int index, E obj)   // inserts obj at position index (0 ≤ index ≤ size),
       // moving elements at position index and higher
       // to the right (adds 1 to their indices) and adjusts size
- E get(int index)
- E set(int index, E obj)   // replaces the element at position index with obj
       // returns the element formerly at the specified position
- E remove(int index)   // removes element from position index, moving elements
       // at position index + 1 and higher to the left
       // (subtracts 1 from their indices) and adjusts size
       // returns the element formerly at the specified position

class java.util.ArrayList<E> implements java.util.List<E>

GO ON TO THE NEXT PAGE.

COMPUTER SCIENCE A

SECTION I

Time—1 hour and 30 minutes

Number of Questions—40

Percent of total exam grade—50%

Directions: Determine the answer to each of the following questions or incomplete statements, using the available space for any necessary scratchwork. Then decide which is the best of the choices given and fill in the corresponding oval on the answer sheet. No credit will be given for anything written in the examination booklet. Do not spend too much time on any one problem.

Notes:
- Assume that the classes listed in the Quick Reference have been imported where appropriate.
- Assume that declarations of variables and methods appear within the context of an enclosing class.
- Assume that method calls that are not prefixed with an object or class name and are not shown within a complete class definition appear within the context of an enclosing class.
- Unless otherwise noted in the question, assume that parameters in the method calls are not `null` and that methods are called only when their preconditions are satisfied.

MULTIPLE CHOICE QUESTIONS   **USE THIS SPACE FOR SCRATCHWORK**

1. Consider the following method:

```
public static int mystery(int a, int b)
{
    if (a <= 0)
        return b;
    else
        return mystery(a - 2, b);
}
```

What value is returned by the call `mystery (12, 5)`?

(A) 5
(B) 6
(C) 12
(D) 60
(E) 1565

GO ON TO THE NEXT PAGE.

2. Consider the following instance variable and method

```
private int[] numList;

//Precondition: numList contains a list of int values in no particular order

public int mystery(int n)
{
    for (int k = 0; k <= numList.length - 1; k++)
    {
        if (n <= numList[k])
            return k;
    }
    return numList.length;
}
```

Which of the follow statements is most accurate about numList following the execution of the following statement?

```
int j = mystery(number);
```

(A) The greatest value in numList is at index j.
(B) The greatest value in numList that is less than number is at index j.
(C) All values in numList from index 0 to j-1 are greater than or equal to number.
(D) All values in numList from index 0 to j-1 are less than number.
(E) All values in numList from index j to numList.length-1 are greater than number.

GO ON TO THE NEXT PAGE.

Questions 3–4 refer to the following incomplete class declaration for a new data type called a Quack.

```
Public class Quack
{
    ArrayList<Object> myData;

    // Constructor initializes myData
    public Quack()
    {  /* implementation not shown */  }

    // Quack.
    public void enquack (Object x)
    {  /* implementation not shown */  }

    // if front is true, returns the object at the front end of the Quack;
    // otherwise returns the object at the back end of the Quack.  Assumes the Quack
    // is not empty.
    public Object dequack (boolean front)
    {  /* implementation not shown */  }

    // Returns true if the Quack has no objects; otherwise returns false.
    public boolean isEmpty ()
    {  /* implementation not shown /*  }

    <designation> ArrayList myData;

    // ... other methods and data not shown
```

3. Which of the following is the best choice for `<designation>` and the best reason for that choice?

   (A) `<designation>` should be `private` so that programs using a `Quack` will not be able to modify `myData` by using methods enquack and dequack, thereby preserving the principle of data stability.

   (B) `<designation>` should be `private` so that programs using a `Quack` can only modify `myData` by using methods such as `enquack` and `dequack`, thereby preserving the principle of information hiding.

   (C) `<designation>` should be `private` as an indication to programs using a `Quack` that `myData` can be modified directly but that it is *better* to modify `myData` only by using methods such as `enquack` and `dequack`, thereby preserving the principle of maximum information dissemination.

   (D) `<designation>` should be `public` because programs using a `Quack` need to know how the `Quack` class has been implemented in order to use it.

   (E) `<designation>` should be `public`. Otherwise, only objects constructed from derived subclasses of a `Quack` will be able to modify the contents of a `Quack`.

4. Which of the following is an effective return statement for `isEmpty` as described in the incomplete declaration above?

   (A) `return (myData.length == 0)`
   (B) `return (size() == 0)`
   (C) `return (myData.size() == 0);`
   (D) `return (myData.length() == 0)`
   (E) `return (myData.size == 0)`

GO ON TO THE NEXT PAGE.

5. Consider the following method definition:

```java
public static int mystery(int n)
{
    if (n <= 1)
        return 2;
    else
        return 1 + mystery(n - 3);
}
```

Which of the following lines of code can replace the line in mystery containing the recursive call so that the functionality of mystery does not change?

(A) `return 1 + ( (n + 2)  /  3) ;`
(B) `return 1 + ( (n + 3)  /  2) ;`
(C) `return 2 + ( (n + 1)  /  3) ;`
(D) `return 2 + ( (n + 2)  /  3) ;`
(E) `return 3 + ( (n + 1)  /  2) ;`

GO ON TO THE NEXT PAGE.

Questions 6–7 refer to the following incomplete class declaration

```
public class DistanceTracker
{
    private int kilometers;
    private int meters;

    /** Constructs a DistanceTracker object
     * @param k the number of kilometers
     * Precondition: k ≥ 0
     * @param m the number of meters
     * Precondition: 0 ≤ m < 1000
     */
    public DistanceTracker (int k, int m)
    {
      kilometer = k;
      meters = m;
    }
    /** @return the number of kilometers
     */
    public int getKilometers()
    { /* implementation not shown*/}
    /** @return the number of meters
     */
    public int getMeters()
    { /* implementation not shown*/}
      /** Adds k kilometers and m meters
       * @param k the number of kilometers
       * Precondition: k ≥ 0
       *@param m the number of meters
     * Precondition: m ≥ 0
     */
    public void addDistance(int k, int m)
    {
      kilometers += k;
      meters += m;
      /* rest of method not shown*/
    }
//Rest of class not shown
    }
```

6. Which of the following code segments can be used to replace /* rest of method not shown */ so the addDistance will correctly increase the distance?

(A) ```
kilometers += meters / 1000
meters = meters % 1000
```
(B) ```
kilometers += meters % 1000
meters = meters / 1000
```
(C) `meters += kilometers % 1000`
(D) `kilometers += meters % 1000`
(E) `meters = meters % 1000`

GO ON TO THE NEXT PAGE.

7. Consider the following incomplete class declaration

```
public class DistanceTrackerSet
{
    Distance Tracker[] set;
    /*Declaration method not shown*/

    public  DistanceTracker total()
    {
       DistanceTracker temp = new DistanceTracker(0, 0);
    for (int k = 0; k < set.length; k++)
       {
           /*missing code segment*/
       }
       return temp;
    }
/*Other methods not shown*/
}
```

Assuming set is properly initialized with DistanceTracker objects and all needed classes are properly imported, which is the following can be used to replace /*missing code segment*/ so that the method returns a DistanceTracker object with the total of all distances stored in set?

(A) `temp.addDistance(temp[k].kilometers, temp[k].meters);`
(B) `set[k].addDistance(temp[k].getKilometers(), temp[k].getMeters());`
(C) `set[k].addDistance();`
(D) `temp += temp.addDistance();`
(E) `temp.addDistance(temp[k].getKilometers(), temp[k].getMeters());`

8. Consider the following method

```
 public List<Integer> nums() {
    List<Integer> values = new ArrayList<Integer>() ;
    for (int i = 0; i < 50; i = i + 5)
       if (i % 4 == 1)
          values.add(i) ;
    return value ;
 }
```

What will return of nums() contain?

(A) `[5, 45]`
(B) `[5, 25, 45]`
(C) `[0, 20, 40]`
(D) `[5, 9, 13, 17, 21, 25, 29, 33, 37, 41, 45]`
(E) `[0, 5, 10, 15, 20, 25, 30, 35, 40, 45]`

GO ON TO THE NEXT PAGE.

9. Consider the following incomplete method `mystery`:

```
public static boolean mystery(boolean a, boolean b, boolean c)
{
    return <expression>;
}
```

What should `<expression>` be replaced with so that `mystery` returns `true` when exactly two of its three parameters are true; otherwise `mystery` returns `false`?

(A)
```
(a  &&  b  &&  !c)  ||
(a  &&  !b  &&  c)  ||
(!a  &&  b  &&  c)
```

(B)
```
(a  && b && !c)  &&
(a  &&  !b && c)  &&
(!a  && b && c)
```

(C)
```
(a | | b | | !c)  &&
(a | | !b | | c)  &&
(!a | | b | | c)
```

(D)
```
(a && b)  ||
(a && c)  ||
(b && c)
```

(E)
```
(a | | b)  &&
(a | | c)  &&
(b | | c)
```

10. Consider the following code segment:

```
int x;
x = 5 - 4 + 9 * 12 / 3 - 10;
```

What is the value of x after the code segment is executed?

(A) 13
(B) 27
(C) 30
(D) -57
(E) -10

11. What is the best way to declare a variable `myStrings` that will store 50 `String` values if each `String` will be no longer than 25 characters?

(A) `ArrayList <String> myStrings[String[50]] ;`
(B) `ArrayList <String> myStrings = new String[50] ;`
(C) `ArrayList <String> myStrings = new String[25] ;`
(D) `String [] myStrings = new String [50, 25] ;`
(E) `String [] myStrings = new String [50] ;`

GO ON TO THE NEXT PAGE.

12. Consider the following code segment

```
List <Integer> scores= new ArrayList<Integer>() ;
scores.add(93) ;
scores.add(97) ;
scores.add(84) ;
scores.add(91) ;
scores.remove(2) ;
scores.add(1, 83) ;
scores.set(3, 99) ;
System.out.println(scores) ;
```

What is the output of the code segment?

(A) [83, 93, 99, 91]
(B) [93, 83, 91, 99]
(C) [83, 94, 91, 99]
(D) [93, 83, 97, 99]
(E) The code throws and ArrayIndexOutofBoundsException

13. Consider the following precondition, postcondition, and signature for the getDigit method:

```
// precondition: n >= 0
//          whichDigit >= 0
// postcondition: Returns the digit of n in
//          the whichDigit position
//          when the digits of n are
//          numbered from right to
//          left starting with zero.
//          Returns 0 if whichDigit  >=
//          number of digits of n.
int getDigit (int n, int whichDigit)
```

Consider also the following three possible implementations of the getDigit method:

```
I.   if (whichDigit == 0)
        return n % 10;
     else
        return getDigit (n / 10, whichDigit - 1) ;
II.  return (n / (int) Math.pow(10, whichDigit) )  % 10;
III. for (int k = 0: k < whichDigit; k++)
        n /= 10;
     return n % 10;
```

Which implementation(s) would satisfy the postcondition of the getDigit method?

(A) I and II
(B) I and III
(C) II and III
(D) I, II, and III
(E) None of the above

GO ON TO THE NEXT PAGE.

14. Consider an array of integers.

    4   10   1   2   6   7   3   5

Assume that SelectionSort is used to order the array from smallest to largest values.

Which of the following represents the state of the array immediately after the first iteration of the outer for loop in the SelectionSort process?

(A) 1   4   10   2   3   6   7   5
(B) 1   2   4   6   10   7   3   5
(C) 1   10   4   2   6   7   3   5
(D) 4   3   1   5   6   7   10   2
(E) 5   3   7   6   2   1   10   4

15. Assume that a program declares and initializes v as follows

```
String [] v;
v = initialize () ;            // Returns an array of
                               // length 10 containing
                               // ten valid strings
```

Which of the following code segments correctly traverses the array *backwards* and prints out the elements (one per line)?

```
 I. for (int k = 9; k >= 0; k --)
        System.out.println(v[k]) ;
II. int k = 0;
    while (k < 10)
    {
        System.out.println(v[9-k]);
        k++;
    }
III. int k = 10;
     while (k >= 0)
     {
         System.out.println(v[k]);
         k -- ;
     }
```

(A) I only
(B) II only
(C) I and II only
(D) II and III only
(E) I, II, and III

GO ON TO THE NEXT PAGE.

16. Consider the following method

```
/**Precondition: @param set  an ArrayList that contains distinct integers
*@param n an int value
*/
public int mystery(List<Integer> set, int n)
{
    for (int k = 0; k < set.length(); k++)
    {
        if (set.get(k) > n)
        {
            return (set.remove(k) + mystery(set, n));
        }
    }
    return 0;
}
```

What is returned by the method call `mystery(set, n)`?

(A) 0
(B) The number of elements of set that are greater than n
(C) The sum of the elements of set that are greater than n
(D) The sum of the elements of set that are less than n
(E) The sum of the elements of set that or less than or equal to n

GO ON TO THE NEXT PAGE.

17. Consider the following two-dimensional array

```
[ [0, 0, 0 ,0]
  [0, 1, 0, 0]
  [0, 1, 2, 0]
  [0, 1, 2, 3] ]
```

Which of the following methods returns this two-dimensional array?

(A)
```
public int[][] nums()
{
  int[][] temp = new int[4][4] ;
  for (int j = 0; j < 4; j++)
  {
      for (int k = 0; k < 4; k ++)
      {
              temp[j][k] = j ;
      }
  }
  return temp ;
}
```

(B)
```
public int[][] nums()
{
  int[][] temp = new int[4][4] ;
  for (int j = 0; j < 4; j++)
  {
      for (int k = 0; k < 4; k ++)
      {
              temp[j][k] = k ;
      }
  }
  return temp ;
}
```

(C)
```
public int[][] nums()
{
  int[][] temp = new int[4][4] ;
  for (int j = 0; j < 4; j++)
  {
      for (int k = j; k < 4; k ++)
      {
              temp[j][k] = k ;
      }
  }
  return temp ;
}
```

GO ON TO THE NEXT PAGE.

```
(D)  public int[][] nums()
     {
       int[][] temp = new int[4][4] ;
       for (int j = 0; j < 4; j++)
       {
           for (int k = 0; k <= j; k ++)
           {
                   temp[j][k] = j ;
           }
       }
       return temp ;
     }
(E)  public int[][] nums()
     {
       int[][] temp = new int[4][4] ;
       for (int j = 0; j < 4; j++)
       {
           for (int k = 0; k <= j; k ++)
           {
                   temp[j][k] = k ;
           }
       }
       return temp ;
     }
```

GO ON TO THE NEXT PAGE.

18. A children's club classifies members based on age according to the table below

Years	Classification
Under 3	Infant
3 to 7 inclusive	Pee-wee
8 to 13 inclusive	Cub
Over 14	Leader

Which of the following methods will correctly take the integer parameter age and return the String Classification?

(A)
```java
public String Classification(int age)
{
    String temp ;
    if (age < 3)
        temp = "Infant" ;
    if (age <= 7)
        temp = "Pee-Wee" ;
    if (age <= 13)
        temp = "Cub" ;
    if (age >= 14)
        temp = "Leader" ;
    return temp;
}
```

(B)
```java
public String Classification(int age)
{
    String temp ;
    if (age < 3)
        temp = "Infant" ;
    if (3 <= age <= 7)
        temp = "Pee-Wee" ;
    if (8 <= age <= 13)
        temp = "Cub" ;
    if (age >= 14)
        temp = "Leader" ;
    return temp;
}
```

(C)
```java
public String Classification(int age)
{
    String temp ;
    if (age < 3)
        temp = "Infant" ;
    else if (age <= 7)
        temp = "Pee-Wee" ;
    else if (age <= 13)
        temp = "Cub" ;
    else if (age > 14)
        temp = "Leader" ;
    return temp;
}
```

GO ON TO THE NEXT PAGE.

```
(D)  public String Classification(int age)
     {
         String temp ;
         if (age < 3)
            temp = "Infant" ;
         else if (age < 7)
            temp = "Pee-Wee" ;
         else if (age < 13)
            temp = "Cub" ;
         else if (age > 14)
            temp = "Leader" ;
         return temp;
     }
(E)  public String Classification(int age)
     {
         String temp ;
         if (age < 3)
            temp = "Infant" ;
         if (age < 7)
            temp = "Pee-Wee" ;
         if (age < 13)
            temp = "Cub" ;
         if (age > 14)
            temp = "Leader" ;
         return temp;
     }
```

GO ON TO THE NEXT PAGE.

For <u>Questions 19–20</u> Consider the method `getGap` with line numbers added for reference. Method `getGap` is intended to find the maximum difference between the indexes of any two occurrence of num in the array arr. The method `getGap` does not work as intended.

For example, if the array arr contains [8, 7, 5, 5, 4, 3, 2, 7, 1, 2, 7], the call getGap(arr, 7) should return 9, the difference between the indexes of the first and last occurrence of 7.

`/**Precondition:` arr contains at least two occurrences of num */

Line 1:	`public int getGap(int[] arr, int num)`
Line 2:	`{`
Line 3:	`    int index1 = -1;`
Line 4:	`    int index2 = -1;`
Line 5:	`    for (int k = 0; k < arr.length; k++)`
Line 6:	`    {`
Line 7:	`        if (arr[k] == num)`
Line 8:	`        {`
Line 9:	`            if (index1 == -1)`
Line 10:	`            {`
Line 11:	`                index1 = k;`
Line 12:	`                index2 = k;`
Line 13:	`            }`
Line 14:	`            else`
Line 15:	`            {`
Line 16:	`                index1 = index2;`
Line 17:	`                index2 = k;`
Line 18:	`            }`
Line 19:	`        }`
Line 20:	`    }`
Line 21:	`    return (index2 - index1);`
Line 22:	`}`

19. The method `getGap` does not work as intended. Which of the following best describes the return of the method `getGap` ?

(A) The difference between the indexes of the last two occurrences of num in arr.
(B) The minimum difference between the indexes of any two occurrences of num in arr.
(C) The difference between the first two occurrences of num in arr
(D) The length of the array arr
(E) The number of occurrences of num in arr

20. Which of the following changes should be made to `getGap` so that the method will work as intended?

(A) Delete the statement at line 4.
(B) Delete the statement at line 11.
(C) Delete the statement at line 12.
(D) Delete the statement at line 16.
(E) Delete the statement at line 17.

GO ON TO THE NEXT PAGE.

Questions 21–23 refer to the following incomplete class declaration used to represent calendar dates.

```
Public class Date
{
    private int month;
        // represents month 0-11
    private int day;
        // represents day of the month
        // 0-31
    private int year;
        // represents the year

    // constructor sets the private data
    public Date (int m, int d, int y)
    { /* implementation not shown */ }

    // postconditions: returns the month
    public int getMonth()
    { /* implementation not shown */ }

    // postcondition: return the day
    public int getDay()
    { /* implementation not shown */ }

    // postcondition: returns the year
    public int getYear()
    { /* implementation not shown */ }

    // postcondition: returns the number of
    //               days which, when
    //               added to this Date
    //               gives newDate
    public int daysUntil (Date newDate)
    { /* implementation not shown */ }

    // postcondition: returns true if
    //               the month, day, and
    //               year of this Date are
    //               are equal to those of
    //               other; otherwise
    //               returns false
    public boolean equals (Date other)
    { /* implementation not shown */ }

    // .. other methods not shown
```

21. Consider the method equals of the Object class.

    Which of the following method signatures is appropriate for the equals method?

    (A) public boolean equals (Object other)
    (B) public int equals (Object other)
    (C) public boolean equals (Date other)
    (D) public int equals (Date other)
    (E) public boolean equals (Date d1, Date d2)

GO ON TO THE NEXT PAGE.

22. Which of the following code segments could be used to implement the equals method of the Date class so that the equals method works as intended?

```
I.   if (month == other.month)
       if (day == other.day)
             if (year == other.year)
                   return true;
     Return false;
II.  if (month == other.getMonth() &&
             day == other.getDay() &&
             year == other.getYear())
       return true;
     else
       return false;
III. return ! ((getMonth()  != other.getMonth())  ||
       (getDay()  != other.getDay())  ||
       (getYear() != other.getYear())) ;
```

(A) I only
(B) II only
(C) I and II only
(D) II and IIII
(E) I, II, and III

23. During the testing of the Date class, it is determined that the class does not correctly handle leap years—although it handles non-leap years correctly.

In which method of the Date class is the problem most likely to be found?

(A) the Date constructor
(B) the getMonth method
(C) the getDay method
(D) the daysUntil method
(E) the equals method

GO ON TO THE NEXT PAGE.

24. Consider the following methods:

```
public static void mystery ()
{
    int [] A;
    A = initialize ();
        // returns a valid initialized
        // array of integers
    for (int k = 0; k < A.length / 2; k++)
        swap (A[k], A[A.length - k - 1]);
}

public static void swap (int x, int y)
{
    int temp;
    temp = x;
    x = y;
    y = temp;
}
```

Which of the following best characterizes the effect of the for loop in the method mystery?

(A) It sorts the elements of A.

(B) It reverses the elements of A.

(C) It reverses the order of the first half of A and leaves the second half unchanged.

(D) It reverses the order of the second half of A and leaves the first half unchanged

(E) It leaves all of the elements of A in their original order.

GO ON TO THE NEXT PAGE.

25. Consider the following code segment:

```
int [][] A = new int [4][3] ;
for (int j = 0; j < A[0].length; j++)
    for (int k = 0; k < A.length; k++)
        if (j == 0)
                A[k][k] = 0;
        else if (k % j == 0)
                A[k][j] = 1;
        else
                A[k][j] = 2;
```

What are the contents of A after the code segment has been executed?

(A) 0 0 0 0
     1 1 1 1
     1 2 1 2

(B) 0 1 1 1
     0 2 2 2
     0 1 2 1

(C) 0 0 0
     1 1 2
     1 1 1
     1 1 2

(D) 0 1 1
     0 2 1
     0 2 2
     0 2 1

(E) 0 1 1
     0 1 2
     0 1 1
     0 1 2

26. Consider the following method:

```
/** @param num an int value such that num >= 0
 */
public void mystery(int num)
{
    System.out.print(num % 100);
    if ((num / 100) != 0)
    {
        mystery(num / 100);
    }
    System.out.print(num % 100);
}
```

Which of the following is printed as a result of the call mystery(456789)?

(A) 456789
(B) 896745
(C) 987654
(D) 456789896745
(E) 896745456789

27. Consider the following method:

```
public static int mystery (int x, int y)
{
    if (x > 0)
        return x;
    else if (y > 0)
        return y;
    else
        return x / y;
}
```

In accordance with good design and testing practices, which of the following is the best set of test cases (x, y) for the method mystery?

(A) (3, 4), (-3, 4), (-3, -4)
(B) (3, 4), (-3, 4), (-3, -4), (-3, 0)
(C) (3, 4), (3, -4), (-3, -4), (-3, 0)
(D) (3, 4), (3, -4), (-3, -4), (-3, 4), (-3, 0)
(E) (3, 4), (2, 5), (3, -4), (-3, 0), (4, 0), (0, 0)

28. Consider the following method.

```
/** Precondition: numList is not empty
 */
private int mystery(int[] numList)
{
    int n = numList.length - 1;
    for (int k : numList)
    {
        if (numList[n] > numList[k])
        {
            n = k;
        }
    }
    return numList[n];
}
```

Which of the following best describes the return of mystery?

(A) The largest value in the array numList
(B) The least value in the array numList
(C) The index of the largest value in the array numList
(D) The index of the least value in the array numList
(E) The number of indexes whose values are less than numList[n]

29. Consider the following method.

```
public int[] editArray(int[] arr, int old, int new)
{
    /*missing code*/
    return arr;
}
```

The method above is intended to replace any instance of old in arr with any instances of new. Which of the following can be used to replace /*missing code*/ to replace any values of old in the array with values of new?

(A)
```
for (int k = 0; k < arr.length; k++)
{
    if (arr[k] = old)
    {
        arr[k] == new;
    }
}
```

(B)
```
for (int k = 0; k < arr.length; k++)
{
    if (arr[k] == old)
    {
        arr[k] = new;
    }
}
```

(C)
```
while (arr[k] == old)
{
    arr[k] = new
}
```

(D)
```
for (int k = 0; k < arr.length; k++)
{
    arr[k] == new;
}
```

(E)
```
while (int k = 0; k < arr.length; k++)
{
    if (arr[k] = old)
    {
        arr[k] == new;
    }
}
```

GO ON TO THE NEXT PAGE.

30. Consider the following two classes.

```
public class SalesPerson
{
    public void sale()
    {
        System.out.print("greet ");
        pitch();
    }
public void pitch()
    {
        System.out.print("pitch ");
    }

}

public class CommissionedSalesPerson extends SalesPerson
{
    public void sale()
    {
        super.sale();
        System.out.print("record ");
    }
    public void pitch()
    {
        super.pitch();
        system.out.print("close ");
    }

}
```

The following code segment is found in a class other than `SalesPerson`.

```
SalesPerson vincent = new CommissionedSalesPerson();
vincent.sale();
```

Which of the following is the best description of the functionality of this code segment?

(A) `greet pitch`
(B) `greet pitch close`
(C) `greet pitch record`
(D) `greet pitch record close`
(E) `greet pitch close record`

GO ON TO THE NEXT PAGE.

31. Consider the following declaration of a class that will be used to represent dimensions of rectangular crates.

```
public class Crate
{
    private int length;
    private int width;
    private int height;

    public Crate(int x, int y, int z)
{

    length = x;
    width = y;
    height = z;
    }

    //other methods not shown
    }
```

The following incomplete class declaration is intended to extend the Crate class so that the color of the crate can be specified.

```
public class ColoredCrate{
    private String color;
    //Constructors not shown
    //Other methods not shown
    }
```

Which of the following possible constructors for ColoredCrate would be considered legal?

I. `public ColoredPoint(int a, int b, int c, String crateColor)`
    ```
    {
        length = a;
        width = b;
        height = c;
        color = crateColor;
    }
    ```
II. `public ColoredPoint(int a, int b, int c, String crateColor)`
    ```
    {
        super (a, b, c)
        color = crateColor;
    }
    ```
III. `public ColoredPoint()`
    ```
    {
        color = "";
    }
    ```

(A) I only
(B) III only
(C) I and II only
(D) I and II only
(E) II and III only

GO ON TO THE NEXT PAGE.

32. Consider the following three proposed implementations of method reverse, intended to return the reverse the order of objects in an `ArrayList`:

I.
```
public static ArrayList<Object> reverse (ArrayList<Object> q)
{
        ArrayList<Object> s = new ArrayList<Object>();
        while (q.size() != 0)
                s.add(0, q.remove(0));
         return s;
}
```

II.
```
public static ArrayList<Object> reverse (ArrayList<Object> q)
{
        ArrayList<Object> s = new ArrayList<Object>(s);
        for (int k = 0; k < q.size(); k++)
                s.add(0, q.remove(0));
        return s;
}
```

III.
```
public static ArrayList<Object> reverse (ArrayList<Object> q)
{
        Object obj;
        if (q.size() != 0)
        {
                obj = q.remove(0);
                q = reverse(q);
                q.add(obj);
        }
        return q;
}
```

Which of the above implementations of method reverse work as intended?

(A) I only
(B) III only
(C) I and II
(D) I and III
(E) I, II, and III

GO ON TO THE NEXT PAGE.

33. Consider the following code segment.

```
List<Integer> values = new ArrayList<Integer>() ;
values.add(5) ;
values.add(3) ;
values.add(2) ;
values.add(2) ;
values.add(6) ;
values.add(3) ;
values.add(9) ;
values.add(2) ;
values.add(1) ;
for (int j = 0; j < values.size(); j++)
{
    if (values.get(j).intValue() == 2)
    {
        values.remove(j);
    }
}
```

What will values contain as a result of executing this code segment?

(A) [5, 3, 2, 2, 6, 3, 9, 2, 1]
(B) [5, 3, 2, 6, 3, 9, 2, 1]
(C) [5, 3, 6, 3, 9, 1]
(D) [2, 2, 2, 5, 3, 6, 3, 9, 1]
(E) The code throws an `ArrayIndexOutOfBoundsException` exception

GO ON TO THE NEXT PAGE.

34. Consider the class Data partially defined below. The completed max1D method returns the maximum value of b, a one-dimensional array of integers. The completed max2D method is intended to return the maximum value c, a two dimensional array of integers.

```
public class Data
{
    /** Returns the maximum value of one-dimensional array b */
    public int max1D(int[] b)
    { /* implementation not shown */}
    /** Returns the maximum value of two-dimensional array c */
    public int max2D(int[] c)
    {
        int max;
        /* missing code */
        returns max
    }
    /* other methods of Data class not shown*/
}
```

Assume that max1D words as intended. Which of the follow can replace /* missing code */ so that max2D works as intended.

```
I.   for (int[] row: c)
     {
         max = max1D(row);
     }
II.  max = max1D(c[0]);
     for (int k = 1; k <= c.length; k++)
     {
         max = max1D(c[k]);
     }
III. max = max1D(c[0]);
     for (int[] row: c)
     {
         if (max < madID(row))
         {
             max = max1D(row);
         }
     }
```

(A) I only

(B) III only

(C) I and II only

(D) II and III only

(E) I, II, and III only

GO ON TO THE NEXT PAGE.

35. Consider the following instance variable, numList, and incomplete method, countZeros. The method is intended to return an integer array count such that for all k, count[k] is equal to the number of elements from numList[0] through numList[k]. For example, if numList contains the values {1, 4, 0, 5, 0, 0}, the array countZeros contains the values {0, 0, 1, 1, 2, 3}.

```
public int[] countZeros(int[] numList)
{
    int[] count = new int[numList.length];
    for (int k : count)
    {
        count[k] = 0;
    }
    /* missing code */
    return count;
}
```

The following two versions of /*missing code*/ are suggested to make the method work as intended.

Version 1
```
for (int k = 0;  j <= numList.length; j++)
{
    for (int j = 0; j <= k; j++)
    {
        if  (numList[j] == 0)
        {
            count[k] = numList[k] + 1;
        }
    }
}
```

Version 2
```
for (int k = 0; k < numList.length; k++)
{
    if  (numList[k] = 0)
    {
        count[k] = count[k - 1] + 1;
    }
    else
    {
        count[k] = count[k - 1];
    }
}
```

Which of the following statements are true?

(A) Both Version 1 and Version 2 will work as intended, but Version 1 is faster than Version 2.

(B) Both Version 1 and Version 2 will work as intended, but Version 1 is faster than Version 2.

(C) Version 1 will work as intended but Version 2 causes an ArrayIndexOutOfBoundsException.

(D) Version 2 will work as intended but Version 1 causes an ArrayIndexOutOfBoundsException.

(E) Version 1 and Version 2 each cause an ArrayIndexOutOfBoundsException.

GO ON TO THE NEXT PAGE.

36. A real estate agent wants to develop a program to record information about apartments for rent. For each apartment, she intends to record the number of bedrooms, number of bathrooms, whether pets are allowed, and the monthly rent charged. Which of the following object oriented program designs would be preferred?

    (A) Use a class Apartment with four subclasses: `Bedrooms`, `Bathrooms`, `PetsAllowed`, and `Rent`.

    (B) Use four classes: `Bedrooms`, `Bathrooms`, `PetsAllowed`, and `Rent`, each with subclass `Apartment`.

    (C) Use of class Apartment with four instance variables `int bedrooms`, `int bathrooms`, `boolean petsAllowed`, and `double rent`.

    (D) Use five unrelated classes: `Apartment`, `Bedrooms`, `Bathrooms`, `PetsAllowed`, and `Rent`

    (E) Use a class Apartment, with a subclass `Bedrooms`, with a subclass `Bathrooms`, with a subclass `PetsAllowed`, with a subclass `Rent`.

37. Consider the following declarations

```
public class Book
{
    boolean hasMorePagesThan(Book b);
    //other methods not shown
}
Public class Dictionary extends Book
{
    //other methods not shown
}
```

Of the following method headings of `hasMorePagesThan`, which can be added to Dictionary so that it will satisfy the Book superclass?

I.   `int hasMorePagesThan(Book b)`
II. `boolean hasMorePagesThan(Book b)`
III. `boolean hasMorePagesThan(Dictionary d)`

    (A) I only
    (B) I and II only
    (C) II only
    (D) II and III only
    (E) I, II, and III

GO ON TO THE NEXT PAGE.

38. Consider the following method.

```
/**Precondition: set contains does not contain any negative values
 */
public int mystery(int[] set, int max)
{
    int m = 0;
    int count = 0;
    for (int n = 0; n < set.length && set[n] < max; n++)
    {
        if (set[n] >= m)
        {
            m = set[n]; //Statement A
        }
        count++; //Statement B
    }
    return count;
}
```

Assume that mystery is called and is executed without error. Which of the following are possible combinations of the number of the value of max, the number of times Statement A is executed and the number of times Statement B is executed?

	Value of max	Executions of Statement A	Executions of Statement B
I	8	2	3
II	3	7	5
III	7	0	4

(A) I only

(B) III only

(C) I and II only

(D) I and III only

(E) I, II, and III

GO ON TO THE NEXT PAGE.

39. The following method is intended to return an array that inserts an integer m at index n, pushing the values of all indexes after n to the index one higher. For example, if the index arr is

4	2	1	3

and the command arr = insert(arr, 5, 2) is called, the method is intended to return

4	2	5	1	3

Line 1	`public int[] insert(int[] arr, int m, int n)`
Line 2	`{`
Line 3	`    int[] temp = new int[arr.length+1];`
Line 4	`    for (int k  = 0; k < arr.length; k++)`
Line 5	`    {`
Line 6	`        if (k < n)`
Line 7	`        {`
Line 8	`            temp[k] = arr[k];`
Line 9	`        }`
Line 10	`        else`
Line 11	`        {`
Line 12	`            temp[k + 1] = arr[k];`
Line 13	`        }`
Line 14	`    }`
Line 15	`    temp[m] = n;`
Line 16	`    return temp;`
Line 17	`}`

The method insert does not work as intended. Which of the following changes will cause it to work as intended?

(A) Change Line 6 to `if (k > n)`
(B) Change Line 6 to `if (k <= n)`
(C) Change Line 12 to `temp[k] = arr[k + 1];`
(D) Change Line 15 to `temp[n] = m;`
(E) Change Line 16 to `return arr;`

GO ON TO THE NEXT PAGE.

40. If X, Y, and Z are integer values, the boolean expression

```
(X > Y)  &&  (Y > Z)
```

can be replaced by which of the following?

(A) `X  >  Z`

(B) `(X  <  Y)  ||  (Y  <  Z)`

(C) `(X <= Y)  ||  (Y  <= Z)`

(D) `! ( (X  <  Y)  ||  (Y  <  Z) )`

(E) `! ( (X  <=  Y)  ||  (Y  <=  Z) )`

END OF SECTION I

**IF YOU FINISH BEFORE TIME IS CALLED,
YOU MAY CHECK YOUR WORK ON THIS SECTION.**

DO NOT GO ON TO SECTION II UNTIL YOU ARE TOLD TO DO SO.

COMPUTER SCIENCE A

SECTION II

Time—1 hour and 30 minutes

Number of Questions—4

Percent of Total Grade—50

Directions: SHOW ALL YOUR WORK. REMEMBER THAT PROGRAM SEGMENTS ARE TO BE WRITTEN IN JAVA™.

Notes:

- Assume that the classes listed in the Java Quick Reference have been imported where appropriate.

- Unless otherwise noted in the question, assume that parameters in method calls are not null and that methods are called only when their preconditions are satisfied.

- In writing solutions for each question, you may use any of the accessible methods that are listed in classes defined in that question. Writing significant amounts of code that can be replaced by a call to one of these methods will not receive full credit.

FREE RESPONSE QUESTIONS

1. A monochrome (black-and-white) screen is a rectangular grid of pixels that can be either white or black. A pixel is a location on the screen represented by its row number and column number.

   Consider the following proposal for modeling a screen and its pixels.

   A black pixel on the screen is modeled by an object of type `Pixel`. The `Pixel` class includes the following private data and methods:

   - `row`—this `int` holds the row number of this pixel
   - `col`—this `int` holds the column number of this pixel
   - `Pixel` constructor—this constructor creates a `Pixel` based on the given row and column
   - `getRow`—this method returns the row number of this pixel
   - `getCol`—this method returns the column number of this pixel

   ```java
   public class Pixel
   {
       private int row;
       private int col;
       public Pixel (int r, int c)
       {row = r; col = c; }
       public int getRow ( )
       {return row; }
       public int getCol ( )
       { return col; }
   }
   ```

GO ON TO THE NEXT PAGE.

A screen is modeled by an object of type Screen. Internally, the screen is represented by an array of linked lists of pixels. The index into the array represents the given row on the screen; the linked list at that element represents the *black* pixels at the various columns in order from smallest to largest column. *White pixels are not stored in the linked list.* A pixel not in the list is assumed to be white.

The Screen class includes the following private data and methods:

- data—The array of linked lists.

- pixelAt—This method returns the pixel at the given location if it exists (i.e., is black) in this Screen. Otherwise, this method returns null.

- pixelOn—This method creates and stores a black Pixel at the appropriate place in the array of linked lists based on the given row and column number.

```
public class Screen
{
    private ArrayList<int>[] data;
    private int numCols;

    // postcondition: data is created with
    //            height elements;
    //            numCols is set to
    //            width
    public Screen (int width, int height)
    {  /* to be implemented in part  (a)  */

    // precondition: 0 <= row <=
    //            data.length-1;
    //            0 <= col <= numCols-1
    //postcondition: returns the pixel at
    //            the given row and col
    //            if it exists (black)
    //            or null if the pixel
    //            doesn't exist (white)
    public Pixel pixelAt (int row, int col)
    { /* to be implemented in part (b) */}

    // precondition: 0 <= row <=
    //            data.length-1;
    //            0 <= col <= numCols -1;
    //            the pixel at row,col
    //            does not exist
    //            in this Screen
    // postcondition: adds the pixel at
    //            the given row and col
    //            so that pixels in a
    //            given row of data are
    //            in increasing column
    //            order
    public void pixelOn (int row, int col)
    {  /*to be implemented in part (c) */ }

    //   . . . constructors, other methods,
    // and other private data not shown
```

GO ON TO THE NEXT PAGE.

(a) Write the constructor for the `Screen` class. The constructor should initialize the private data of the `Screen` class as appropriate.

Complete the constructor for the Screen class below.

```
// postcondition: data is created with
//          height elements; numCols
//          is set to width
public Screen (int width, int height)
```

(b) Write the `Screen` method pixelAt. Method `pixelAt` should return the pixel at the given row and column of the screen if that pixel exists (i.e., is black). Otherwise pixelAt should return null.

Complete method `pixelAt` below.

```
//precondition: 0 <= row <=
//          data.length-1;
//          0 <= col <= numCols-1
// postcondition: returns the pixel at
//          the given row and col
//          if it exists (black)
//          or null if the pixel
//          doesn't exist (white)
public Pixel pixelAt (int row, int col)
```

(c) Write the `Screen` method pixelOn. Method `pixelOn` should modify this `Screen` so that a pixel is stored at the given row and column.

Complete method `pixelOn` below.

```
// precondition: 0 <= row <=
//          data.length-1;
//          0 <= col <= <= numCols-1;
//          the pixel at row,col
//          does not exist
//          in this Screen
// postcondition: adds the pixel at
//          the given row and col
//          so that pixels in a
//          given row of a data are
//          in increasing column
//          order
public void pixelOn (int row, int col)
```

GO ON TO THE NEXT PAGE.

2. A toy collector is creating an inventory of her marble collection. A marble set specifies the color and number of a particular group of marbles from her collection. The declaration of the `MarbleSet` class is shown below.

```
public class MarbleSet
{
    /** Constructs a new MarbleSet object */
    public MarbleSet(String color, int numMarbles)
    {   /* implementation not shown*/   }

    /** @return the color of the set of marbles
     */
    public String getColor()
    {   /* implementation not shown*/   }

    /** @return the number of marbles in the set
      */
     public int getNumber()
     { /* implementation not shown*/   }

    // There may be instance variables, constructors, and methods that are not shown.
}
```

The `MarbleCollection` class documents all sets of marbles in the collection. The declaration of the `MarbleCollection` class is shown below.

```
public class MarbleCollection
{
    /** This is a list of all marble sets */
    private List<MarbleSet> sets;

    /** Constructs a new MarbleSet object */
    public MarbleCollection()
    {   sets = new ArrayList<MarbleSet>();        }

    /** Adds theSet to the marble collection
     * @param theSet the marble set to add to the marble collection
     */
    public void addSet(MarbleSet theSet)
    {   sets.add(theSet);      }

    /** @return the total number of marbles
      */
     public int getTotalMarbles()
     { /* to be implemented in part (a)*/       }
    /** Removes all the marble sets from the marble collection that have the same
    color as
     * marbleColor and returns the total number of marbles removed
     * @param marbleColor the color of the marble sets to be removed
     * @return the total number of marbles of marbleColor in the marble sets removed
     */
    public int removeColor(String marbleCol)
     { /* to be implemented in part (b)*/       }
```

GO ON TO THE NEXT PAGE.

(a) The `getTotalMarbles` method computes and returns the sum of the number of marbles. If there are no marble sets, the method returns 0.

```
Complete method  getTotalMarbles below
/** @return the sum of the number of marbles in all marble sets
 */
public int getTotalMarbles()
```

(b) The `removeColor` updates the marble collection by removing all the marble sets for which the color of the marbles matches the parameter `marbleCol`. The marble collection may contain zero or more marbles with the same color as the `marble-Col`. The method returns the number of marbles removed.

For example after the execution of the following code segment

```
MarbleCollection m = new MarbleCollection();
m.addSet(new MarbleSet("red", 2);
m.addSet(new MarbleSet("blue", 3);
m.addSet(new MarbleSet("green", 3);
m.addSet(new MarbleSet("blue", 4);
m.addSet(new MarbleSet("red", 1);
```

the contents of the marble collection can be expressed with the following table.

"red" 2	"blue" 3	"green" 3	"blue" 4	"red" 1

The method call `m.removecolor("red")` returns 3 because there were two red marbel sets containing a total of 3 marbles. The new marble collection is shown below.

"blue" 3	"green" 3	"blue" 4

The method call `m.removecolor("purple")` returns 0 and makes no modifications to the marble collection.

Complete the method `removeColor` below.

```
/** Removes all the marble sets from the marble collection that have the same
*color as  marbleColor and returns the total number of marbles removed
* @param marbleColor the color of the marble sets to be removed
* @return the total number of marbles of marbleColor in the marble sets removed
*/
    public int removeColor(String marbleCol)
```

GO ON TO THE NEXT PAGE.

3. A binary, or base two, integer is a number consisting of digits that are either 0 or 1. Digits in a binary integer are numbered from right to left starting with 0.

The decimal value of the binary integer is the sum of each digit multiplied by 2^d where d is the number of the digit.

For example, the decimal value of the binary integer 1011010 is

$$(0 * 2^0) + (1 * 2^1) + (0 * 2^2) + (1 * 2^3) + (1 * 2^4) + (0 * 2^5) + (1 + 2^6)$$

$$= 0 + 2 + 0 + 8 + 16 + 0 + 64$$

$$= 90$$

A decimal integer can be converted into its corresponding binary integer according to the following algorithm:

- Calculate the remainder when the decimal integer is divided by 2. This is the rightmost digit of the corresponding binary integer

- Divide the decimal integer by 2 using integer division. If the result is 0, stop. Otherwise repeat the algorithm using the new value of the decimal integer

The digits produced will be in right-to-left order in the binary integer.

For instance, the decimal integer 90 can be converted into its corresponding binary integer as follows:

90 % 2 = 0	(the rightmost digit)
90 / 2 = 45 45 % 2 = 1	(the second digit from the right)
45 / 2 = 22 22 % 2 = 0	(the third digit from the right)
22 / 2 = 11 11 % 2 = 1	(the fourth digit from the right)
11 / 2 = 55 % 2 = 1	(the fifth digit from the right)
5 / 2 = 22 % 2 = 0	(the sixth digit from the right)
2 / 2 = 11 % 2 = 1	(the leftmost digit)
1 / 2 = 0	

Consider the design of a class that represents an arbitrary length non-negative binary integer.

The operations on this class include

- constructing an empty binary integer with value zero
- constructing a binary integer from an arbitrary non-negative decimal integer
- returning a binary integer that represents the result of adding another binary integer to this binary integer
- returning the result of converting this binary integer to a `String`
- returning a positive integer if this binary integer is less than another binary integer, zero if it is equal, and a negative integer if it is less

GO ON TO THE NEXT PAGE.

In addition, the binary integer class should fully implement the Comparable interface.

(a) Write the definition of a binary integer class called BinaryInt, showing the appropriate data definitions, constructors, and method signatures. You should *not* write the implementations of the constructor or any of the methods you define for the BinaryInt class.

(b) Using the signature you wrote in part (a), write the implementation for the operation that constructs a BinaryInt from an arbitrary decimal integer.
In writing this method, you may call any of the methods in the BinaryInt class (as you defined it in part (a)). Assume that these methods work as specified.

(c) Using the BinaryInt class (as you defined it in part (a)), complete the following method, Test, that adds the following pairs of decimal integers in binary and outputs the larger of the two binary sums. Test is *not* a method of the binary integer class.

Pair 1: 2,314,279,623 and 3,236,550,123. Pair 2: 3,412,579,010 and 2,128,250,735.

In writing this method, you may call any of the methods BinaryInt (as you defined it in part (a)). Assume that these methods work as specified.

Complete method Test below.
```
public static void Test ()
```

GO ON TO THE NEXT PAGE.

4. A Parabola is a graph defined by the equation $y = ax^2 + bx + c$, where a, b, and c are all integers and a is non-zero. The x-value of the axis of symmetry of a parabola is defined by the double $-b/2a$. A point is a pair of integer values, x and y. A point is defined to be on Parabola if it satisfies the equation of Parabola. Consider the examples in the table below:

Equation	Axis of symmetry ($-b/2a$)	Is point (4, 3) on parabola?
$y = 2x^2 - 6x - 5$	$-(-6)/2(2) = 1.5$	Yes, $3 = 2(4)^2 - 6(4) - 5$
$y = 4x^2 + 2x - 3$	$-2/2(4) = -0.25$	No, 3 $\neq$ 4(4)^2 + 2(4) $-$ 3

The following code code segment is from a method outside the class `Parabola` and demonstrates how the `Parabola` class can be used to represent the two equations above

```
Parabola par1 = new Parabola (2, -6, -5);
double axis1 = par1.getAxis(); //assigns 1.5 to axis1
boolean onGraph1 = par1.isOnGraph(4, 3); //assigns true to onGraph1

Parabola par2 = new Parabola (4, 2, -2);
double axis2 = par2.getAxis(); //assigns -0.25 to axis2
boolean onGraph2 = par2.isOnGraph(4, 3); //assigns false to onGraph2
```

Write the `Parabola` class. The constructor class of `Parabola` must take three integer parameters that represent a, b, and c, successively. You may assume as a precondition that a be a non-zero integer. You must include a `getAxis` method that returns the x-coordinate of the axis of symmetry as a double and a `isOnGraph` method that takes a point represented by two integer parameters, x and y, and returns true is the point is on the `Parabola` and returns false if it is not. Your class methods must be able to return the values indicated in the examples above. You can ignore any overflow issues.

STOP

END OF EXAM

Chapter 12
Practice Test 2:
Answers and
Explanations

PRACTICE TEST 2 ANSWER KEY

1. A		21. A	
2. D		22. D	
3. B		23. D	
4. C		24. E	
5. C		25. E	
6. A		26. E	
7. D		27. D	
8. B		28. B	
9. A		29. B	
10. B		30. E	
11. E		31. E	
12. D		32. C	
13. D		33. B	
14. C		34. B	
15. C		35. E	
16. C		36. C	
17. E		37. C	
18. C		38. A	
19. A		39. D	
20. D		40. E	

PRACTICE TEST 2 EXPLANATIONS

Section I: Multiple-Choice Questions

1. **A** This problem is actually quite simple to answer because the value of b never changes. Eventually a will be equal to zero and the value of b will be returned by each call to mystery.

2. **D** Plug in values. For example, let numList = {3, 5, 8, 2, 1, 9} and number = 6. (Note that numList need not be in any particular order.) When mystery is called, number is stored as the parameter n, so n = 6. Enter the for loop. In the first iteration of the for loop, k = 0. The condition on the if statement is (n <= numList[k]). Since it is not the case that 6 <= numList[0] = 3, skip the if statement and end this iteration of the for loop. Increment k, so k = 1. Go to the if statement again. Since it is not the case that 6 <= numList[1] = 5, skip the if statement and end this iteration of the for loop. Increment k again, so k = 2. Go to the if statement. Since it is the case that 6 <= numList[2] = 8, execute the if statement and return the value of k, which is 2. Since mystery(6) returns 2, j = 2. Check each answer and eliminate any that are false.

    Choice (A) is incorrect. The value at index 2 is 8, which is not the greatest value.

    Choice (B) is incorrect. The value greatest value in numList that is less than 6 is 5, which in not at index 2.

    Choice (C) is incorrect. All the values in numList from 0 to 2 – 1 = 1 are less than number not greater.

    Choice (D) is true for this set of values, so keep (D).

    Choice (E) is incorrect. Some of the numbers from index 2 through 5 are greater than 6 but not all.

    Choice (D) is the only correct answer. Since the numbers are not in order, so assumption can be made about the indexes after j but the indexes prior to j must contains lesser values in order for the if statement containing the return not the be executed.

3. **B** In general, data fields of a class are designated private in order to hide the implementation of the class. This ensures that the functionality of the class—as seen by the programmer using the class—does not change if the implementation changes. Choice (B) is correct.

    Choice (A) is incorrect. Methods of a class are able to access the private data of their class.

    Choice (C) is incorrect. Data fields that are designated as private cannot be modified outside their class.

    Choice (D) is incorrect. A program does not need to know how a class is implemented in order to use it.

Choice (E) is incorrect. The methods enquack and dequack are public and accessible to any program using the Quack class. These methods modify the contents of a Quack.

4. **C** The isEmpty method has to return true if myData contains no elements and false otherwise. If myData contains no elements, then the size is 0. The term length is used for arrays rather than ArrayLists, so eliminate (A) and (D). Since size is an ArrayList method rather than a variable, size() must be used instead of size, so eliminate (E). Also, since size() is an ArrayList method rather than a Quack method, the ArrayList myData must be referenced, so eliminate (B). The correct answer is (C).

5. **C** The fastest way to solve this problem is to make a table of values for mystery(n) and see which gives answer that match those given by original method.

Note that we can stop filling in answers for a particular choice as soon as one of the answers does not match the answer given by the original method.

n	Original	(A)	(B)	(C)	(D)	(E)
2	3	2	3	3	3	4
3	3	–	4	3	4	–

After checking two values, only (C) provides answers that are the same as the original method. Choice (C) is correct.

6. **A** The addDistance method adds the parameter k to the number of kilometers and m to the number of meters. This might appear to be sufficient, but every 1000 meters should be converted to 1 kilometer. Determine which answer choice correctly does this. Consider one possible case. Let kilometers = 3 and meters = 2300. 2300 meters should be converted to 2 kilometers and 300 meters, leaving an end result of kilometers = 5 and meters = 300. Eliminate any answer choice that doesn't give this result.

Choice (A) adds meters / 1000 to kilometers. Remember that integer division in Java is performed by dropping any remainder and rounding toward 0. Therefore meters / 1000 = 2300 / 1000 = 2, so 2 is added to kilometers to get 5. This is correct, so far. The second statement sets meters equal to meters % 1000, which the remainder when meters is divided by 1000. This sets meters = 300, which is also correct, so keep (A).

Choice (B) adds meters % 1000 to kilometers. Thus, kilometers = 3 + 300 = 303. Since this is not correct, eliminate (B).

Choice (C) adds kilometer % 1000 to meters. 3 % 1000 = 3, so meters would equal 2300 + 3 = 2303. This is not correct, so eliminate (C).

Choice (D) adds meters % 1000 to kilometers, so kilometers = 3 + 300 = 303, which is incorrect, so eliminate (D).

Choice (E) sets meters = meters % 1000 = 300, which is correct. However, it doesn't change the value of kilometers, which incorrectly remains 3, so eliminate (E).

Therefore, the correct answer is (A).

7.　**D**　Go through each answer choice one at a time.

Choice (A) may appear to be correct. However, remember that kilometers and meters are private variables (as are all variables in AP Computer Science). Therefore, they cannot be directly accessed by another class. Eliminate (A).

Choice (B) correctly accesses these variables by using the public getKilometers and getMeters methods. However, these values are added to set[k]. Therefore, this would simply double each of the distances without adding anything to temp. Since temp is the value that is returned, eliminate (B).

Choice (C) uses set[k].addDistance(). However, the method advance requires two integer parameters, so eliminate (C).

Eliminate (D) for the same reason.

Choice (E) correctly accesses kilometers and meters via getKilometers and getMeters from set[k]. These values are also correctly added to temp, the DistanceTracker to be returned, via its addDistance method. Therefore, the correct answer is (E).

8.　**B**　Follow the method coding, one line at a time. First create the empty ArrayList of type Integer called values. Now go through the for loop. First, let i = 0. Look at the condition in the if statement. i%4, i.e. the remainder when i is divided by 4, equals 0. Since this value does not meet the condition, do not execute the if statement. Since 0 is not in the ArrayList, eliminate any choices that include 0: (C) and (E). Now, add 5 to i to get i = 5. Since i%4 = 1, execute the statement and add 5 to the ArrayList. Now, add 5 again to get i = 10. Since i%4 = 2, do not execute the statement. Note that the value of i has skipped over 9, which is one of the integers in (D). Since i will never equal 9, eliminate (D). Add 5 again to get i = 15. Since i%4 = 3, do not execute the statement. Add 5 again to get i = 20. Since i%4 = 0, do not execute the statement. Now, add 5 to i to get i = 25. Since i%4 = 1, execute the statement and add 25 to the ArrayList. Since 25 is not included in (A), eliminate this choice. The correct answer, therefore, is (B).

9.　**A**　To have the correct return <expression> must be true when exactly two of the Boolean variables are true and exactly one is false. There are three possible ways for this to happen: if a and b are true but c is false, if a and c are true but b is false, and if b and c are true but a is false. Put these three into proper Java Boolean terminology. In Java "and" is represented by &&, "or" is represented by ||, and "not" is represent by !. The first case, a and b, are true but c is false and expressed by a && b &&!c. (Note that in logic, there is no distinction between "and" and "but".) The second case, a and c are true but b is false and expressed by a && !b && c. The third case, b and c are true but a is false and expressed by !a && b && c. Since <expression> should be true is *any* of these cases are true, these should be combined as a "or" statement: (a && b && !c) || (a && !b && c) || (!a && b && c). The correct answer is (A).

Therefore, the correct answer is (A).

10. **B** This problem tests your knowledge of operator precedence in expressions. Multiplication and division are performed before addition and subtraction operations that are at the same precedence level, which are performed in left-to-right order.

Apply these rules to the code segment in the question

$$
\begin{aligned}
X \quad &= 5 - 4 + 9 * 12 / 3 - 10 \\
&= 5 - 4 + (9 * 12) / 3 - 10 \\
&= 5 - 4 + 108 / 3 - 10 \\
&= 5 - 4 + (108 / 3) - 10 \\
&= 5 - 4 + 36 - 10 \\
&= (5 - 4) + 36 - 10 \\
&= 1 + 36 - 10 \\
&= (1 + 36) - 10 \\
&= 37 - 10 \\
&= 27
\end{aligned}
$$

Choice (B) is correct.

11. **E** String objects are dynamic in the sense that they do not have a maximum length (other than one imposed by a limit of available memory!), so the mention of this limit is just a red herring. Therefore, (C) and (D), which appear to refer to a 25-character String limit, can be eliminated immediately.

Choice (A) can be eliminated because it is not valid Java code.

Choice (B) can be eliminated because an array of Strings is being instantiated and then incorrectly assigned to an ArrayList object.

Choice (E) correctly declares and creates an array of 50 Strings.

12. **D** Go through each line of coding one at a time. First, create the empty ArrayList<Integer> scores. Then add the integer 93. The ArrayList is [93]. Then, add the integer 97. Since the add method with one parameter adds the integer parameter to the end of the list, the list is now [93, 97]. Similarly, add 84 to get [93, 97, 84], and add 91 to get [93, 97, 84, 91]. Now, remove the integer at index 2, and move following elements to the left. Since the indexes start with 0, the index 2 refers to the 84. The list is now [93, 97, 91]. Now execute the line scores.add(1, 83). When the add method has 2 parameters, the first parameter is the index to which the second parameter is inserted. Therefore, 83 is inserted at index 1, and, without deleting any items, all succeeding items are pushed to the right. Therefore, the list is now [93, 83, 97, 91]. Now, execute scores.set(3, 99); The first parameter,

3, is the index to which the second parameter, 99, must replace the existing integer. Therefore, the list is now [93, 83, 97, 99]. System.out.println(scores) output this list. Therefore, the correct answer is (D).

13. **D**   Implementation I is correct. This implementation recursively finds the correct digit by noting that the rightmost digit of n can be found by taking the remainder when n is divided by 10 (the base case). Other digits of n can be found by dividing n by 10 and finding the digit one place to the right (the recursive case). Eliminate any choice that does not include Implementation I: (C) and (E).

Implementation II is correct. The pow method calculates $10^{whichDigit}$. Dividing n by this number gives a number whose rightmost digit is the target digit. Taking the remainder of this number divided by 10 returns the correct digit. Eliminate any choice that does not include Implementation II: (B).

Implementation III is correct. The loop has the same effect as dividing n by $10^{whichDigit}$. The implementation then returns the correct digit by taking the remainder of this number divided by 10. Eliminate any choice that doesn't include Implementation III: (A).

The correct answer is (D).

14. **C**   SelectionSort begins at index 0 and swaps that element with the least element in the rest of the array. The item in the rest of the array with the least value is 1 at index 2. Swap the 4 from index 0 with the 1 from index 2, and leave all other elements the same. The result is (C).

15. **C**   Statement I is correct. This is the most straightforward way of traversing the array backwards and printing out the values. The for loop causes k to take on values from 9 down to 0 and print out the kth element of v. Eliminate any choice that does not include Statement I: (B) and (D).

Statement II is also correct. Although k takes on values from 0 up to 9, the array index 9-k gives the correct indices of 9 down to 0. Eliminate any choice that does not include Statement II: (A).

Statement III is incorrect. The first time through the loop, k will have a value of 10, which will raise an ArrayIndexOutOfBounds exception. Eliminate any choice that does include Statement III: (E).

Choice (C) is the correct answer.

16. **C**   To answer this question, invent a set and an integer n. Let set = {4, 2, 5, 3, 1} and let n = 3. Now go through the method call. Begin with the for loop, which initalizes k = 0. Since k than set.length() = 5, execute the for loop, which includes an if statement. The condition on the if is that set.get(k) > n. Remember that indexes begin with 0, so set.get(k) = set.get(0) = 4. This is greater than n = 3, so execute the if statement, which is to return (set.remove(k) + mystery(set, n)). The remove method of ArrayList not only removes the element but also returns it at the specified index. Therefore, this returns 4 + mystery(set, 3) with the new set: {2, 5, 3, 1}. Note that the return

statement ends the execution of the method, so there will not be a need to continue with the for loop. However, in this case, it also calls the method recursively, so execute the new method call for mystery(set, 3). Once again, start with the for loop, which initializes k = 0, which is less than set. length() = 4, so execute the for statement again. The condition on this if statement, this time, is not met since set.get(k) = 2 < n = 3. Increment k to get k = 1. Since this is less than 4, execute the for statement. This time, the if condition is met, since set.get(1) = 5 > 3, so execute the statement. Remove 5 from set but also return 5 + mystery(set, 3) with the new set being {2, 3, 1}. Insert this into the original return to get 4 + 5 + mystery(set, 3). Execute the new method call. Once again, start with the for loop. k = 0 < set.length() = 3, so execute the for statement again. The condition on this if statement is not met since set.get(k) = 2 < n = 3. Increment k to get k = 1. This is also less than set.length() = 3, so execute continue the loop. The condition on this if statement is not met since set.get(k) = 3, which is equal to but not less than the value of n. Increment k to get k = 2. This is less than set.length() = 3, so continue. The condition on this if statement is not met since set.get(k) = 1 < n = 3. Increment k to get k = 3. Since this is not less than set.length () = 3, terminate the for loop. return 0 and insert this into the original return to get a return of 4 + 5 + 0 = 9. Now go through the answer choices and eliminate anything that is not 9.

Choice (A) is 0, so eliminate this choice.

Choice (B) is the number of elements greater than n. If n = 3 and there are two elements greater than 3, eliminate this choice.

Choice (C) is the sum of the elements greater than n. Since the elements greater than n are 4 and 5, which have a sum of 9, keep this choice.

Choice (D) is the sum of the elements that are less than n. The elements less than 3 are 2 and 1, which have a sum of 3, so eliminate this choice.

Choice (E) is the sum of the elements that are less than or equal to n. The elements less than or equal to 3 are 2, 3, and 1, which have a sum of 6, so eliminate this choice, too. The correct answer is (C).

17. **E** Each of the answer choices creates a 4-by-4 two-dimensional array called temp and returns that array. The question, therefore, becomes which correct fills the array. Choice (A) creates a for loop with initial value int j = 0. Since j <= 3, continue with the for loop to get to a new for loop with initial value int k = 0.

Since k < 4, continue with this for loop to reach the statement temp[j][k] = j; This assigns temp[0][0] = 0. Remember that all indexes begin with 0, so temp[0][0] refers to the first row, first column. This is the correct value for this element, so continue. Increment the value of k to get k = 1. This is still less than 4, so continue with this inner for loop. Assign temp[j][k] = j, so temp[0][1] = 0. Because this is the first row, second column, which contains a 0, continue. Increment the value of k again to get k = 2. This is still less than 4, so continue with this inner for loop. Assign temp[j][k] = j, so temp[0][2] = 0. Since this is the first row, third column, which contains a 0, continue.

Increment the value of k again to get k = 3. This is still less than 4, so continue with this inner for loop. Assign temp[j][k] = j, so temp[0][3] = 0. Because this is the first row, fourth column, which contains a 0, continue. Increment the value of k to get k = 4. As this is not less than 4, end the inner for loop. Return to the outer for loop and increment j to get j = 1. Begin the inner for loop with initial value k = 0. Since this is less than 4, enter this for loop. Assign temp[j][k] = j, so temp[1][0] = 1. This element refers to the second row first column, which does not have a value of 1. This is incorrect, so eliminate (A). Go onto (B).

Similarly, (B) begins with the same for loop for the j values *and* the same for loop for the k values. Therefore the statement temp[j][k] = k assigns temp[0][0] = 0 (since k is also 0). This is correct, so continue. Increment the value of k to get k = 1. Since this is less than 4, continue the inner for loop. Now, the statement temp[j][k] = k assigns temp[0][1] = 1. This is not the value in this position, so eliminate (B). Go onto (C).

Choice (C) has the same outer for loop, so initialize the value of j to be 0. The inner for loop initializes k = j, so k = 0. This is less than 4, so execute the statement. Thus, temp[j][k] = k assigns temp[0][0] = 0. As this is the correct value, continue. Increment k to get k = 1. Since this is less than 4, continue the inner for loop. Now, the statement temp[j][k] = k assigns temp[0][1] = 1. Since this is not the value in this position, eliminate (C). Go onto (D).

Choice (D) has the same outer for loop, so initialize the value of j to be 0. The inner for loop initializes k = 0. The condition on the inner for loop is k <= j. This is true, so enter the inner for loop. Execute temp[j][k] = j to get temp[0][0] = 0. Since this is the correct value, continue. Increment the value of k to get k = 1. As k is greater than j, end the inner for loop. Go back to the outer for loop and increment j to get j = 1. This is still less than 4, so continue with the outer for loop and go to the inner for loop, which gives k initial value 0. Because k is less than or equal to j, execute temp[j][k] = j to get temp[1][0] = 1. This is not the correct value, so eliminate (D).

Go to (E). Choice (E) has the same outer for loop, so give j initial value 0. Now, go to the inner for loop and give k initial value 0. The condition on the inner for loop is k is less than or equal to j. This is true, so enter the inner for loop. Execute temp[j][k] = j to get temp[0][0] = 0. This is the correct value, so continue. Increment the value of k to get k = 1. Since k is greater than j, end the inner for loop. Go back to the outer loop and increment j to get j = 1. This is still less than 4, so continue with the outer for loop and go to the inner for loop, which gives k initial value 0. Since k is less than or equal to j, execute temp[j][k] = k to get temp[1][0] = 0. This is still the correct value, so continue. Increment the value of k to get k = 1. Since k is still less than or equal to j, continue the inner for loop and execute temp[j][k] = k to get temp[1][1] = 1. Once again, this is the correct value, so continue. Increment k to get k = 2, which is greater than the value of j, so end the inner for loop and return to the outer for loop. Increment j to get j = 2. Because this is less than 4, continue to the inner for loop. Initialize k = 0. Because k is less than or equal to j, execute temp[j][k] = k to get temp[2][0] = 0. This is the correct value, so continue. Increment k to get k = 1. Since k is less than or equal to j, execute temp[j][k] = k to get temp[2][1] = 1. This is the correct value, so continue.

Increment k to get k = 2. Since k is less than or equal to j, execute temp[j][k] = k to get temp[2][2] = 2. This is the correct value, so continue. Increment k to get k = 3. Because this is greater than the value of j, end the inner for loop and return to the outer for loop. Increment j to get j = 3. Since this is less than 4, continue to the inner for loop, which gives k initial value 0. As k is less than or equal to j, execute temp[j][k] = k to get temp[3][0] = 0. This is the correct value, so continue. Increment the value of k to get k = 1. Since k is still less than or equal to j, continue the inner for loop and execute temp[j][k] = k to get temp[3][1] = 1. This is the correct value, so continue. Increment k to get k = 2. Because k is less than or equal to j, execute temp[j][k] = k to get temp[3][2] = 2. This is the correct value, so continue. Increment k to get k = 3. Since k is less than or equal to j, execute temp[j][k] = k to get temp[3][3] = 3. This is the correct value, so continue. Increment k to get k = 4. Because this is greater than j, end the inner for loop and return to the outer for loop. Increment j to get j = 4. Since this is not less than 4, end the outer for loop. Remember that type int is initialized by default as 0. Therefore, any element whose value has not been specifically assigned nor modified has value 0. This is consistent with the given array. Therefore, (E) is correct.

18.   **C**   Go through each answer choice one at a time.

Choice (A) creates an empty String temp. Then, if the age is less than 3, temp is set equal to "infant". This is correct. Then, if the age is less than or equal to 7, the temp is set equal to "Pee-wee". This appears to be correct. However, this instruction will apply not only to those from 3 to 7 but also to those less than 3. Therefore, those less than 3 will be incorrectly labeled "Pee-wee". Therefore, eliminate (A).

Choice (B) also creates an empty String temp. Then, if the age is less than 3, temp is set equal to "Infant". This is correct. However, the next if condition, (3 <= age <= 7), is not a valid statement formation in Java. Therefore, eliminate (B).

Choice (C) creates an empty String temp. Then, if the age is less than 3, temp is set equal to "Infant". This is correct. The next statement is an else if (age <= 7). This may appear to be the same problem as (A). However the else means that this instruction will not be executed if the original condition was met. Therefore, this statement does not apply to any age less than 3. Therefore, for the remaining ages that are less than or equal to 7, the String temp will be assigned the value "Pee-Wee". This is correct, so far. Next is another else if statement. Similarly, for all ages less than or equal to 7, this statement will not be executed. For the remaining ages that are less than or equal to 13, the String temp will be assigned the value "Cub". Then, there is another else if statement. Ignore all ages less than or equal to 13. If age is greater than or equal to 14, which is all remaining ages, then the String temp is assigned "Leader". This is correct. Finally, the method returns the correctly assigned String temp. This is correct. Check the two remaining answers to be sure.

Choice (D) begins like the other three. Empty String temp is created and if the age is less than 3, temp set equal to "Infant". Next, there is an else if (age < 7). Because of the else, this is correctly not executed for ages less than 3. However, because the operator is < and not <=, it is not executed for those equal to 7. The table says that all those from 3 to 7 *inclusive* should be assigned to "Pee-Wee". Since those who are exactly 7, would not get this assignment, eliminate (D).

Choice (E) makes both the mistake of (A), not using the else, and the mistake of (D), not using <=. Therefore, eliminate (E).

The correct answer is (C).

19. **A** Consider the results of executing the example given. Let arr contain [8, 7, 5, 5, 4, 7, 2, 7, 1, 2, 7]. Call getGap(arr, 7). Set index1 and index2 equal to -1. Now execute the for loop. for(int k = 0; k < arr.length; k++) executes the for loop for each index of arr and calls that index k. Start with k = 0. The condition on the if statement is (arr[k] == num). Since arr[0] is equal to 8 and not 7, do not execute the if statement. The if statement is the entirety of the for loop, so go to k = 1. Because arr[1] = 7, execute the if statement, which begins with a new if statement with the condition (index1 == -1). This is true, so execute the if statement and ignore the else statement. Set index1 = 1 and index2 = 1. Now, increment k to get k = 2. Since arr[2] = 5, do not execute the if statement and increment to get k = 3. As arr[3] = 5, do not execute the if statement and increment to get k = 4. Because arr[4] = 4, do not execute the if statement and increment to get k = 5. Since arr[5] = 7, execute the if statement. Look at the condition of the inner if statement, (index1 == −1). This is now false, so execute the else statement. Set index1 equal to index2, which is 1. Then set index2 equal to k, which is 5. Now, go to k = 6. Since arr[6] = 2, do not execute the if statement and increment to get k = 7. Because arr[7] = 7, execute the if statement. Look at the condition of the inner if statement, (index1 == −1). This is false, so execute the else statement. Set index1 equal to index2, which is 5. Set index2 equal to k, which is 7. Now, go to k = 8. Since arr[8] = 1, do not execute the if statement and go to k = 9. As arr[9] = 2, do not execute the if statement and go to k = 10. Because arr[10] = 7, execute the if statement. Look at the condition of the inner if statement, (index1 == −1). Since this is false, execute the else statement. Set index1 equal to index2, which is 7. Then set index2 equal to k, which is 10. Now, go to k = 11, which is equal to arr.length, so end the for loop. Now execute the return statement, which is return (index2 − index1). This returns 10 − 7 = 3. Now go through the answer choices to see which are equal to 3. Choice (A) is the difference between the indexes of the last two occurrences of num. The last two occurrences of 7 are at index 7 and index 10. Since this difference is 3, keep this answer choice.

Choice (B) is the minimum difference between two occurrences of num. The least difference is between the 7's at indexes 5 and 7. Since the difference is 2, eliminate (B).

Choice (C) if the difference between the first two occurrences in arr. The first two occurrences are at index 1 and 5, which have a difference of 4, so eliminate (C).

Choice (D) is the length of the array arr, which is 11, so eliminate (D).

Choice (E) is the number of occurrence of arr, which is 4, so eliminate (E).

The correct answer is (A).

20. **D** The method is intended to determine the maximum difference between the indexes of any two occurrences of num in arr. In order for this to happen, index1 must be the index of the first occurrence of num and index2 must be the last occurrence. Index1 is given the index of the first occurrence at line 11. Index2 is given the index of the last occurrence at the final execution of line 17. This is correct. However, the reason the method does not work as intended is that the value of index1 is change at line 16. Therefore, this statement should be deleted. The correct answer is (D).

21. **A** The Object class equal method is called with boolean return and Object parameter, so the call will have to use this exactly. The only choice that does this is (A).

22. **D** Only Statement II and III are correct.

   Statements I calls variables other.month, other.day, and other.year. However, these variables are private and, thus, can only be recognized within other.

   Statement II combines the three tests into one if statement condition and returns true if that condition is satisfied.

   Statement III returns the opposite of checking if any one of the month, day, or year are not equal. This is an application of DeMorgan's law (see question 40 for another example).

23. **D** The daysUntil method is the only method that needs to know about leap years in order to work properly. For example: the number of days between February 27 and March 2 is different according to whether or not the year is a leap year.

   All of the other methods do not depend on whether the year is a leap year.

24. **E** In Java, parameters methods are passed by value. Thus, the values of any arguments in the code that calls the method are not changed by calling the method.

   In this question—despite its misleading name—the swap method does not change the arguments of the code that calls swap.

   Because swap has no effect, (E) is correct: The elements of A are left in their original order.

25. **E** To solve this problem, first eliminate (A) and (B) as they represent two-dimensional arrays that have 3 rows and 4 columns, not 4 rows and 3 columns as indicated in the code segment.

   Note that k iterates through the rows and j iterates through the columns.

   Second, examine the value at A[1][0]. This value is set when k = 1 and j = 0. Because j has the value 0, A[1][0] should be set to 0. This eliminates (C).

   Finally, examine the value at A[1][1]. This value is set when k = 1 and j = 1. Because k % j has the value 0, A[1][1] should be set to 1. This eliminates (D).

   Choice (E) is correct.

26. **E**   Execute the recursive call on step at a time. When mystery(456789) is called, the first executed line is System.out.print(num % 100). In Java, the % symbol refers to the remainder when the first term is divided by the second. Since num = 456789, the remainder when dividing by 100 is the last two digits, 89. Therefore, the program will print 89. Eliminate any choice that does not print 89: (A), (C), and (D). Now go to the if statement, for which the condition is (num / 100 != 0). Since 456789 / 100 = 4567 (rounding toward 0), execute the if statement, which is mystery(num / 100), i.e. mystery(4567). Execute this method call. The first executed line of mystery 4567 is System.out.print(num % 100), i.e. System.out.print(4567 % 100). Since the remainder of 4567 % 100 is 67, the program prints 67 and displays 8967. Now go to the if statement, which is if (num / 100 != 0). Since 4567 / 100 (rounded toward 0) is 45, execute the if statement, mystery (num / 100), i.e. mystery(45). The first executed line of mystery(45) is System.out.print(num % 100), i.e. System.out.print(45 % 100). Since the remainder of 45 / 100 is 45, the program prints 45 and displays 896745. This is (B). Check to see whether anything else is printed. The if statement says if (num / 100 != 0). Since 45 / 100 (rounding toward 0) is 0, don't execute the if statement. Go to the next statement, which is System.out.print(num % 100). Since num % 100 is 45, print 45. More is printed than what is indicated by (B), so eliminate (B). The correct answer is (E). [Note that the program will complete the execution of mystery(4567) and print 67, then complete mystery(456789) and print 89, giving the output indicated by (E).]

27. **D**   A good set of test data exercises every conditional test in the code including cases that generate errors.

In the method mystery, a good set of test cases must include, at the minimum, data that allow each of the return statements to be executed.

x > 0 and y = <anything>

x <= 0 and y > 0

x <= 0 and y < 0

x <= 0 and y = 0 (the error condition)

Only (D) meets all four of these criteria.

28. **B**   Test the method using a particular array of integers. For example, consider the array {2, 3, 6, 0, 1}. Execute the method with this array as the parameter numList. Initialize n = numList.length – 1 = 5 – 1 = 4. Now go to the for loop, which is an enhanced for loop. Go through each index of numList and one at a time, assign each index to k. Let k = 0. The condition on the if statement is (numList[n] > numList[k]). Since numList[4] = 1 is not greater than numList[0] = 2, skip the if statement. Increment k to get k = 1. Go to the if statement. Since numList[4] = 1 is not greater than numList[1] = 3, skip the if statement. Increment k to get k = 2. Go to the if statement. Since numList[4] = 1 is not greater than numList[2] = 6, skip the if statement. Increment k to get k = 2. Go to the if statement. Since numList[4] = 1 is greater than numList[3] = 0, execute the if statement. Set n = k = 3.

The correct answer, therefore, is (B). Increment k to get k = 4. Go to the if statement. Since num-List[4] = 1 is not greater itself, skip the if statement. Since that is the last index of numList, end the for loop. Now return numList[n] = numList[3] = 0. This is not the largest value in the array, so eliminate (A). This is the least value in the array, so keep (B). This is not the index of the largest value in the array, so eliminate (C). This is not the index of the least value in the array, so eliminate (D). This is not the number of indexes whose values are less than numList[n], so eliminate (E). The correct answer is (B).

29. **B** Go through each choice one at a time and determine whether each will give the intended result: replacing any instances of old with instances of new. Choice (A) may look good initially. However, the condition of the if statement uses the assignment "=" rather than the Boolean "==". Similarly, the if statement itself uses the Boolean rather than the assignment. Therefore, this is not proper syntax. Eliminate choice (A).

Choice (B) uses a for loop of go through each index of arr. Then, if the value at any index is equal to old, it is changed to new. Keep this choice.

Choice (C) uses a while loop that terminates at the first index for while the value is not old. Since there may be some instances later, this is not correct. Eliminate (C).

Choice (D) uses a for loop to go through each index of arr but changes all values to new rather than using a conditional statement. Eliminate (D).

Similar to (D), (E) uses a while loop that terminates at the first instance of an index whose value is not old. Eliminate (E). Therefore, the correct answer is (B).

30. **E** The SalesPerson vincent is a CommissionedSalesPerson, so follow the coding of the CommissionedSalesPerson. Execute Vincent.sale() by following the CommissionedSalesPerson method sale(). Since the first command is System.out.print("greet "), the output must begin with this word. The next command is pitch(). Even though is called by the super class, since vincent is a CommissionedSalesPerson, default to the CommissionedSalesPerson pitch() method. The first command is super.pitch(). Now go to SalesPerson pitch(), which has one command: System.out.print("pitch "), so the second word of the output must be pitch. Now complete the execution of CommissionedSalesPerson pitch(), which includes one addition command: System.out.print("close "). Since the next word of the output must be "close", eliminate (A), (C), and (D). Now complete the execution of the CommissionedSalesPerson sale() method, which has one remaining command: System.out.print("record "). Since the next and final word of the output must be "record", eliminate (B). The correct answer is (E).

31. **E** Go through each of the possible constructors and determine whether each is legal. Constructor I takes three integers and a String as parameters. It then assigns the three integers to height, width, and length, respectively. However, these are private variables in another class, even one which in-

herits from the superclass. Therefore, this is illegal. Eliminate any choices that includes I: (A), (C), and (D). Constructor II also takes three integers and a String as parameters. It correctly assigns the integers to the private variables using the constructor method. It then assigns the String to the color, which is part of, and therefore accessible by, the subclass. Therefore, this is legal. Eliminate any choice that does not include II: (B). Only one choice remains. To see why constructor III is legal, realize that a constructor need not give each variable a value to be legal. The correct answer is (E).

32. **C** Consider each possible reverse method. Test using an array integer with elements 1, 2, and 3. The end result should be 3, 2, and 1. Start with I. This method takes the ArrayList<Object> q as a parameter. It creates a new ArrayList<Object> s. Go to the while loop. The condition is that q.size() != 0. Since the size of q is 3, enter the while loop. The lone statement in the while loop is s.add(0, q.remove(0)). This elements the object returned by q.remove(0) to s at index 0. The method call q.remove(0) removes the Object at index 0, moving all object at later indexes to the left in order to fill in the gap and return the removed object. In this case, the object at index 0 of q is the Integer 1. This object is removed from q, leaving the list with two Objects: 2 and 3. The Integer 1 is also added to the list s at index 0, leaving s as a list with one Object: 1. Now, q.size() = 2. Since it is still not 0, execute the while loop again. Remove the Object of q at index 0, leaving it with one Object: 3. Add the removed object to the s at index 0, moving Objects at later indexes to the right, leaving it with two Objects: 2 and 1. Since q.size() now equals 1, execute the while loop again. Once again remove the object from q at 0 and add it to s at 0. Thus, the Integer Object 3 is removed from q, leaving it with no objects, and added to s, leaving it with 3 Objects: 3, 2, and 1. Since q.size() is now equal to 0, do not execute the while loop again. Return the ArrayList s, which is 3, 2, 1. Since this is the reverse of the original, I works as intended. Eliminate any choice that does not include I: (D).

Now look at II. This method creates a new ArrayList<Object> s. Go to the for loop. The for loop initializes k = 0. The condition is that k < q.size(). Since q is the Integers 1, 2, and 3, q.size() = 3, so execute the for loop. The lone command in the for loop is s.add(0, q.remove(0)). When there is only one parameter, the add() adds the Object parameter to the end. Therefore, this removes 1 from the list q and adds it to the list s. Thus q has the Objects 2 and 3, and s has the Object 1. Increment k to get k = 1. Since q.size() is now 2, the for loop condition is still true, so execute the for loop. The command s.add(0, q.remove(0)) removes the Object 2 from q and adds it to the end of s. Thus, the list q has the Object 3 and s has the Objects 1 and 2. Increment k to get k = 2. Since q.size() is now 1, the for loop condition is loop. Do not execute the for loop again. Return s, which is 2 and 1. Since this is not the reversal of the original, eliminate any choice that includes II: (B) and (E).

Finally, look at III. This method creates an Object obj. The if statement has the condition that q.size() != 0. Since q is the list 1, 2, and 3, q.size() is 3 and the condition is true, so execute the if statement. The first command is obj = q.remove(0). This assigns the Object at index 0, the

Integer 1, to obj and removes it from q. The next command is the recursive call reverse(q). Execute the call for the ArrayList<Object> q with Integer Objects 2 and 3. The a new Object obj is created that is independent from the old and only exists in this execution of reverse. Since q.size() is still not 0, execute the if statement. Execute the command obj = q.remove(0) by removing 2 from q and assign obj with 2. Now execute the recursive call reverse(q) with q now the list with only the Integer 3. Now create new Object obj. Since q.size() is 1, execute the if statement. The command obj = q.remove(0) removes the Integer 3 from q as assigns it to obj, leaving q with no Objects. The recursive call reverse(q) uses the empty ArrayList q. This method call creates a Object obj. Since q.size() is 0, skip the if statement and execute the return statement by returning an empty ArrayList. Going back to the previous remove call q is assigned this empty ArrayList. The next command is q.add(obj). Since, in this call, obj is 3, 3 is added to the end the q, resulting in the list with Integer 3. This list is returned to the previous call of the method. In this call, obj = 2. This obj is added to the end of the list, leaving the list with Integers 3 and 2. This list is returned to the prior call. In this call obj = 1, so 1 is add to q to get a list with Integers 3, 2, and 1. This list is returned. There is no prior call so the final return is a list with Integers 3, 2, and 1. Since this is the reverse, this version of the method works as intended. Eliminate (A). The correct answer is (C).

33. **B** Go through each line of code one at a time. This will be especially important in this example since remove() method changes the indexes. First, create values, an empty ArrayList of Integers. Next add 5 to the list. Then, add 3 to the end. And then add 2 to the end. Next, add another 2 to the end. Then, add 6 to the end. And then add 3 to the end. Next, add 9 to the end. Then, add to the end, and then add 1 to the end. The List now contains [5, 3, 2, 2, 6, 3, 9, 2, 1]. Now, go to the for loop. Initialize j = 0. Since values.size() returns the number of elements in the list, values.size() = 9. Since j < values.size(), execute the for loop. Since values.get(j) returns the element at index j, value.get(j) = 5. (Remember that the indexes begin with 0.) As this is not equal to 2, do not execute the instruction in the if statement. Now add 1 to j to get j = 1. This is still less that values.size(), so execute the for loop. This time, value.get(j) = 3. Since this is not equal to 2, do not execute the instruction in the if statement. Now add 1 to j to get j = 2. This is still less that values.size(), so execute the for loop. This time, value.get(j) = 2, so execute the instruction in the if statement. The statement values.remove(j) removes the element at index j and moves each of the following elements to the previous index. Therefore the List now contains [5, 3, 2, 6, 3, 9, 2, 1]. Note that values.size() is now 8. Now add 1 to j to get j = 3. This is still less that values.size(), so execute the for loop. Execute value.get(j). However, remember that the List has change. The element that is at index 3 is no longer the second 2 but rather the 6. Since this is not equal to 2, do not execute the instruction in the if statement. Now add 1 to j to get j = 4. This is still less that values.size(), so execute the for loop. This time, value.get(j) = 3. Since this is not equal to 2, do not execute the instruction in the if statement. Add 1 to j to get j = 5. This is still less that values.size(), so execute the for loop. This time, value.get(j) = 9. Since this is not equal to 2, do not execute the instruction in the if statement.

Add 1 to j to get j = 6. This is still less that values.size(), so execute the for loop. This time, value. get(j) = 2, so execute the instruction in the if statement. Remove the 2. The List now contains [5, 3, 2, 6, 3, 9, 1]. Note that values.size() is now 7. Add 1 to j to get j = 7. Since this is no longer less that values.size(), stop executing the for loop. The final version of the List is [5, 3, 2, 6, 3, 9, 1]. The correct answer is (B).

34. **B** Check options I, II, and III one at a time. I uses the shortened for loop notation. Remember that two dimensional array c is actually an array a one dimensional arrays, i.e. an array of the rows of the two dimensional array. Therefore, for(int[] row: c) goes through each one dimensional array in the two dimensional array c and refers to it as the variable row. In the for loop, it sets the int max equal to the return of the 1Dmax(row), which is the maximum value of each row. However, since it automatically changes it, the result will simply be the maximum value of the last row rather than the maximum value of the two dimensional array. Therefore, I does not work as intended. Eliminate any answer that includes I: (A), (C), and (E). Now try II. However, II also automatically changes the value of max at every row. Therefore, it would also result in the max being set at the maximum value of the value row, rather than the maximum value of the whole two dimensional array. Eliminate any answer choice that includes II: (D). Only one choice remains. To see why III works, not that sets the value of max at the maximum value of c[0], which is the first row, and only changes the value if max is less than the maximum value of a particular row. Therefore, the correct answer is (B).

35. **E** Use the numList given as a test for each version. Try Version 1. The outer for loop initiates k = 0. The inner for loop initiates j = 0. Go to the if statement, which says if (numList[j] = 0). Since numList[0] is not 0, skip the if statement. Increment j to get j = 1. Because j > k, end the inner for loop and increment k to get k = 1. The inner for loop initiates j = 0. Go to the if statement, which says if (numList[j] = 0). As numList[0] is not 0, skip the if statement. Increment j to get j = 1. Since numList[1] is not 0, skip the if statement. Increment j to get j = 2. Since j > k, terminate the inner for loop and increment k to get k = 2. The inner for loop initiates j = 0. Go to the if statement, which says if (numList[j] = 0). Since numList[0] is not 0, skip the if statement. Increment j to get j = 1. Because numList[1] is not 0, skip the if statement. Increment j to get j = 2. As numList[2] is 0, execute the if statement, which says that count[k] = count[k] + 1, so count[0] = 0 + 1 = 1. Increment j to get j = 3. Since j > k, end the inner for loop and increment k to get k = 3. The inner for loop initiates j = 0. Go to the if statement, which says if (numList[j] = 0). Since numList[0] is not 0, skip the if statement. Increment j to get j = 1. Because numList[1] is not 0, skip the if statement. Increment j to get j = 2. As numList[2] is 0, execute the if statement, which says that count[k] = count[k] + 1, so count[3] = 0 + 1 = 1. Increment j to get j = 3. Since numList[3] is not 0, skip the if statement and increment j to get j = 3. Because j > k, end the inner for loop and increment k to get k = 4. The inner for loop initiates j = 0. Go to the if statement, which says if (numList[j] = 0). As numList[0] is not 0, skip the if statement. Increment j to get j = 1. Since numList[1] is not 0, skip the if statement. Increment j to get j = 2. Because numList[2] is 0, execute the if statement, which says that count[k] = count[k] + 1, so count[4] = 0 + 1 = 1. Increment j to get j = 3. Since

numList[3] is not 0, skip the if statement and increment j to get j = 4. As numList[4] is 0, execute the if statement, which says that count[k] = count[k] + 1, so count[4] = 1 + 1 = 2. Increment j to get j = 5. Because j > k, end the inner for loop and increment k to get k = 5. The inner for loop initiates j = 0. Go to the if statement, which says if (numList[j] = 0). Since numList[0] is not 0, skip the if statement. Increment j to get j = 1. As numList[1] is not 0, skip the if statement. Increment j to get j = 2. Because numList[2] is 0, execute the if statement, which says that count[k] = count[k] + 1, so count[5] = 0 + 1 = 1. Increment j to get j = 3. Since numList[3] is not 0, skip the if statement and increment j to get j = 4. As numList[4] is 0, execute the if statement, which says that count[k] = count[k] + 1, so count[5] = 1 + 1 = 2. Increment j to get j = 5. Because numList[5] is 0, execute the if statement, which says that count[k] = count[k] + 1, so count[5] = 2 + 1 =3. Increment j to get j = 6. Since j > k, end the inner for loop and increment k to get k = 6. The inner for loop initiates j = 0. Go to the if statement, which says if (numList[j] = 0). As numList[0] is not 0, skip the if statement. Increment j to get j = 1. Because numList[1] is not 0, skip the if statement. Increment j to get j = 2. Since numList[2] is 0, execute the if statement, which says that count[k] = count[k] + 1. This would attempt to execute count[6] = count [6] + 1. However, because the count has 6 elements, the highest index is 5, so this would throw an ArrayIndexOutOfBounds exeception. Eliminate the choices that says Version 1 works as intended: (A), (B), and (C).

If Version 2 works as intended, the answer is (D); otherwise the answer is (E). Test Version 2. The for loop initiates k = 0. Go to the if statement, which says if(numList[k] = 0). Since numList[0] is not 0, do not execute the if statement but instead execute the else, which says count[k] = count[k - 1]. This attempts to execute count[0] = count[-1]. However, since there are not negative indexes, this also causes an ArrayIndexOutOfBoundsException. Therefore, the answer is (E).

36. **C** Go through each choice one at a time.

Choice (A) correctly assigned Bedrooms, Bathrooms, PetsAllowed, and Rent to the class Apartment. However, making each of these four a class is unneccesary, since they each only require on value. Eliminate (A).

Choice (B) assigns the subclass Apartment to each of the classes Bedroom, Bathroom, PetsAllowed, and Rent. However, these four are characteristics of an apartment rather than an apartment being a characteristic of these four. Therefore, an Apartment class should contain these four attributes rather than the other way around. Eliminate (B).

Choice (C) is similar to choice (A) but bedrooms, bathrooms, petsAllowed, and rent are simple variables, which is a more minimal design. Keep this choice.

Choice (D) makes the five unrelated. These characteristics should be related as the number of bedrooms, the number of bathrooms, whether pets are allowed, and the rent are all characteristics of an apartment. Therefore, eliminate (D).

Choice (E) creates a chain of subclasses. This makes Rent a characteristic of whether pets are allows, which is a characteristic of the number of bathrooms, which is a characteristic of the number of bedrooms. This is not correct, so eliminate (E).

Therefore, the correct answer is (C).

37. **C** If a method in a subclass has the same name as a method in a superclass, it must have exactly the same method heading. I and III have different headings, but II has the same. Therefore, only II can be added. The correct answer is (C).

38. **A** The question asks for possible combinations of max and the number of executions of each of the marked statements. Look to see how, if at all, the three relate to each other. Statement A and Statement B are both contained within the for loop. However, Statement A is contained within an if statement in the for loop and Statement B is not. Therefore, for each iteration of the for loop, Statement B will be executed but Statement A may not be. Therefore, the number of executions of Statement A cannot exceed the number of executions of Statement B. In Combination II, the number of executions of A does exceed the number of executions of B, so eliminate any choice that includes Combination II: (C) and (E).

The value of max relates to the elements contained within the array set, but there does not seem to be a direction connection to the indexes, so there does not seem to be any connection between this value of the number of executions of the two marked statements. Test the two remaining combinations with particular examples to determine whether they are valid. To test Combination I, find a way for Statement A to be executed twice and Statement B to be executed three times. This means that the for loop has to be executed three times and the if condition would have to be false one time. To make sure the if for loop is executed three times, keep at values in set less than max and make sure that set.length = 3. To make sure that the if condition is false once, make sure that the value of m is greater than the value of set[k] exactly one time. Let max = 8 and set = {1, 2, 1}. Set m and count equal to 0. Enter the for loop, which sets k = 0. Since 0 is less than set.length, which is 3, and set[0] is less than max, execute the for loop. Since set[0], which is 1, is greater than or equal to m, which is 0, execute the if statement, which sets m equal set[0], which is 1. Statement A is executed the first time. The if statement ends and Statement B is executed the first time. At the end of the for loop, increment k to get k = 1. Since 1 is less than set.length, which is 3, and set[1] is less than max, execute the for loop. Since set[1], which is 2, is greater than or equal to m, which is 1, execute the if statement, which sets m equal set[1], which is 2. Statement A is executed for the second time. The if statement ends and Statement B is executed for the second time. At the end of the for loop, increment k to get k = 2. Since 2 is less than set.length, which is 3, and set[2] is less than max, execute the for loop. Since set[2], which is 1, is less than m, which is 1, do not execute the if statement. Skip to after the if statement, where Statement B is executed the third time. Increment k to get k = 3. Since k is not less than set.length, end the for loop. Thus max = 8, Statement A is executed twice and Statement B is executed three times, so Combination I is valid. Eliminate any choice that does not include Combination I: (B).

Now, attempt to find a valid combination of Combination III. In this case, the for loop has to be executed four times without the if condition ever being true. To makes sure the for loop is executed four times, let set.length equal 4 with every value less than max. To make sure the if condition is always false make sure the value of m is always greater than the value of set[k] for all k. However, m is initialized at 0 and the precondition indicates that set has no negative values. Since all non-negative values are greater than or equal to 0, the if condition would have to be true at at least at the first execution of the for loop. Therefore, Combination III is not valid. Eliminate any choice that includes III: (D). The correct answer is (A).

39. **D** The method is intended to insert an int at a given index, pushing ints to the right. In the returned array, indexes 0 through n-1 should contain the same values as the indexes 0 through n-1 of the original array, the index n should contain the value m, and the indexes n+1 and above should contain the same values as the indexes n and above in the original array. Go through each of the choices.

Choice (A) changes the condition on the if statement to (k > n). The consequent on the if statement is to set temp[k] = arr[k]. The values should only be copied to the same index for indexes less than n, so eliminate (A).

Similarly, the value at index n in arr should be pushed to index n+1 in the return array. Therefore, the inequality sign should not be changed to <=. Eliminate (B).

Choice (C) would not only places values at the wrong indexes but would also cause an ArrayIndexOutOfBoundException. When k = arr.length – 1, the command temp[k] = arr[k+1] would call arr[arr.length]. Since indexes begin at 0, the last index of an array is always one less than the length of the array. Thus the index equal to the length of the array is out of bounds. Eliminate (C).

Making the change is (D) would cause the int m to be placed at index n in the temp array. This is the intention of the method, so keep (D).

Choice (E) returns arr instead of temp. Since no changes are made directly to arr, the return of this method would be an unaltered copy of the original array. Since this is not intended, eliminate (E).

The correct answer is (D).

40. **E** The easiest way to solve this problem is to use DeMorgan's law. This states that

```
!(p && q) is equivalent to !p || !q
```

Or, negating both sides

```
P && q is equivalent to !(!p || !q).
```

In this problem, set p to (X > Y) and q to (Y > Z).

```
!p becomes (X <= Y) and !q becomes (Y <= Z).
```

Finally, !(!p || !q) becomes !((X <= Y) || (Y <= Z)).

Therefore, (E) is correct.

Note that although (A) appears to be correct because it follows the transitive property of inequality, consider the two Boolean equations after setting X to 6, Y to 8, and Z to 4.

(6 > 8) && (8 > 4) is false, but 6 > 4 is true.

Section II: Free Reponse Questions

1. (a)
```
public Screen(int  width, int height)

{
    numCols = width;
    data = new ArrayList<Pixel>[height];
    for (int k = 0; k < height; k++)
        data[k] = new ArrayList<Pixel>;
}
```
   (b)
```
public Pixel pixelAt(int row, int col)

{
    ArrayList<Pixel> theRow = data[row];
    for (int k = 0; k < theRow.size; k++)
    {
        Pixel p = theRow.get(k);
        If (p.getCol() == col)
            return p;
    }
    return null;
}
```
   (c)
```
public void pixelOn(int row, int col)

{
    Pixel newPx1 = new Pixel(row, col);
    Pixel p;
    ArrayList<Pixel> theRow = data[row];
    int index = 0;
    for (int k = 0; k < data[row].size(); k++)
        {
            if (col > data[row].get(k).getCol())
                index++;
        }
    data[row].add(index, p);
}
```

2. (a) Sample Answer # 1:

```
public int getTotalMarbles()
{
    int marbles = 0;
    for (int k = 0; k < sets.length(); k++)
    {
        marbles += sets.get(k).getNumber();
    }
    return marbles;
}
```

Sample Answer # 2:

```
public int getTotalMarbles()
{
    int marbles;
    for (int k : sets)
    {
        marbles = marbles + sets.get(k).getNumber();
    }
    return marbles;
}
```

The goal of the method is to return the sum of the total number of marbles and return 0 if there are no marbles. Begin by declaring an int type to store the total number of marbles counted thus far. In this case, we called it marbles. Give marbles initial value 0, since no marbles have been counted so far. Note that this is optional, since the default value on type int is 0. Now, create a for loop for to go through each element in the ArrayList sets. To do this, use either a standard for loop or an enhanced for loop. For the standard for loop, the first index is 0, so, in the for loop statement, initialize int k = 0, to represent the index of the ArrayList. Increase the index by 1 until the index is equal to the length of the ArrayList. (Note that to count the length, begin with one rather than 0, so the last array element has index length() – 1.) The for statement becomes (int k = 0; k < sets.length(); k++). To use an enhanced for loop, simply use for (int k: sets). This automatically goes through each index of sets and calls each index k. Note that if sets is empty, sets.length() = 0, so the for loop will not be executed. In this case, the method will return the initial value of marbles, which is 0. This fulfills the requirement for that case. If the ArrayList is not empty, then for each index, the number of marbles in that index's MarbleSet should be added to marbles. To do this execute either marbles = marbles + sets.get(k).getNumber() or the shortcut notation marbles += sets.get(k).getNumber(). Note that sets[k].getNumber() is not valid, since set[k] denote an element of a simple array rather than an ArrayList. This is all that is needed of the for loop. Close the for loop, and return the value of marbles.

(b)   Sample Answer # 1:

```java
public int removeColor(String marbleCol)
{
  int num = 0;
  for (int k = 0; k < sets.length(); k++)
  {
     if (sets.get(k).getColor().equals(marbleCol))
     {
          num += sets.get(k).getNumber();
          sets.remove(k);
     }
  }
  return num;
}
```

Sample Answer # 2:

```java
public int removeColor(String marbleCol)
{
  int num;
  for (int k : sets)
  {
     if (sets.get(k).getColor().equals(marbleCol))
     {
          num = num + sets.get(k).getNumber();
          sets.remove(k);
     }
  }
  return num;
}
```

Sample Answer # 3:

```java
public int removeColor(String marbleCol)
{
  int num = 0;
  for (int k = 0; k < sets.length(); k++)
  {
     if (sets.get(k).getColor().equals(marbleCol))
     {
          num += sets.remove(k).getNumber();
     }
  }
  return num;
}
```

The method requires an integer return. Let the first statement of the method be to create this integer and the final be to return it. We have called this integer num. Since no marbles have been counted yet, num can be initialized as int num = 0 or simply as int num since the default initial value of an int is 0. Now, go through each MarbleSet in the MarbleCollection using a for loop. This could be done using a standard for loop, for (int k = 0; k < sets.length(); k++). Remember that the index for an ArrayList begin with 0 but the length() is determined by counting beginning with 1, so the final element of the ArrayList is at index length() − 1. The following enhanced for loop can also be used as shorthand: for (int k: sets). Action should only be taken in the event that the color of the MarbleSet matches marbleCol, so use an if statement. The condition should be sets. get(k).getColor().equals(marbleCol). Note that sets[k].getColor().equals(marbleCol) is not valid since sets[k] is the index for a simple array rather than an ArrayList. Therefore, the get method of the ArrayList class is needed. Also note that sets.get(k).getColor() == (marbleCol), since the == operator uses the Object definition, which requires that the two be the same Object rather than simply have the same information. Therefore the equals method of the String class is needed. Should the if condition be meet, two goals are to be met. The first is that the number of marbles in the set be added to num. This can be either either by the statement num = num + sets.get(k).getNumber() or the shortcut notation num += sets.get(k).getNumber(). The other goal is that the MarbleSet be removed. This can be done using the remove method of the ArrayList class with the statement sets. remove(k). Note that the remove method returns the removed element. Therefore, the two goals could also be done in one statement: num = num + sets.remove(k).getNumber() or num += sets. remove(k).getNumber(). Remember to close the if statement, then remember to close the for loop. Return num.

3. (a)
```
public class BinaryInt

{
  private ArrayList<int> digits;
  public BinaryInt()
  ( /* implementation not needed */ )
  public BinaryInt (int decimalValue)
  ( /* implementation not needed */ )
  public BinaryInt add (BinaryInt other)
  ( /* implementation not needed */ )
  public String toString()
  ( /* implementation not needed */ )
  public int compareTo(BinaryInt other)
  ( /* implementation not needed */ )

}
```

(b)
```java
public BinaryInt(int decimalValue)
{
    digits = new ArrayList<int>();
    while (decimalValue > 0)
    {
        digits.add(0, new Integer(decimalValue % 2));
        decimalValue / = 2;
    }
}
```

(c)
```java
public static void Test()
{
    BinaryInt a1 =
        new BinaryInt(2314279623);
    BinaryInt a2 =
        new BinaryInt(3236550123);
    BinaryInt aSum = a1.add(a2);
    BinaryInt b1 =
        new BinaryInt(3412579010);
    BinaryInt b2 =
        new BinaryInt(2128250735);
    BinaryInt bSum = b1.add(b2);
    if (aSum.compareTo(bSum) > 0)
        System.out.print(aSum.toString());
    else
        System.out.print(bSum.toString());
}
```

4.   Possible Solution # 1:

```java
public class Parabola
{

    private int a;
    private int b;
    private int c;

    public Parabola(int a; int b; int c)
    {
        this.a = a;
        this.b = b;
        this.c = c;
    }

    public double getAxis()
    {
        return (double) (-1 * b / (2*a));
    }

    public boolean isOnGraph(int x, int y)
    {
        return (y == a*x*x + b*x + c);
    }
}
```

Possible Solution # 2:

```java
public class Parabola
{

    private int a;
    private int b;
    private int c;

    public Parabola(int myA, int myB, int C)
    {
        a = myA;
        b = myB;
        c = myC;
    }

    public double getAxis()
    {
        int num = -1 * b;
        int den = 2 * a;
        double axis = (double)(num / den);
return axis;
    }

    public boolean isOnGraph(int x, int y)
    {
        int rightSide = a*x*x + b*x + c;
        boolean onGraph = (y == rightSide);
return (onGraph);
    }
}
```

The class should have three integer instance variables, *a*, *b*, and *c*. The constructor class has to take in three integer parameters to represent these instance variables. This can be done two different ways. One possible way is to call the parameter variables in the declaration something other than a, b, and c. When you do this, you can simply set the instance variables equal to the parameters, as shown in Possible Solution # 2. This can also be accomplished by also calling the parameter variables. However, in this case, in order set the instance variables equal to the parameter, refer to the instance variables using the Keyword this, as shown in Possible Solution # 1. Now define the getAxis method. This method needs no parameters but must return a double equal to $-b/2a$. Remember that the expression $-b/2a$ is not proper Java coding. To negative an integer, multiply it by -1, so $-b$ must be represent by $-1 * b$. Also, a Java complier would interpret 2a as an undeclared variable rather than 2 times a, so $2a$ must be represented by 2*a. Thus, $-b/2a$ must be represent in Java as $(-1 * b / (2*a))$. This can be done in one line, as in Possible Solution # 1, or in several steps, as in Possible Solution # 2. In either case, remember to cast the division of two integers as a double. Otherwise, the compiler will recognize this as integer division, which will drop an remainder and round down to the nearest integer rather than return a double. Now create the method isOnGraph. This must take two integer parameters, x and y, and return a boolean. It should return true if the values *x* and *y* satisfy the equation $y = ax^2 + bx + c$. Remember that raising a number to an exponent is the same as multiplying it by itself, so this can be rewritten as $y = axx + bx + c$. To test this in Java, uses the boolean equal sign, ==, and the multiplication sign, *, to make the boolean statement y == a*x*x + b*x + c. This can be done in one line, as in Possible Solution # 1, or in several steps, as in Possible Solution # 2.

The Princeton Review®

Completely darken bubbles with a No. 2 pencil. If you make a mistake, be sure to erase mark completely. Erase all stray marks.

1.

YOUR NAME: _____
(Print)   Last   First   M.I.

SIGNATURE: _____   DATE: __ / __ / __

HOME ADDRESS: _____
(Print)   Number and Street

_____
City   State   Zip Code

PHONE NO.: _____

IMPORTANT: Please fill in these boxes exactly as shown on the back cover of your test book.

2. TEST FORM

_____

6. DATE OF BIRTH

Month		Day		Year	
○ JAN					
○ FEB	⓪	⓪	⓪	⓪	
○ MAR	①	①	①	①	
○ APR	②	②	②	②	
○ MAY	③	③	③	③	
○ JUN		④	④	④	
○ JUL		⑤	⑤	⑤	
○ AUG		⑥	⑥	⑥	
○ SEP		⑦	⑦	⑦	
○ OCT		⑧	⑧	⑧	
○ NOV		⑨	⑨	⑨	
○ DEC					

3. TEST CODE

⓪	Ⓐ	Ⓙ	⓪	⓪
①	Ⓑ	Ⓚ	①	①
②	Ⓒ	Ⓛ	②	②
③	Ⓓ	Ⓜ	③	③
④	Ⓔ	Ⓝ	④	④
⑤	Ⓕ	Ⓞ	⑤	⑤
⑥	Ⓖ	Ⓟ	⑥	⑥
⑦	Ⓗ	Ⓠ	⑦	⑦
⑧	Ⓘ	Ⓡ	⑧	⑧
⑨			⑨	⑨

4. REGISTRATION NUMBER

⓪ ⓪ ⓪ ⓪ ⓪ ⓪ ⓪
① ① ① ① ① ① ①
② ② ② ② ② ② ②
③ ③ ③ ③ ③ ③ ③
④ ④ ④ ④ ④ ④ ④
⑤ ⑤ ⑤ ⑤ ⑤ ⑤ ⑤
⑥ ⑥ ⑥ ⑥ ⑥ ⑥ ⑥
⑦ ⑦ ⑦ ⑦ ⑦ ⑦ ⑦
⑧ ⑧ ⑧ ⑧ ⑧ ⑧ ⑧
⑨ ⑨ ⑨ ⑨ ⑨ ⑨ ⑨

7. GENDER

○ MALE
○ FEMALE

The Princeton Review®

5. YOUR NAME

First 4 letters of last name   FIRST INIT   MID INIT

Ⓐ Ⓐ Ⓐ Ⓐ   Ⓐ Ⓐ
Ⓑ Ⓑ Ⓑ Ⓑ   Ⓑ Ⓑ
Ⓒ Ⓒ Ⓒ Ⓒ   Ⓒ Ⓒ
Ⓓ Ⓓ Ⓓ Ⓓ   Ⓓ Ⓓ
Ⓔ Ⓔ Ⓔ Ⓔ   Ⓔ Ⓔ
Ⓕ Ⓕ Ⓕ Ⓕ   Ⓕ Ⓕ
Ⓖ Ⓖ Ⓖ Ⓖ   Ⓖ Ⓖ
Ⓗ Ⓗ Ⓗ Ⓗ   Ⓗ Ⓗ
Ⓘ Ⓘ Ⓘ Ⓘ   Ⓘ Ⓘ
Ⓙ Ⓙ Ⓙ Ⓙ   Ⓙ Ⓙ
Ⓚ Ⓚ Ⓚ Ⓚ   Ⓚ Ⓚ
Ⓛ Ⓛ Ⓛ Ⓛ   Ⓛ Ⓛ
Ⓜ Ⓜ Ⓜ Ⓜ   Ⓜ Ⓜ
Ⓝ Ⓝ Ⓝ Ⓝ   Ⓝ Ⓝ
Ⓞ Ⓞ Ⓞ Ⓞ   Ⓞ Ⓞ
Ⓟ Ⓟ Ⓟ Ⓟ   Ⓟ Ⓟ
Ⓠ Ⓠ Ⓠ Ⓠ   Ⓠ Ⓠ
Ⓡ Ⓡ Ⓡ Ⓡ   Ⓡ Ⓡ
Ⓢ Ⓢ Ⓢ Ⓢ   Ⓢ Ⓢ
Ⓣ Ⓣ Ⓣ Ⓣ   Ⓣ Ⓣ
Ⓤ Ⓤ Ⓤ Ⓤ   Ⓤ Ⓤ
Ⓥ Ⓥ Ⓥ Ⓥ   Ⓥ Ⓥ
Ⓦ Ⓦ Ⓦ Ⓦ   Ⓦ Ⓦ
Ⓧ Ⓧ Ⓧ Ⓧ   Ⓧ Ⓧ
Ⓨ Ⓨ Ⓨ Ⓨ   Ⓨ Ⓨ
Ⓩ Ⓩ Ⓩ Ⓩ   Ⓩ Ⓩ

---

1. Ⓐ Ⓑ Ⓒ Ⓓ Ⓔ
2. Ⓐ Ⓑ Ⓒ Ⓓ Ⓔ
3. Ⓐ Ⓑ Ⓒ Ⓓ Ⓔ
4. Ⓐ Ⓑ Ⓒ Ⓓ Ⓔ
5. Ⓐ Ⓑ Ⓒ Ⓓ Ⓔ
6. Ⓐ Ⓑ Ⓒ Ⓓ Ⓔ
7. Ⓐ Ⓑ Ⓒ Ⓓ Ⓔ
8. Ⓐ Ⓑ Ⓒ Ⓓ Ⓔ
9. Ⓐ Ⓑ Ⓒ Ⓓ Ⓔ
10. Ⓐ Ⓑ Ⓒ Ⓓ Ⓔ

11. Ⓐ Ⓑ Ⓒ Ⓓ Ⓔ
12. Ⓐ Ⓑ Ⓒ Ⓓ Ⓔ
13. Ⓐ Ⓑ Ⓒ Ⓓ Ⓔ
14. Ⓐ Ⓑ Ⓒ Ⓓ Ⓔ
15. Ⓐ Ⓑ Ⓒ Ⓓ Ⓔ
16. Ⓐ Ⓑ Ⓒ Ⓓ Ⓔ
17. Ⓐ Ⓑ Ⓒ Ⓓ Ⓔ
18. Ⓐ Ⓑ Ⓒ Ⓓ Ⓔ
19. Ⓐ Ⓑ Ⓒ Ⓓ Ⓔ
20. Ⓐ Ⓑ Ⓒ Ⓓ Ⓔ

21. Ⓐ Ⓑ Ⓒ Ⓓ Ⓔ
22. Ⓐ Ⓑ Ⓒ Ⓓ Ⓔ
23. Ⓐ Ⓑ Ⓒ Ⓓ Ⓔ
24. Ⓐ Ⓑ Ⓒ Ⓓ Ⓔ
25. Ⓐ Ⓑ Ⓒ Ⓓ Ⓔ
26. Ⓐ Ⓑ Ⓒ Ⓓ Ⓔ
27. Ⓐ Ⓑ Ⓒ Ⓓ Ⓔ
28. Ⓐ Ⓑ Ⓒ Ⓓ Ⓔ
29. Ⓐ Ⓑ Ⓒ Ⓓ Ⓔ
30. Ⓐ Ⓑ Ⓒ Ⓓ Ⓔ

31. Ⓐ Ⓑ Ⓒ Ⓓ Ⓔ
32. Ⓐ Ⓑ Ⓒ Ⓓ Ⓔ
33. Ⓐ Ⓑ Ⓒ Ⓓ Ⓔ
34. Ⓐ Ⓑ Ⓒ Ⓓ Ⓔ
35. Ⓐ Ⓑ Ⓒ Ⓓ Ⓔ
36. Ⓐ Ⓑ Ⓒ Ⓓ Ⓔ
37. Ⓐ Ⓑ Ⓒ Ⓓ Ⓔ
38. Ⓐ Ⓑ Ⓒ Ⓓ Ⓔ
39. Ⓐ Ⓑ Ⓒ Ⓓ Ⓔ
40. Ⓐ Ⓑ Ⓒ Ⓓ Ⓔ

The Princeton Review®

Completely darken bubbles with a No. 2 pencil. If you make a mistake, be sure to erase mark completely. Erase all stray marks.

1.

YOUR NAME: _____
(Print)   Last   First   M.I.

SIGNATURE: _____   DATE: ___/___/___

HOME ADDRESS: _____
(Print)   Number and Street

_____
City   State   Zip Code

PHONE NO.: _____

IMPORTANT: Please fill in these boxes exactly as shown on the back cover of your test book.

2. TEST FORM

3. TEST CODE

0	Ⓐ	Ⓙ	0	0
1	Ⓑ	Ⓚ	1	1
2	Ⓒ	Ⓛ	2	2
3	Ⓓ	Ⓜ	3	3
4	Ⓔ	Ⓝ	4	4
5	Ⓕ	Ⓞ	5	5
6	Ⓖ	Ⓟ	6	6
7	Ⓗ	Ⓠ	7	7
8	Ⓘ	Ⓡ	8	8
9			9	9

4. REGISTRATION NUMBER

0	0	0	0	0	0	0
1	1	1	1	1	1	1
2	2	2	2	2	2	2
3	3	3	3	3	3	3
4	4	4	4	4	4	4
5	5	5	5	5	5	5
6	6	6	6	6	6	6
7	7	7	7	7	7	7
8	8	8	8	8	8	8
9	9	9	9	9	9	9

6. DATE OF BIRTH

Month	Day		Year	
◯ JAN				
◯ FEB	0	0	0	0
◯ MAR	1	1	1	1
◯ APR	2	2	2	2
◯ MAY	3	3	3	3
◯ JUN		4	4	4
◯ JUL		5	5	5
◯ AUG		6	6	6
◯ SEP		7	7	7
◯ OCT		8	8	8
◯ NOV		9	9	9
◯ DEC				

7. GENDER

◯ MALE
◯ FEMALE

The Princeton Review®

5. YOUR NAME

| First 4 letters of last name | | | | | FIRST INIT | MID INIT |

Ⓐ Ⓐ Ⓐ Ⓐ   Ⓐ Ⓐ
Ⓑ Ⓑ Ⓑ Ⓑ   Ⓑ Ⓑ
Ⓒ Ⓒ Ⓒ Ⓒ   Ⓒ Ⓒ
Ⓓ Ⓓ Ⓓ Ⓓ   Ⓓ Ⓓ
Ⓔ Ⓔ Ⓔ Ⓔ   Ⓔ Ⓔ
Ⓕ Ⓕ Ⓕ Ⓕ   Ⓕ Ⓕ
Ⓖ Ⓖ Ⓖ Ⓖ   Ⓖ Ⓖ
Ⓗ Ⓗ Ⓗ Ⓗ   Ⓗ Ⓗ
Ⓘ Ⓘ Ⓘ Ⓘ   Ⓘ Ⓘ
Ⓙ Ⓙ Ⓙ Ⓙ   Ⓙ Ⓙ
Ⓚ Ⓚ Ⓚ Ⓚ   Ⓚ Ⓚ
Ⓛ Ⓛ Ⓛ Ⓛ   Ⓛ Ⓛ
Ⓜ Ⓜ Ⓜ Ⓜ   Ⓜ Ⓜ
Ⓝ Ⓝ Ⓝ Ⓝ   Ⓝ Ⓝ
Ⓞ Ⓞ Ⓞ Ⓞ   Ⓞ Ⓞ
Ⓟ Ⓟ Ⓟ Ⓟ   Ⓟ Ⓟ
Ⓠ Ⓠ Ⓠ Ⓠ   Ⓠ Ⓠ
Ⓡ Ⓡ Ⓡ Ⓡ   Ⓡ Ⓡ
Ⓢ Ⓢ Ⓢ Ⓢ   Ⓢ Ⓢ
Ⓣ Ⓣ Ⓣ Ⓣ   Ⓣ Ⓣ
Ⓤ Ⓤ Ⓤ Ⓤ   Ⓤ Ⓤ
Ⓥ Ⓥ Ⓥ Ⓥ   Ⓥ Ⓥ
Ⓦ Ⓦ Ⓦ Ⓦ   Ⓦ Ⓦ
Ⓧ Ⓧ Ⓧ Ⓧ   Ⓧ Ⓧ
Ⓨ Ⓨ Ⓨ Ⓨ   Ⓨ Ⓨ
Ⓩ Ⓩ Ⓩ Ⓩ   Ⓩ Ⓩ

1. Ⓐ Ⓑ Ⓒ Ⓓ Ⓔ
2. Ⓐ Ⓑ Ⓒ Ⓓ Ⓔ
3. Ⓐ Ⓑ Ⓒ Ⓓ Ⓔ
4. Ⓐ Ⓑ Ⓒ Ⓓ Ⓔ
5. Ⓐ Ⓑ Ⓒ Ⓓ Ⓔ
6. Ⓐ Ⓑ Ⓒ Ⓓ Ⓔ
7. Ⓐ Ⓑ Ⓒ Ⓓ Ⓔ
8. Ⓐ Ⓑ Ⓒ Ⓓ Ⓔ
9. Ⓐ Ⓑ Ⓒ Ⓓ Ⓔ
10. Ⓐ Ⓑ Ⓒ Ⓓ Ⓔ

11. Ⓐ Ⓑ Ⓒ Ⓓ Ⓔ
12. Ⓐ Ⓑ Ⓒ Ⓓ Ⓔ
13. Ⓐ Ⓑ Ⓒ Ⓓ Ⓔ
14. Ⓐ Ⓑ Ⓒ Ⓓ Ⓔ
15. Ⓐ Ⓑ Ⓒ Ⓓ Ⓔ
16. Ⓐ Ⓑ Ⓒ Ⓓ Ⓔ
17. Ⓐ Ⓑ Ⓒ Ⓓ Ⓔ
18. Ⓐ Ⓑ Ⓒ Ⓓ Ⓔ
19. Ⓐ Ⓑ Ⓒ Ⓓ Ⓔ
20. Ⓐ Ⓑ Ⓒ Ⓓ Ⓔ

21. Ⓐ Ⓑ Ⓒ Ⓓ Ⓔ
22. Ⓐ Ⓑ Ⓒ Ⓓ Ⓔ
23. Ⓐ Ⓑ Ⓒ Ⓓ Ⓔ
24. Ⓐ Ⓑ Ⓒ Ⓓ Ⓔ
25. Ⓐ Ⓑ Ⓒ Ⓓ Ⓔ
26. Ⓐ Ⓑ Ⓒ Ⓓ Ⓔ
27. Ⓐ Ⓑ Ⓒ Ⓓ Ⓔ
28. Ⓐ Ⓑ Ⓒ Ⓓ Ⓔ
29. Ⓐ Ⓑ Ⓒ Ⓓ Ⓔ
30. Ⓐ Ⓑ Ⓒ Ⓓ Ⓔ

31. Ⓐ Ⓑ Ⓒ Ⓓ Ⓔ
32. Ⓐ Ⓑ Ⓒ Ⓓ Ⓔ
33. Ⓐ Ⓑ Ⓒ Ⓓ Ⓔ
34. Ⓐ Ⓑ Ⓒ Ⓓ Ⓔ
35. Ⓐ Ⓑ Ⓒ Ⓓ Ⓔ
36. Ⓐ Ⓑ Ⓒ Ⓓ Ⓔ
37. Ⓐ Ⓑ Ⓒ Ⓓ Ⓔ
38. Ⓐ Ⓑ Ⓒ Ⓓ Ⓔ
39. Ⓐ Ⓑ Ⓒ Ⓓ Ⓔ
40. Ⓐ Ⓑ Ⓒ Ⓓ Ⓔ

NOTES

NOTES

International Offices Listing

China (Beijing)
1501 Building A,
Disanji Creative Zone,
No.66 West Section of North 4th Ring Road Beijing
Tel: +86-10-62684481/2/3
Email: tprkor01@chol.com
Website: www.tprbeijing.com

China (Shanghai)
1010 Kaixuan Road
Building B, 5/F
Changning District, Shanghai, China 200052
Sara Beattie, Owner: Email: sbeattie@sarabeattie.com
Tel: +86-21-5108-2798
Fax: +86-21-6386-1039
Website: www.princetonreviewshanghai.com

Hong Kong
5th Floor, Yardley Commercial Building
1-6 Connaught Road West, Sheung Wan, Hong Kong
(MTR Exit C)
Sara Beattie, Owner: Email: sbeattie@sarabeattie.com
Tel: +852-2507-9380
Fax: +852-2827-4630
Website: www.princetonreviewhk.com

India (Mumbai)
Score Plus Academy
Office No.15, Fifth Floor
Manek Mahal 90
Veer Nariman Road
Next to Hotel Ambassador
Churchgate, Mumbai 400020
Maharashtra, India
Ritu Kalwani: Email: director@score-plus.com
Tel: + 91 22 22846801 / 39 / 41
Website: www.score-plus.com

India (New Delhi)
South Extension
K-16, Upper Ground Floor
South Extension Part–1,
New Delhi-110049
Aradhana Mahna: aradhana@manyagroup.com
Monisha Banerjee: monisha@manyagroup.com
Ruchi Tomar: ruchi.tomar@manyagroup.com
Rishi Josan: Rishi.josan@manyagroup.com
Vishal Goswamy: vishal.goswamy@manyagroup.com
Tel: +91-11-64501603/ 4, +91-11-65028379
Website: www.manyagroup.com

Lebanon
463 Bliss Street
AlFarra Building - 2nd floor
Ras Beirut
Beirut, Lebanon
Hassan Coudsi: Email: hassan.coudsi@review.com
Tel: +961-1-367-688
Website: www.princetonreviewlebanon.com

Korea
945-25 Young Shin Building
25 Daechi-Dong, Kangnam-gu
Seoul, Korea 135-280
Yong-Hoon Lee: Email: TPRKor01@chollian.net
In-Woo Kim: Email: iwkim@tpr.co.kr
Tel: + 82-2-554-7762
Fax: +82-2-453-9466
Website: www.tpr.co.kr

Kuwait
ScorePlus Learning Center
Salmiyah Block 3, Street 2 Building 14
Post Box: 559, Zip 1306, Safat, Kuwait
Email: infokuwait@score-plus.com
Tel: +965-25-75-48-02 / 8
Fax: +965-25-75-46-02
Website: www.scorepluseducation.com

Malaysia
Sara Beattie MDC Sdn Bhd
Suites 18E & 18F
18th Floor
Gurney Tower, Persiaran Gurney
Penang, Malaysia
Email: tprkl.my@sarabeattie.com
Sara Beattie, Owner: Email: sbeattie@sarabeattie.com
Tel: +604-2104 333
Fax: +604-2104 330
Website: www.princetonreviewKL.com

Mexico
TPR México
Guanajuato No. 242 Piso 1 Interior 1
Col. Roma Norte
México D.F., C.P.06700
registro@princetonreviewmexico.com
Tel: +52-55-5255-4495
+52-55-5255-4440
+52-55-5255-4442
Website: www.princetonreviewmexico.com

Qatar
Score Plus
Office No: 1A, Al Kuwari (Damas)
Building near Merweb Hotel, Al Saad
Post Box: 2408, Doha, Qatar
Email: infoqatar@score-plus.com
Tel: +974 44 36 8580, +974 526 5032
Fax: +974 44 13 1995
Website: www.scorepluseducation.com

Taiwan
The Princeton Review Taiwan
2F, 169 Zhong Xiao East Road, Section 4
Taipei, Taiwan 10690
Lisa Bartle (Owner): lbartle@princetonreview.com.tw
Tel: +886-2-2751-1293
Fax: +886-2-2776-3201
Website: www.PrincetonReview.com.tw

Thailand
The Princeton Review Thailand
Sathorn Nakorn Tower, 28th floor
100 North Sathorn Road
Bangkok, Thailand 10500
Thavida Bijayendrayodhin (Chairman)
Email: thavida@princetonreviewthailand.com
Mitsara Bijayendrayodhin (Managing Director)
Email: mitsara@princetonreviewthailand.com
Tel: +662-636-6770
Fax: +662-636-6776
Website: www.princetonreviewthailand.com

Turkey
Yeni Sülün Sokak No. 28
Levent, Istanbul, 34330, Turkey
Nuri Ozgur: nuri@tprturkey.com
Rona Ozgur: rona@tprturkey.com
Iren Ozgur: iren@tprturkey.com
Tel: +90-212-324-4747
Fax: +90-212-324-3347
Website: www.tprturkey.com

UAE
Emirates Score Plus
Office No: 506, Fifth Floor
Sultan Business Center
Near Lamcy Plaza, 21 Oud Metha Road
Post Box: 44098, Dubai
United Arab Emirates
Hukumat Kalwani: skoreplus@gmail.com
Ritu Kalwani: director@score-plus.com
Email: info@score-plus.com
Tel: +971-4-334-0004
Fax: +971-4-334-0222
Website: www.princetonreviewuae.com

Our International Partners

The Princeton Review also runs courses with a variety of
partners in Africa, Asia, Europe, and South America.

Georgia
LEAF American-Georgian Education Center
www.leaf.ge

Mongolia
English Academy of Mongolia
www.nyescm.org

Nigeria
The Know Place
www.knowplace.com.ng

Panama
Academia Interamericana de Panama
http://aip.edu.pa/

Switzerland
Institut Le Rosey
http://www.rosey.ch/

All other inquiries, please email us at
internationalsupport@review.com